'I was asked some years ago if I could capture the essence of Jung's psychology in a phrase. My mind went blank and time seemed to drag out. But then it came: *everything belongs*. There is nothing in human experience or in human behavior that is not the proper purview for reflection through the Jungian lens. Douglas Thomas' book, *The Deep Psychology of BDSM and Kink: Jungian and Archetypal Perspectives on the Soul's Transgressive Necessities*, is an exquisite example of this belongingness of what most might generally feel should be left to the nether regions of human behavior. Yet, what Doug makes abundantly clear is that the human soul seeks expression, relationship and incarnation in even the most hellish of forms, even those where human evil is at the very edge. In looking at what some may consider forbidden topics, Doug has done a deep service not only to depth psychology by bringing these topics out of the closet and into full light of day, but also to those members of the BDSM and kink communities, enabling them to find soulful meaning in their activities, so rejected by the general collective. Practitioners of depth psychology, as well as partitioners of erotic choices far outside what is considered 'normal,' will benefit from a close reading of Doug's magnificent offering. It is indeed a gift.'

Russell Lockhart, *author:* Words as Eggs: Psyche
in Language and Clinic *(1983)*, Psyche Speaks:
A Jungian Approach to Self and World *(1982)*

'Psychology is transformed by *The Deep Psychology of BDSM and Kink*, which explores alternative sexualities as integral to soul. Drawing from *The Red Book*, Douglas Thomas frees C. G. Jung from his compulsory heterosexist mode of individuation, and reveals kink sexualities in psychic dynamics described by James Hillman. The book shows that archetypes are deeply implicated in BDSM and kink through spiritual themes such as suffering, the underworld, evil, ecstasy and death. Depth Psychology needs this book to conjoin sexuality with the sacred, see the body's dreamworld and, ultimately, to understand kink in collective cultural relationships. This book is a must.'

Susan Rowland, PhD, *author:* Jung: A Feminist Revision (*2002*), The Sacred Well Murders *(2022)*

'Those of us grappling for decades, clinically and personally, with the meaning of sexualities like BDSM will no doubt welcome Thomas's book as a big breath of fresh air a long time coming. His whip-smart approach to the transgressive ways and compelling means of sexual dominance and erotic submission manages throughout to lay bare all the potentially rich archetypal dimensions of this form of erotic encounter, and does so for both academic and kinkster alike. Discriminating without being judgmental, at all times alive to the power and the glory of sex in the psyche, Thomas illuminates a place many of us know intimately.'

Robert Hopcke, *author:* Jung, Jungians, and Homosexuality (*1991*)

The Deep Psychology of BDSM and Kink

This fascinating volume investigates how the concept of soul is connected to BDSM and kink, exploring the world of alternative sexualities through the psychology of C. G. Jung and James Hillman as readers are guided on a provocative and lively journey through darker aspects of the sexual imagination.

Contextualized both in sexual history and contemporary events, the book unveils surprising points of correspondence between the tortured fantasy-images of Jung's *The Red Book* and the modern world of BDSM and describes from Hillman's psychology a soul-centered perspective that affirms the psychological value of fantasy-images animating our human lives. The book also considers the collective archetypal sources of historical trauma which have provided inspiration to some of the more disquieting aspects of BDSM and details how the deep psychology of BDSM creates a space in the modern world to ethically engage these practices. Kinksters and BDSM practitioners will discover a psychological language that clarifies and affirms why these activities and relationships can be so intensely intimate, pleasurable, and transformative.

Psychotherapists and enthusiasts of Jungian and archetypal psychology will find fresh insights here that support the practice of BDSM as a form of individuation and a path for bringing soul into the world.

Douglas Thomas has a private Jungian-based psychotherapy practice in Pasadena, California, where he specializes in work with dreams, LGBTQ+ issues, and alternative sexualities. He also teaches as adjunct faculty at Pacifica Graduate Institute in Santa Barbara, California. Dr. Thomas has written articles for the *Journal of Jungian Scholarly Studies* and *International Journal of Jungian Studies*. His essay "My Kinky Shadow: The Poetics of the Sadomasochistic Other" was published last year in Routledge's *The Spectre of the Other in Jungian Psychoanalysis*. For more information, visit Dr. Thomas's website at Drdouglasthomas.com.

The Deep Psychology of BDSM and Kink

Jungian and Archetypal Perspectives on the Soul's Transgressive Necessities

Douglas Thomas

Routledge
Taylor & Francis Group

LONDON AND NEW YORK

Designed cover image: © Metropolitan Museum of New York City Open Access Initiative

First published 2024
by Routledge
4 Park Square, Milton Park, Abingdon, Oxon OX14 4RN

and by Routledge
605 Third Avenue, New York, NY 10158

Routledge is an imprint of the Taylor & Francis Group, an informa business

© 2024 Douglas Thomas

British Library Cataloguing-in-Publication Data
A catalogue record for this book is available from the British Library

Library of Congress Cataloging-in-Publication Data
Names: Thomas, Douglas (Psychotherapist), author.
Title: The deep psychology of BDSM and kink : Jungian and archetypal
    perspectives on the soul's transgressive necessities / Douglas Thomas.
Description: Abingdon, Oxon ; New York, NY : Routledge, 2024. | Includes
    bibliographical references and index.
Identifiers: LCCN 2023012422 (print) | LCCN 2023012423 (ebook) |
    ISBN 9781032122090 (hardback) | ISBN 9781032122076 (paperback) |
    ISBN 9781003223597 (ebook)
Subjects: LCSH: Sex (Psychology) | Bondage (Sexual behavior)—Psychological
    aspects. | Sadomasochism—Psychological aspects. | Jungian psychology. | Soul.
Classification: LCC BF175.5.S48 T46 2024 (print) | LCC BF175.5.S48 (ebook) |
    DDC 155.3—dc23/eng/20230623
LC record available at https://lccn.loc.gov/2023012422
LC ebook record available at https://lccn.loc.gov/2023012423

ISBN: 978-1-032-12209-0 (hbk)
ISBN: 978-1-032-12207-6 (pbk)
ISBN: 978-1-003-22359-7 (ebk)

DOI: 10.4324/9781003223597

Typeset in Casion Pro
by Apex CoVantage, LLC

For Guy Baldwin

For the Leather Gods, who forged a world of honor and transgression

And for the Nature Spirits who found a home there

Contents

ACKNOWLEDGMENTS

To everyone who contributed to the creation of this book, I offer my heart-felt thanks.

The book first started to take shape during a monthlong writing retreat at the Roundstone Guest Lodge in Limpopo, South Africa. My friend and colleague Elizabeth Nelson was an ideal traveling companion and sounding board. There is also deep gratitude for the generous hospitality of the Roundstone staff under the direction of Delmar and Cecile Pretorius. The experience of the South African land and the animals that made their home there was unforgettable and invaluable. The chthonic magic there helped the writing emerge.

My husband, Dan Poirier, has been a constant source of support and advice at each stage of this project. He helped edit early drafts of the manuscript and gave candid feedback and advice on how to address the many challenges that were a regular feature of the writing process.

Matthew Fike provided expert assistance with the editing process.

In the later stages of revisions, Christine Downing was an ideal reviewer. She possessed the perfect combination of knowledge of the BDSM community through several close friendships and a distinguished career as an author and scholar well-acquainted with depth psychology. Her many deeply perceptive suggestions were a major contribution to this book. I am also profoundly grateful to Christine for writing the foreword to this volume.

Others who contributed to the review process were Susan Rowland, Robert Hopcke, Russell Lockhart, and Glenn Slater. I am grateful to each of them for pointing out the strengths of this book and its relevance to the fields of depth psychology and human sexuality.

This book features excerpts from interviews with several members of the BDSM and kink communities. Their voices add dimension and intimacy that bring the world of BDSM to life. Thank you to Moth Meadows, Miss Dion, Mister Blue and BlueFrost, Doc Coral, and Master Jess and boi Kaseem for sharing so deeply the personal details of your lives.

Finally, there are members of the BDSM and kink communities whom I am fortunate to count among my friends and colleagues. To Guy Baldwin, Caroline Shahbaz, Peter Chirinos, Skip Chasey, and Rick Levine, thank you for your friendship, your encouragement, and your advice.

FOREWORD
Christine Downing

When Douglas Thomas asked me if I would be willing to look at a chapter of his almost-completed book on depth psychological understandings of transgressive sexualities, I immediately said, "Yes, and I want to see the whole book, not just a chapter."

I knew how much we needed just this book, partly because of my friendship with John McConnell, whom I first met when he was a gay graduate student involved in a committed Master/slave relationship. John went on to become a psychotherapist, whose practice focused on patients engaged in "spicy sex" and power-differentiated relationships. Two years ago, shortly before his death, he gave a talk about these diverse sexualities to the local San Diego chapter of the APA division that focuses on "Diversity and Inclusion." Addressing these fellow professionals, he invoked Freud, he brought in Greek mythology, and he expected a welcoming and interested audience. Instead, people walked out, they screamed invectives, no one wanted to stay around and talk. He was heartbroken.

I know he would have loved *The Deep Psychology of Kink and BDSM* and its exploration of alternative sexualities from a depth psychological perspective. Douglas's book, directed in part to the same audience, fellow professionals, aims to help them overcome the discomfort, the tendency to stigmatize and pathologize that was so evident in the reception to John's presentation. It offers no clinical guidelines, only an encouragement to psychotherapists to help their kinky patients explore the subjective meaning of their sexuality—*and* to do their own soul work, to explore what lies behind their suspicion or rejection, to move beyond seeing participants in kink as radically other.

The book is also directed at BDSM participants themselves, designed to encourage them to explore what lies behind their pull to engage in transgressive sexuality, to step back and look at their experience more consciously, to engage in introspection, reflection, ethical appraisal.

The book encourages both to adopt a depth psychological way of looking.

It is also directed to persons already interested in Jung and Hillman, who might be curious about how their theories can illuminate a context neither ever directly addressed. Although Douglas also brings in other thoughtful theorists, such as Winnicott, Gadamer, Huizinga, Bataille, and Kristeva, his deep appreciation of what he has learned from Hillman illuminates the whole book.

This archetypal perspective issues in a book that not only offers readers a deeper understanding of those pulled to honor what Douglas calls the "transgressive necessities of soul" by participating in kink but also a deeper understanding of ourselves. Indeed, we might even close the book sensing that in some way, "they" do it for "us."

That is a radical proposal, but I believe it is made possible by the tone of Douglas's book, which beautifully communicates a sympathetic understanding of BDSM practitioners, without romanticizing them. It also expresses empathy toward those made uncomfortable by some aspects of kink practices, inviting them to acknowledge the discomfort and to explore what might lie behind it.

As the book articulates what it means to adopt a depth psychological perspective, it, of course, begins with Freud, who taught us to look at alternative sexualities, not as perversions, not as pathologies, but simply as variations, and who also made us aware of how much of our sexuality is unconscious. All of us, Freud believed, have both active and passive sexual aims, the most extreme version of which, the version that appears in myths and in our dreams and fantasies, is sadism and masochism. Thus, he subtly introduces the idea that in our unconscious, in our imaginations, we are all sadists and masochists.

But Doug's understanding of depth psychology is more attuned to what Jung and Hillman added by their more evident focus on the imaginal and the archetypal, by their focus on the soul rather than the person, on the whole of our psyche, including especially its shadowed unconscious aspects—and by their insistence that what the soul loves is images: fantasies, metaphors, and myths. He returns again and again to Hillman's affirmation, "We do not make our fantasies, they make us."

The soul, Doug goes on to remind us, is drawn to underworld experience, to suffering, submission, and death—something most of us repress. But for some—for BDSM practitioners—the draw becomes conscious, becomes imperative, becomes fate. Those underworld fantasies "make" them; they represent "transgressive *necessities* of soul." To engage in transgressive sexuality is to participate in an archetypal pattern, although Doug acknowledges that not all participants would understand themselves in this way.

When talking about kink and BDSM, we are talking about an intentionally, consciously, transgressive counterculture. Yes, of course, there have been individuals engaged in sadomasochistic practices and relationships always and everywhere, but kink and BDSM as constituting communities with rules is relatively new. The authority transfer, the structured imbalance, is voluntary, negotiated, consensual. The participants are counterparts, not opposites; there is real intimacy between them. Doug goes to great effort throughout the book to emphasize this.

My friend John's own experience of BDSM was through a series of long-established Master/slave relationships. I witnessed his deep grief as two of his partners died of AIDS; his last partner is still bereft. I had a real sense that for John being Master was a responsible, caring role, that the partners (whom I came to know) felt that being John's slave answered a deep soul need, allowed them to be who they really were, who they were in a sense "fated" to be. Among the parts of Doug's book that moved me most was the inclusion of several extended interviews with other long-term Master/slave relationships where this was also true.

But for many involved in kink, it means not a primary committed relationship but more occasional participation in "scenes," where the fantasy aspect is more clearly visible. Throughout his book, Doug scatters lists that help us vividly imagine these scenes as rituals, as deliberately fashioned ordeals, as initiation. When we read of

> The submissive gesture of lips pressed against a boot, the smell of cured leather, the sound of rattling chains, the other-worldly silence of mummification, the repetitive blows of a flogger striking

bare flesh, the reddening warmth of skin stinging from repeated
slaps by a gloved hand

Or of "rope/chain/plastic wrap/hood/gimp suit," we are led not to abstract
ideas about violence or bondage but to powerful images of what it's really
like to be flogged or chained. We are helped to experience that Doug is
writing about the embodiment, the actual enactment, the *living* of fantasies,
the *surrender* to fantasies.

We come to understand that to participate in kink is to obey the soul's
call to actualize the feelings and thoughts associated with sadism and masochism, to bring soul into the world through suffering, endured and inflicted,
to actualize the paradoxical confluence of suffering and pleasure. We come
to recognize that there is something thrilling about the sense of violating
taboos, of eroticizing the immoral, of engaging in something forbidden,
something ordinarily viewed as evil.

The depth psychological perspective helps reveal why these scenes, which
bring together ecstatic pleasure and terror, can have such numinous, transformative power: they evoke the archetypal, the mythic. One engages in
kink for the sake of transcendent experience. Doug's discussion of Dionysus, the Greek god associated with ecstatic experience, clarifies how the
escape from ego boundaries and social conventions, going to extremes, testing one's limits, can lead one to feel connected to something larger than
one's personal identity. Indeed, this god—and he is a god—seems to preside
over all aspects of kink experience. Dionysus is the Lord of Souls, who has
himself journeyed to the Underworld, confronted death, and returned. As
the god of theater, he is clearly present in the play space of BDSM's scenes,
in the role-play, the masks, the costumes, the scripts.

Doug goes to great lengths to remind us that these are *contained* enactments of fantasies, that there is aftercare, a scripted transition out of the
other world of the scene. The scene takes place in a place and time set aside
from one's ordinary life. And yet . . .

And yet, he suggests, participants may return to the ordinary world
changed. What happened happened in a world set apart, and yet it happened. Addressing participants themselves, he advises, "If you want the
most out of your kink, treat it as psychological work. Step back; reflect."
Participation in kink can be a path leading to integration, to growth. Reflection, introspection, can issue in self-revelation and transformation.

After all the pages devoted to play, to suffering, to evil, to death, the book ends (as I think it must) with love, with a testimony to the deep intimacy and trust that comes to exist between the two partners—whether engaged in a long-term committed relationship or in the play space of a scene. To point to the archetypal aspect of kink, Doug once again turns to classical mythology, to the myth of Psyche and Eros and to those associated with Persephone, the goddess who rules over the Underworld, the world of soul.

As I reflect on my own reading and rereading of this amazing book, I find myself remembering most vividly what Doug writes about submission, about the archetypal figure of the submissive:

> The archetypal figure that has forever been a part of the human psyche in the collective unconscious. The archetypal figure emerges from the depths and seizes us, captivates us, and has the potential to guide us along the path of individuation. (Perhaps the way of the archetypal submissive is the catalyst for personal growth and transformation for all of us.)

This book, I discovered, is, indeed, about all of us, about me.

Christine Downing

PREFACE

Douglas Thomas

This book considers a central question: *How is the psychological notion of the soul pertinent to the activities and relationships of BDSM and kink?* What follows is a depth psychological exploration of modern intentionally transgressive sexualities. Sometimes referred to as radical sexualities or alternative sexualities, these terms refer to a range of activities and relationships that are interrelated in some combination of eroticism, sexual expression, and a structured imbalance of authority. BDSM stands for bondage and discipline, Domination and submission, and sadism and masochism.[1] Kink is a loosely defined umbrella term that refers generally to a range of fetish-based interests and activities.

The Deep Psychology of BDSM and Kink was born out of psychological curiosity. My own personal curiosity led me to examine in depth how the psychological ideas of C. G. Jung and James Hillman could contribute fresh perspectives and insights to support BDSM participants and mental health professionals alike. Many of the elements of kink and BDSM resemble images and themes that are present in world mythology and dreams. The similarities suggest that radical sexualities are powerful, pleasurable, and transformative because they are connected to deeper, sometimes ominous, archetypal structures in the psyche. Curiosity itself belongs to a fundamental psychic substrate, as many of the myths from classical Greece remind us. The curiosity of the mythic Psyche as she enters the darkened bed chamber holding a lamp and knife over her sleeping lover, fearing he might be a

monster, is an apt metaphor to hold and guide this journey into places that
are obscure, troubling, and often difficult to speak of. The classical myth tells
a tale of desire, longing, secrecy, mystery, domination, submission, danger,
suffering, degradation, endurance, mortal peril, and ultimate union. Where
Psyche and Eros converge, we can anticipate the emergence of these themes,
and they are certainly present in the chapters that follow.

There is also a hope here that archetypal curiosity will engage you as the
reader. If you are someone who enjoys the pleasure and excitement of kink
and BDSM, this book may spark your curiosity to reflect more deeply on
your experience as a poetic expression of soul, particularly in its tortured
or cruel aspects. If you are someone fascinated by the ideas of Jung and
Hillman, perhaps it will pique your interest to read how depth psychology
reveals the inner world of radical sexuality. If you experience both curiosity
and discomfort toward BDSM and kink, perhaps you will find a deeper
understanding that renders these activities and relationships less foreign
than you might have previously imagined. If you are a mental health professional, perhaps you will feel intrigued by the suggestion that within the
intentionally transgressive sexualities of kink and BDSM, there is a *telos* or
deeper purpose that is drawing people forward in their individuation process. As the historically negative professional attitudes toward sadomasochism evolve, the time is ripe for clinicians to cultivate greater psychological
curiosity toward the topic and its practitioners.

Historically, from the early days of psychology starting with Richard von
Krafft-Ebing's[2] *Psychopathia Sexualis*, sadomasochism and related forms of
what today we would refer to as alternative sexualities were regarded as
perversions and pathological disorders. In the final years of the nineteenth
century, Sigmund Freud pioneered the field of depth psychology, which
introduced the concept of the unconscious. He proposed that what society
condemned as perversions were in fact variations in human sexuality (i.e.,
referencing sexuality's polymorphous nature) and that which was esteemed
as "normal" sexuality was but one of those variations. Freud developed a
more nuanced understanding of sadomasochism as a fusion of destructive and pleasurable impulses that are common to everyone—an aspect of
the psyche with which we all must contend. Jung and Hillman developed
their own theories of the psyche as an autonomous unseen collective force
that appears through primordial fantasy-images. By imagining psyche as
soul, they created room for a more poetic and metaphorical approach to

understanding human experience and the hidden forces that draw the soul toward erotic underworld experiences.

Where we are at our most unconscious, the soul is at work, speaking through our peculiar habits, our sexual secrets, our visceral reactions and extreme emotions. And so it is reasonable to pursue a line of questioning here that posits at the beginning that in BDSM and kink, where we find arguably the most extreme, the most intense, and the most imaginative expressions of human sexuality, the soul is at work, seeding the imagination with its extravagant fantasies. Society has changed, and what was once perceived as unhealthy is now becoming part of a fulfilling and meaningful life for people who are professionally successful and who enjoy loving intimate relationships, two of Freud's primary criteria for a healthy life. Yet despite the Diagnostic and Statistical Manual of the American Psychiatric Association[3] having removed behaviors related to BDSM and kink as de facto disorders, there remains a lingering negative bias in the profession that views them as inherently disturbed and undesirable. I hope the present discussion will provide a fresh clinical perspective that will lead to more affirming and supportive therapeutic care for BDSM and kink practitioners. I also hope it will provide a broader readership with a view of BDSM that will show its relevance to understanding some of the deeper currents at work in our own souls.

Suffering is a central topic of this discussion. Our ideas and fantasies about suffering and our orientation toward it as a state of soul find expression in our personal and collective attitudes toward alternative sexualities. BDSM has adopted suffering as a kind of lingua franca, developing a nuanced and sophisticated vocabulary, which has evolved into a true logos of pathos, rather than a pathology. On some level, whether they are conscious of it or not, people who participate in BDSM activities and relationships acknowledge suffering as an essential agent of paradoxical pleasure and psychological transformation. However, suffering is an integral part of the human condition beyond the confines of the dungeons and playrooms of BDSM's practitioners. This book will propose that alternative sexualities are a creative response to suffering as an integral part of the human condition. Jung believed that suffering was essential to the individuation process. Hillman regarded suffering as one of the ways soul comes into the world (what the poet John Keats referred to as the vale of soul-making). The pull toward suffering and transgression is something deep in all of us.

Based on interviews with particular individuals who are part of the BDSM community, and based on my own interests and experiences, there won't be equal consideration given to all varieties of BDSM or all kinks. As a psychological exploration, this book will place particular emphasis on exploring the various forms of Domination and submission that are practiced and on the role played by sadomasochism in "scenes" (the well-chosen term for structured BDSM encounters) and in life. It is a bias that I acknowledge at the outset. Authority transfer is an extreme form of relationship with an extreme set of practices, making it particularly effective for illustrating psychological ideas.

Among the most important themes in *The Deep Psychology of BDSM and Kink* is the premise that elaborate fantasies of erotic violence, cruelty, and degradation originate in the primordial depths of the psyche. They are emissaries of the soul's transgressive necessities. We all encounter them internally. They are not inherently positive or negative in value because they are archetypal. BDSM and kink have established a set of carefully developed structures and practices to create a resilient container to consciously engage with these forces in their absolute otherness. At its root, *BDSM is a conscious exercise in the eroticization of alterity.*

Notes

1 Oxford English Dictionary (n.d.).
2 Krafft-Ebing, R. (1886/2011).
3 American Psychiatric Association (2013).

References

American Psychiatric Association. (2013). *Diagnostic and statistical manual of mental disorders* (5th ed.). American Psychiatric Association.
Krafft-Ebing, R. (2011). *Psychopathia sexualis* (F. S. Klaf, Trans.). Arcade Publishing. (Original work published 1886)
Oxford English Dictionary. (n.d.). *BDSM.* Retrieved August 5, 2017, from www.oed.com

PART ONE
PSYCHOLOGICAL PERSPECTIVES

1

CONFRONTATION WITH THE EROTIC UNCONSCIOUS

Introduction

The scene. This single word has the power to open the gates to the world of imagination, a place that the French anthropologist Henri Corbin[1] called the *mundus imaginalis* and that C. G. Jung and James Hillman referred to as the soul or the unconscious. Imagination and images are of vital importance to both BDSM and depth psychology, the two subjects whose convergence is the focus of the present discussion. The scene connotes the setting of a theatrical production, the place revealed to us once the lights have dimmed and the curtain is pulled back. The scene is the setting of the play, and *play* is essential both to BDSM and to psychological life. The scene is the location of the stage picture, and it is also the location in the imagination where the drama occurs. Practitioners of BDSM have found the perfect word to describe the other-worldly space that is created through their activities: people get together and do a scene.

The drama of BDSM emerges through scenes. And what stories they tell: tales of shadowy subterranean spaces, dungeons, cages, shackles, chains, ropes, whips, floggers, instruments of abuse and torture, naked bodies, faceless hooded figures, foreboding fierce beings of power and control, and other-worldly silhouettes of base submission. They are tales of intense contradictory emotions and sensations: fear and desire, restriction and liberation, torment and delight, humiliation and exhilaration, devotion and dread. The scene is the place where the players reveal and fulfill their longings, inhabit the hidden parts of their own nature, and enter into dream and trance. Sometimes they discover ecstatic states of transformation, and sometimes they encounter the limits that hold us between life and death.

How is soul involved in the scenes of BDSM and kink? That is the question that guides the present inquiry. Those familiar with the psychology of Jung and Hillman, the two authors whose ideas provide the psychological foundation for the discussion that follows, will likely notice the similarities between the scenes of BDSM and the mythic archetypal characteristics of what these writers referred to as soul. Both Jung and Hillman favored the word *soul* over the more foreign-sounding erudite *psyche*. Soul connotes the realm of the unconscious; the hidden, mythic Underworld of the unseen and the unknown; the source of the poetic imagination and its descriptive metaphorical power; and the place where dreams, myth, and imagination all find their source. The conceptualization of soul is lyrical, and the suggestion here is that the soul is the originator of the scene, the invisible *metteur en scène*, who dreams up the tableau and directs the drama of the inner life.

A depth psychological perspective finds that soul is deeply implicated in the scenes of BDSM play. Depth psychologist Thomas Moore[2] saw the connection when he wrote his groundbreaking book *Dark Eros*. He argued that the Marquis de Sade's graphic tales of sexual torture are psychologically potent and valuable because they confront us with the most hidden necessities of the soul's erotic imagination. Rather than characterizing Sade, whose name lives on in the word sadism, as an extravagant deviant, Moore made the case that he was "a conduit of an underworld mythology."[3] Nearly a decade before Moore's book, Jungian therapist, Lyn Cowan,[4] found a similar connection between masochism and the archetypal forces of soul. Cowan and Moore both found an unusual convergence between the deep psyche and sadomasochism: the peculiar fantasies that blend calibrated cruelty and humiliation with primal sexuality are mythic scenes of the soul's own making. The strange shadowy tales that unfold in the scenes of BDSM are expressed in psyche's nocturnal mythic vernacular, the language of soul.

It is rare to find the BDSM practitioner who thinks of a scene as a disclosure of soul. It is also rare to find the depth psychologist who recognizes kinky sex and BDSM relationships as a form of underworld mythology. And yet the world of BDSM and the Underworld of soul are intertwined. They are like two serpents wrapped around a common centering staff, an image which is the symbolic emblem of Hermes, that great ancient god of communication and translation between worlds. Hermes was also the god of the crossroads. His staff or caduceus is a fitting symbol to invoke at the beginning: Hermes invites the reader to dwell at the crossroads where BDSM and soul intersect. For practitioners of BDSM, depth psychology provides a new mode of seeing and describing the deeper hidden dimensions of what it means to do a scene and to forge a bond of trust and intimacy with a partner. For depth psychology, BDSM illuminates and enlivens the ideas of Jung and Hillman by providing the tangible dimension of physical bodies in active relationship. The scenes of BDSM and kink give form and expression to the timeless stories that bring soul into the world.

BDSM: An Overview[5]

According to the *Oxford English Dictionary*,[6] the term BDSM appeared in the early 1990s as an abbreviation for bondage and discipline, domination and submission, and sadism and masochism. Each initial describes an essential aspect of a wide range of behaviors, activities, and relationships that combine sexuality, eroticism, and structured interaction or play, usually involving some form of extreme physical or mental challenge. For some, the term emphasizes the activities (such as restraining the partner with handcuffs, ropes, or chains to restrict mobility and impose control). For others, the emphasis is on identity and lifestyle (a couple creating a household based on dynamics of domination and submission, such as Master and slave).[7] For some, BDSM is an occasional pleasurable recreation; for others, it signifies a life of meaning, purpose, and value. BDSM activities and relationships often emphasize a consensually agreed-upon unequal power dynamic between partners, sometimes referred to as an authority exchange, authority transfer, or authority imbalance. The other popular term for a wide range of unconventional sexual interests is kink or kinky.

A Brief History

Although the modern definition of BDSM goes back only a few decades, sadomasochistic practices have existed throughout history. Frescoes in the Villa of Mysteries in the ancient city of Pompeii depict a scene of ritual scourging, and there are written accounts of sexual encounters involving pain, suffering, and degradation from the Italian Renaissance to the present. Flagellation has been a particularly frequently reported activity across cultures and historical periods. There is a well-documented consensual Master/slave relationship between Arthur Munbee and Hannah Cullwick in Victorian England, and in the United States, there is evidence of a gay SM subculture dating back to at least the 1930s.[8]

However, World War II was perhaps the most influential period for the rise of the modern BDSM movement. The increased concentration of returning veterans in urban centers at the end of the war contributed to the establishment of organizations and loosely affiliated groups who enjoyed participating in sadomasochistic activities. Such nascent communities were more prevalent in the U.S. than in Great Britain or the European continent. In the 1950s and 1960s, an invisible network of leather bar patrons, gay motorcycle club members, and publishers, readers, and advertisers of fetish publications gradually formed away from public view. This network was the beginning of modern BDSM, which gradually became more visible in the 1970s.[9]

The 1946 magazine *Bizarre* was the first modern publication to cater to sadomasochistic interests. After several U.S. Supreme Court decisions in the 1960s eased the restrictions of obscenity laws, both gay and straight publications with SM content began to proliferate. During the same decade, successful professional female Dominants (Dominatrices) became more common, partly as a result of the widely distributed publications and networks that formed around them.[10]

American gay "leather" culture developed over the same period. Many of the returning gay G.I.s settled in urban centers, and some were drawn to motorcycle culture as an expression of their newfound freedom, including sexual freedom. Motorcycle gangs, biker bars, and motorcycle clubs became venues for self-exploration and self-expression. S&M was the accepted term for the kind of sexuality some early leathermen enjoyed.[11] However, leather was not synonymous with sadomasochism. In fact, "Most leathermen were not sadomasochists," according to Stephen Stein,[12] but "leather" also became a convenient euphemism that some men used to state their interest in S&M. The Satyrs, founded in Los Angeles in 1954, was the first gay motorcycle club. The number of clubs grew dramatically through the 1960s and 1970s, and leather bars constituted a cultural thread that led to BDSM sex clubs in the 1970s. In that same decade, "a nationwide leather culture and iconography developed, celebrated in art, literature, film and a growing number of . . . contests hosted by bars."[13] In 1979, Chicago's "Mr. Gold Coast" competition developed into the International Mr.

Leather (IML) contest, which remains an iconic annual leather/BDSM event, among the largest in the world.

The 1970s saw the onset of a social-political movement around BDSM as a lifestyle. "The new literature, gay and straight, encouraged the transition from an older, secret, atomized community of BDSM enthusiasts to an open, organized community, which actively sought to teach, connect with, and educate newcomers."[14] The first publicly advertised organizations formed: The Eulenspiegel Society in New York City in 1970 and the Society of Janus in San Fransciso in 1974. Other organizations such as the Chicago Hellfire Club, established in 1971, remained private and elite, with membership limited to gay men experienced in heavy BDSM. Play parties were held in private homes as far back as the 1940s and no doubt earlier than that. What came to be known as "The Great Parties" developed in the 1970s around the nation's premiere BDSM organizations. "Parties were a performative space in which tops and bottoms demonstrated their skills, endurance and other qualities."[15]

Drummer magazine was established in 1975, a gay publication that focused on leather and BDSM. It "helped create the very leather/SM culture it covered."[16] The serialized publication of John Preston's novel, *Mr. Benson*, in *Drummer* (1979–1980) codified many of the iconic elements of gay Master/slave relationships as part of leather culture and BDSM.

For LGBTQ-identified BDSM practitioners, most gay and lesbian organizations in the 1970s shunned their community and disallowed its participation in pride events. Mainstream society looked upon BDSM with such disdain that the gay movement feared it might be risking its agenda for greater social legitimacy and equality by affirming radical sexualities. During this same period, writers Adrienne Rich, Susan Sontag, and Ti-Grace Atkinson put forward various rationalizations for their disapproval of sadomasochism, such as deeming it unhealthy, misogynistic, and sociopathic. Historian Peter Tupper wrote, "In the late 1970s and 1980s, lesbian-feminists adopted Sontag's thesis and frequently invoked fascism, or other forms of violent authoritarianism, in their [critiques against] lesbian sadomasochism."[17] He continued, "the connection between sadomasochistic sexuality and fascist politics was seen as a given, without much in the way of support. Sadomasochism was said to be both the beginning of the slippery slope to fascism and its driving psychology."[18] Samois, the first all-female BDSM organization, established in 1978, confronted feminist critiques of their activities head-on and defended "women's right to engage in any sexual activities they desired."[19] Its members argued that the perverse and subversive nature of BDSM actually undercut patriarchy. The controversy came to be known as "The Feminist Sex Wars."[20] Samois went on to help establish the first women's BDSM group in Europe in the Netherlands in 1979. Although it folded only four years after its inception, Samois had an important impact on the BDSM movement in the 1980s. The writings and activism of its members contributed to a more thoughtful and persuasive style of advocacy and more effective political skill.[21]

In the 1980s and 1990s, the targeting of the BDSM community with legal threats and police raids helped galvanize a shared identity and resulted in increased public education efforts and political activism. Tension developed between community members who cherished the identity of sexual outlaw and those who sought greater public acceptance and legitimacy. Although the importance of consent as an essential characteristic of modern BDSM had been promoted as early as 1961, guidelines for negotiating consent became increasingly codified during these years. As part of a continued campaign to gain mainstream acceptance and inclusion, organizations increasingly focused on the issue of safety, which included discouraging play while under the influence of alcohol or drugs. Similarly, a national campaign focused on distinguishing BDSM from domestic violence and physical abuse.[22]

Gay Male S/M Activists (GMSMA) was formed in New York City in 1980 with an open roster and no qualification requirements. In 1983, the GMSMA originated the phrase "safe, sane, and consensual" (SSC), which "became a guide to an entire generation of kinksters."[23] GMSMA formed a national network of chapters and qualified as a contingent in the 1987 March on Washington. "By 1986, more than 100 BDSM organizations operated in cities across the United States and Canada."[24]

Not surprisingly, the spread of AIDS in the 1980s intensified the characterizations of BDSM as dangerous and unhealthy. "The era of 'great parties' ended,"[25] and negative portrayals and censorship in the media increased. In response, the leather community organized to face the AIDS crisis: the first International Mr. Leather (IML) competition in Chicago became an AIDS fundraiser, and titleholders in the 1980s regularly served as spokespeople for AIDS-related issues. The first national conference that included both gay and lesbian leatherfolk in the same event took place in 1986. The

National Leather Association (NLA) and Living in Leather (LIL), the two host organizations, both valued education, training, and social activism during the AIDS crisis as fundamental elements of an emerging leather culture. By the end of the decade, titleholders were expected to be activists and fundraisers as well as paragons of the leather ideal.

In Britain, public BDSM clubs and organizations appeared later than in the United States. In 1987, the British police launched Operation Spanner, a campaign to arrest and prosecute sadomasochists and BDSM publications and videos. The subsequent trials and convictions led to a supportive international collaboration with the NLA in the U.S. to raise legal defense funds and provide literature on "safe, sane, and consensual" as a legal defense. The incident marked the beginning of a closer international affiliation between BDSM organizations.[26]

In the 1970s and 1980s, the terms Master and slave (M/s) appeared infrequently in leather publications. The notion of a full-time extreme authority transfer involving ownership and total control of the submissive was regarded as a fringe phenomenon.[27] Practitioners in M/s relationships reported feeling isolated and stigmatized by critics in the leather community, who viewed their commitment to a 24/7 lifestyle with skepticism. To some outside the M/s community, the idea of a full-time identity based on extreme authority transfer sounded like an impossible fantasy—more the stuff of erotic fiction than the banality of daily life. In response to the feelings of stigma and isolation, Masters and slaves Together (MAsT) was founded in 1987 and saw significant growth in the late 1990s. "It hosted its first national conference in 1999, established chapters in several cities, and created an International Master/slave Contest," which continues to the present day.[28] The organization currently has 101 active chapters, including Spanish-speaking chapters in Puerto Rico and in Costa Rica.[29] Chapters in other countries include Australia, New Zealand, and Sweden. The annual Master/slave conference in Washington, D.C., is a major national event sponsored by Master Taíno's Training Academy (MTTA).

In 1997, Susan Wright established the National Coalition for Sexual Freedom (NCSF), which has become the leading advocacy group for the BDSM community as well as other sexual minorities. NCSF played a significant role in working with the American Psychiatric Association to modify the clinical definitions of sexual sadism, sexual masochism, and fetishism in the *Diagnostic and Statistical Manual of Mental Disorders* (DSM) by stating that they could not be considered mental illnesses unless they caused significant functional impairment and distress. More recently, NCSF has had an active role in consulting with the American Law Institute (ALI) in updating the Model Penal Code (MPC) on sexual assault to decriminalize consensual BDSM when explicit prior consent has been given by both parties.[30]

The rise of the Internet provided greater visibility, and easily accessible information resulted in a decreased reliance on local BDSM organizations and publications. Practitioners became less stigmatized, and partners were increasingly easy to find. Many organizations disbanded, specialty publications folded, and millions of people joined online sites like FetLife compared to the hundreds or thousands that had belonged to the organizations of an earlier era. By 2020, FetLife had almost 9 million users.[31] The Internet has also facilitated the expansion of BDSM fantasy material in a safe, mostly consequence-free environment. For most kinks and fetishes, people can now bring their curiosity, their creativity, and their imagination to their online encounters without the kind of legal and professional vulnerability that characterized the pursuit of BDSM activities in past decades. Specialty fetish niches such as *furries* (fantasy-based human-animal hybrids that can include elaborate costumes) and *vore* (erotic fantasies of being eaten) developed online.[32]

BDSM in the Present Moment

For people outside the world of BDSM, the images of what transpires within that world can provoke visceral feelings of discomfort. The elements of cruelty, degradation, usurpation, and coercion can arouse fear and disgust. To some extent, that is the point—the paradoxical convergence of discomfort and pleasure is a fundamental characteristic of BDSM. However, popular references to BDSM in fashion, film, television, and music videos frequently exploit viewer discomfort for its shock value. Conversely, for those who view themselves as members of the BDSM community, there is a highly evolved system of communication to facilitate negotiation and consent prior to engaging in a scene. The attention to clear communication is apparent in the use of terms such as "safe, sane, and consensual,"[33] or "risk aware consensual kink,"[34] that commonly appear in introductory literature about BDSM. Author and BDSM activist Raven

Kaldera emphasized the role of conscious intent and clear communication in Master/slave relationships:

> What we're doing has never been done before in history. We're creating relationships of unequal power that are not only consensual, but negotiated down to the last detail. We work on going into these relationships mindfully and thoughtfully. We use them to improve each other. We put a huge emphasis on the happiness of both people, and on their mutual responsibility for creating that happiness. And we communicate all the time about how things are going—there are no great cultural injustices in our institutions of consensual slavery that must remain unspoken lest the whole edifice fall down.[35]

The countercultural aspect of BDSM is one of its potential strengths. Although practitioners of BDSM find pleasure in the transgression of cultural taboos, nobody is coerced into abusive situations to do anything they haven't agreed to in advance. The intent to avoid harm and to support self-determination underlies the elaborate process of negotiation and consent as well as the iconic safe word that can immediately end a scene.

The data on the number of people interested in kink suggest that, contrary to long-held professional opinions, these behaviors and relationships are neither atypical nor unusual. Curiosity about BDSM is apparent in the runaway success of E. L. James's[36] *Fifty Shades of Grey* trilogy: it has sold 125 million copies worldwide, and the movie based on the first book has grossed more than 500 million dollars.[37] Although the success of the *Fifty Shades* franchise suggests a cultural shift toward greater acceptance of alternative sexualities, members of the BDSM community have sharply criticized the inaccuracies of the stories and films (the absence of clear communication, negotiation, and prior consent to BDSM activities has been particularly troubling for many in the community). The general public appears to be both tantalized and misinformed about the details of BDSM culture.[38]

What is known about the people who engage in these activities and relationships? Individuals of all sexual and affectional orientations, all gender identities, and a broad range of social, racial, and ethnic groups identify as devotees of BDSM and kink.[39] In 1993, *The Janus Report on Sexual Behavior* estimated that up to 14% of men and 11% of women in the United States engaged in some form of BDSM behavior. More recently, a Canadian study with 1,040 subjects selected from the general population found that 45.6% of the sample expressed interest in at least one paraphilic behavior as defined by the *DSM*-5, and 33.9% had engaged in such behaviors at least once.[40]

Paraphilia and *paraphilic* are terms that are part of an established clinical language to describe activities that are typically part of kink and BDSM but are deemed to be at the edge of so-called normative sexuality. While not inaccurate, the language is problematic; it originates in the cultural tendency to marginalize and pathologize these behaviors and relationships. The latest edition of the *DSM* (the 2013 *Diagnostic and Statistical Manual of the American Psychiatric Association*), which is widely regarded as the professional standard for the assessment and diagnosis of mental disorders, unequivocally states that individuals may engage in alternative sexualities without meeting the criteria for a mental disorder. It was a significant development in the mental health field to differentiate between the healthy exploration of BDSM and clinically recognized mental disorders. However, the attitudes and practices of many clinicians do not yet reflect the recent signs of progress.

Many mental health professionals retain a negative view of BDSM due to the work of one early researcher: Richard von Krafft-Ebing. Roughly a century before the term BDSM entered the vernacular, Krafft-Ebing[41] published *Psychopathia Sexualis* in 1886 as a forensic reference book, describing what he deemed to be pathological forms of sexual behavior. Widely regarded as a landmark in psychiatric writing, the book popularized the terms sadism and masochism based on the historical lives and fictional writings of Sade and Leopold von Sacher-Masoch. As an early pioneer in the field of depth psychology, Sigmund Freud perpetuated Krafft-Ebing's views by describing sadomasochism as "the most common and the most significant of all the perversions."[42] However, Freud was presenting a more nuanced understanding of human sexuality, in which his use of the term *perversion* designated *variation*. What others called "normal" sexuality, Freud regarded as but one variation of sexual expression. By referring to sadomasochism as common and significant, he was asserting that all of us must contend with these prominent internal psychosexual forces. Unfortunately, subsequent generations of mental health practitioners frequently mischaracterized and oversimplified Freud's assessment until recently.[43]

In general, the mental health profession has done a poor job of developing clinical competency around alternative sexualities. Several studies have interviewed BDSM practitioners about their experiences in therapy, and participants frequently reported stigma, therapeutic bias, and inadequate care by clinicians.[44] A lack of education paired with a lack of psychological curiosity places psychotherapists at a disadvantage to understand and serve members of the BDSM community. However, there is reason for some optimism. In addition to Goerlich's[45] contribution, recent publications from psychoanalytic authors indicate that clinicians' historically negative bias and deficit in competency are improving.[46]

Those who are unfamiliar with the world of BDSM might argue that there surely must be some underlying trauma or some characterological disorder that would explain why individuals seek out sadomasochistic sex or engage in degrading acts of domination and submission for pleasure. Confronted with the unconventional and overtly transgressive nature of BDSM activities and relationships, it is common for people with more mainstream tastes to question the mental health of people in the lifestyle, labeling them as sick or disordered. Research over the past 20 years does not support that conclusion, according to kink-affirming authors Shahbaz and Chirinos. Their summary of the existing psychometric data found that, as a group, BDSM practitioners have scored above average for subjective well-being, mindfulness, "communication skills, imagination, self-awareness," and openness to new experiences.[47] The best available research does not support the impression that, as a group, kinksters are mentally disordered. Regarding the question of trauma, two studies found no evidence that childhood trauma or abuse caused people to enjoy BDSM activities and relationships later in life.[48] To be clear, some practitioners have had early traumatic experiences, but many have not, and clinical studies have not found a causal relationship between those experiences and a person's enjoyment of BDSM.

In addition to research on BDSM's prevalence and psychometric data on practitioners, a third area of research has investigated the biological changes brought on by participating in BDSM activities. In 2009, Brad Sagarin and his team found in two separate studies that SM practices, when performed as a consensual and pleasurable activity, resulted in positive effects that included lowered levels of the stress hormone cortisol and increased feelings of intimacy between participants.[49] More recent research has confirmed empirically that the consensual practice of BDSM results in pleasurable altered states of consciousness.[50] Subjects in the dominant role met objective criteria for going into a flow state during scenes, and for those in the submissive position, descriptions of time distortion, reduced pain, and feelings of floating and peacefulness (sometimes called "subspace") were consistent with Arne Dietrich's[51] hypothesis of transient hypofrontality (a term describing decreased activity in the frontal lobes of the brain). Psychobiology and empirical testing of theories of brain functioning have provided valuable methods to validate objectively the pleasurable and sometimes transformative experiences reported by practitioners of BDSM. The effects are real, measurable, and often beneficial.

Over 20 years of research provides data that challenge enduring perceptions of BDSM as inherently unhealthy. Rather than finding relationships that are abusive and harmful, researchers have found couples and partners who feel intense trust and intimacy with each other. Rather than finding predatory anti-social individuals who exploit the self-victimizing tendencies of trauma survivors, researchers have found practitioners as a group to be well-adjusted, happy, emotionally resilient people. Yet paradoxically, in order for BDSM to retain its vitality, it needs to remain an unsettling fringe phenomenon. It derives much of its erotic power from the transgressive thrill of violating cultural norms. Reducing social stigma through objective empirical research serves an invaluable function in support of social justice, but it would be a mistake to imagine that it legitimizes or mainstreams the movement in the eyes of the collective or, even more to the point, in the eyes of the movement itself. The BDSM catalog is not composed of clean, wholesome activities. The data from psychometric testing and psychobiology will not make kink less outrageous. These activities are deeply meaningful and life-giving to practitioners, precisely because they constitute a way of discovering vitality in the shadows of collective culture and in the personal psyche. To put it more simply, if it's normal, it's not kinky.

What is missing from all this research is the more poetic notion of psyche as soul. The rigorous experimental scientific approach to understanding BDSM, which has been so effective at disproving long-held misperceptions about practitioners and their activities, needs the enrichment that comes from an approach rooted in the imagination. Throughout three decades of invaluable research and kink-affirming psychological discourse about BDSM, soul's presence as an agent of intensity and meaning has been ignored. It is time to restore soul to the conversation, to notice the director behind the scenes.

What Does *Soul-Centered* Mean?

For readers who are partial to the certainty and precision of the natural science tradition, the appearance of the word *soul* may raise some concerns. What exactly does it mean? As a starting point, the word indicates something that is neither definite nor precise yet at the same time is essential and extremely valuable. Hillman endorsed this imprecision when he wrote, "The soul is a deliberately ambiguous concept resisting all definition in the same manner as do all ultimate symbols which provide the root metaphors for the systems of human thought."[52] Soul draws us into an unusual amalgamation of thought, feeling, and intuition. It defies specificity and logic. Often the word implies depth, intensity of feeling, and the essence of one's being. Soul is related to symbol, metaphor, and imagination. It is familiar to us through the depth we feel in our lived experiences, through our poetic turns of phrase, and through the mysteries that shape us.

Soul-centered psychology is radically different from the quantitative empirical rigors of natural science. Hillman was interested in the systems of human thought that shape and direct our interpretations of reality. In his view, empirical science is a thought system that interprets and describes reality in a particular way and trains us to interpret reality according to the certainties of mathematical and quantitative truth. But this model is only one interpretation among many. Hillman was fond of demonstrating various ways to step outside systems of thought to observe how they become habits of mind, turn invisible, and become unconscious. Building on Jung's investigations of the psyche, what he found in the unconscious dimensions of our thought systems were images.

What would it mean, then, to take a soul-centered approach to understanding kink and BDSM? *The concept of soul includes modes of perception and reflection that are at once expansive and profoundly intimate.* The expansiveness comes from the archetypal nature of soul. We find the particulars of our personal struggles reflected in larger universal thematic patterns. Recurring patterns appear in myths, legends, fairy tales, poems and novels, movies, even in advertising, as well as in our personal emotions, thoughts, and behaviors. They provide a collective context for what appear to be our unique personal experiences. At the same time, profound intimacy develops from paying exquisite attention to the particular images that inhabit our inner lives, the images that live in our own imagination. Here, too, the concept of soul is present as an ultimate symbol of our deep interiority. Intimacy and imagination are allusions to soul.

As noted earlier, those who are attracted to BDSM activities typically value the imaginative aspects of fantasy, play, and creativity that are so vividly present in many scenes. To be soul-centered in exploring these activities and relationships would be to recognize the sexual imagination and its images as *emanations of soul*, at once archetypal and deeply intimate.

Above all, *to be soul-centered is to be simultaneously non-literal and image-focused*. The activities characteristic of BDSM and the relationship dynamics between practitioners appear as a process of symbol creation. Much of the misperception of BDSM activities and the people who enjoy them has to do with a literalized understanding of the scene. To be soul-centered is to be non-literal, which means that there is an unspoken understanding that the scene is itself a kind of somber poetry. The many guidelines and safeguards of consensual, negotiated BDSM exist in part to protect partners from the effects of literalization (i.e., "real harm" and "real abuse"). The agreement to hard and soft limits negotiated in advance, the use of safe words, the presence of dungeon monitors at play parties, and the general concern regarding safety and risk awareness are all examples of a tacit understanding that a protective container is being constructed around the scene. The BDSM container holds the potent fantasy-images, but if they escape and assume a literal form, they can inflict trauma and devastation. BDSM is a soul-centered phenomenon because it values the de-literalized expression of fantasy-images within an established container.

We usually think of humans as pleasure-seeking and pain-avoidant beings. When Sacher-Masoch[53] wrote *Venus in Furs*, he introduced the world to a protagonist who sought the exquisite pleasure of humiliation and suffering at the feet of the woman he loved. By pairing the pain of humiliation with erotic pleasure, masochism unites that which we seek with that which we avoid. For those who savor the conundrum, there is no contradiction. Yet pain that brings pleasure is a de-literalization of what we conventionally think of as pain. By holding together two seemingly contradictory impulses, masochism is a deliberately ambiguous concept. Similarly, degradation that brings a sense of fulfillment and vitality appears paradoxical, even impossible, unless degradation is de-literalized—a living symbol of something that is simultaneously destructive and life-giving. To adopt a soul-centered approach to understanding these paradoxical states is to allow the deliberate ambiguity of the contradiction to stand. To be soul-centered is to be non-literal.

At the same time, to be soul-centered is to be image-focused. Jung regarded the psyche as essentially a meaningful structured series of images.[54] Hillman[55] along with Rafael Lopez-Pedraza and other archetypal psychologists adopted one of Jung's famous admonitions, "Stick with the image," to emphasize that image is the subject and soul of psychology.[56] For Jung,[57] image described more than the visual pictures conjured by the mind. It also described the apperception of any form of sensory stimulus. Accordingly, the psyche constitutes visual images, auditory images, tactile images, olfactory images, and gustatory images. To be soul-centered is to stick with these images. In the case of BDSM, doing so means that the realm of the senses is the realm of soul. The fascination with the sensorial, which ranges from sensory deprivation in various forms to playing with the extremes of sensation and sensitivity, acquires new value as a fascination with soul-images. The submissive gesture of lips pressed against a boot, the smell of cured leather, the sound of rattling chains, the other-worldly silence of mummification, the repetitive blows of a flogger striking bare flesh, the reddening warmth of skin stinging from repeated slaps by a gloved hand—all have the potential to carry complex layers of meaning as psychic images. It bears repeating: to be soul-centered is to be non-literal and image-focused.

A soul-centered approach encourages a metaphorical style of imagining. The value of metaphor lies in its power to render in visually rich language the aspects of an experience that elude a more literal description. When someone is at the end of her rope, when a thief has been caught red-handed, when a friend pours his heart out to a confidante, when a political opponent is dealt a crushing blow, when she stabbed him in the back after he bared his soul, it is the metaphor that makes the impact. However, metaphor is something more than a rhetorical or poetic device. It is a style of imagining that discovers meaning in the interactions between the surrounding world and the world within. A metaphorical style recognizes that the business of understanding ourselves and the world we inhabit involves something more than the opaque concrete details that make up the tedium of our lives. Psychology begins by noticing what is missing, what is hidden, what is essential but intangible. A special kind of de-literalized language is needed to describe the ambiguity of introspection. Deliberately ambiguous, the descriptive power of metaphor is well suited to the logos of soul, and a metaphorical style of imagining enables soul to have presence, influence, and subtle body.

A metaphorical style of imagining in turn implies a *"poetic basis of mind."*[58] Poetic does not mean sentimental nor does it mean inscrutable. It refers to a way of thinking that allows for layers of meaning, one that encourages an aesthetic readiness to be surprised and moved by images, words, sounds, and gestures. Poetry creates a world through metaphor as symbol. It involves a layering or piling up of meaning. A poetic basis of mind adopts these characteristics to develop a mode of introspection based on aesthetic sensitivity. When the basis of mental activity is poetic, images are real and alive yet not literally so, and symbols gain potency by allowing the known to coexist with the unknown in the same moment.

A focus on poetics directs attention to the act of creation. When BDSM is converted from a noun into an adjective, what is being created becomes more apparent. To speak of the BDSM lifestyle, BDSM relationships, BDSM sex, or BDSM philosophy is to suggest that the initials are referencing the creation of a world. A poetic basis of mind envisions BDSM as a psychological world, which has come into existence through the clothing and the gear, through the activities, through the relationships, through the rules and protocols, through the imagination itself. The world of BDSM is bigger than the sum of its kinky parts because it is not literal. A soul-centered approach understands that the world in question is not located in Los Angeles, New York, London, or Berlin. It provides access to that world independent of geography as a place of abundant creativity and complexity.

BDSM: What Is Archetypal?

A soul-centered approach to BDSM provides a new perspective that complements the empirical scientific research and social science research of the past 20 years. The next two chapters will explore the psychology of Jung and Hillman in more detail. Central to the ideas of these two depth psychologists are the concepts of the archetype and the archetypal. For those familiar with the writings of Jung and Hillman, archetypes are familiar territory. However, as Jung himself noted, "the concept of the archetype has given rise to the greatest misunderstandings and—if one may judge by the adverse criticisms—must be presumed to be very difficult to comprehend."[59]

Further, the archetypal dimension of BDSM may not be readily apparent to all readers. Therefore, a few introductory remarks are in order.

The Jungian scholar Edward Edinger called Jung's formulation of the archetypal unconscious his "most basic and far-reaching discovery."[60] Although it is a fair assessment, Jung himself was also right: the concept has led to misunderstandings and is fairly difficult to comprehend. Fundamentally, archetypes are the primordial (meaning earliest or primeval) images that form the contents of the collective unconscious.[61] But once again, the *images* in question are not lifeless pictures or abstractions. The archetype is an active invisible agent that is providing form and pattern to a particular style of perception and psychological experience. For example, a queen is not an archetype, but when one adopts a regal attitude and perceives the world with sovereign authority, the archetype of *the Queen* is emerging and giving form and pattern to the person's experience.

How are archetypes relevant to BDSM? Kinksters sometimes describe their activities as fantasy role-play. Jung's theory of the archetypes provides a psychological structure that takes fantasy seriously. It provides a way of understanding more clearly what is so powerful and often so enjoyable about BDSM. When partners sense something awakening deep within that overtakes their everyday identity, the resulting intensity of the scene signals an archetypal emergence from the collective unconscious. The dynamic between Dominant and submissive is an archetypal pattern that has appeared throughout history all over the world, sometimes with devastating consequences. In BDSM, the archetypal pattern is held consciously in the context of a negotiated, consensual encounter. When practitioners engage consciously with archetypal dynamics, BDSM has the potential to be psychologically transformative, both for individuals and for the collective.

In a Master/slave relationship, each person is also relating to an archetype of *Master* and *slave*.[62] The archetypes provide an animating spark that brings to life the psychological patterns already present in each person's mind. What was perhaps always a masterly or slavish aspect of the individual's personality reaches fuller expression through the archetype to provide a path of psychological exploration, self-discovery, and self-realization.

Each archetype has both a light or positive aspect and a somber, chthonic, and partly unfavorable aspect.[63] In other words, every archetype, like the psyche itself, is inherently value neutral, capable of manifesting in a variety of ways. The archetypes that constellate in the world of BDSM are neither positive nor negative in and of themselves. Their value is determined by how they are expressed in the scene.

Archetypes function as translators between the physical and the mental.[64] In BDSM, the physical ordeals that people endure carry symbolic meaning because archetypes are translating physical pain and suffering into a psychological experience. Archetypes facilitate the symbolic function of the psyche. Because of their relationship with symbols, archetypes are relevant to both psychology and mythology. There will be more to say about the mythic connection momentarily.

One of the hallmarks of an archetypal encounter is its numinous quality. Henri Ellenberger described it as "a feeling of awe and shuddering before an unapproachable Being that is a living energy and 'totally other.'"[65] Lionel Corbett's description of the numinous may sound surprisingly familiar to practitioners of BDSM who have had transformative experiences during scenes:

> We feel stunned, astonished, and filled with wonder because we have been addressed by something uncanny, not of our ordinary world, something very difficult to put into words. We may be cowed by the experience because its sheer force overpowers us, making us feel very small. Or we may feel entranced, captivated, and transported. Contact with the numinosum . . . may also produce a profound sense of union or oneness with the world and with other people.[66]

It is the primordial archetype that triggers or constellates numinous experience. For submissives who enter what is referred to as "subspace" or for Dominants who "unleash the beast" during particularly intense scenes, the concept of the word *numinous* may provide a psychological language that powerfully expresses the impact and the significance of what happens to them.

As one of the leading psychological minds in the generation after Jung, Hillman placed the concept of the archetype at the center of his approach. In developing the concept, he found a distinction between the *archetype* as a noun and the *archetypal* as an adjective. The difference has profound implications. Hillman, observed that the word *archetypal* "rather than pointing *at* something . . . points *to* something, and this is *value*. . . . By archetypal psychology we mean a psychology of value."[67] Moore provided further clarification:

> Archetypal psychology is not a psychology of archetypes. Its primary activity is not matching themes in mythology and art to similar themes in life. Rather, the idea is to see every fragment of life and every dream as myth and poetry.[68]

Consequently, it is a psychology "rooted not in science but in aesthetics and imagination. . . . It strives for depths, resonance, and texture in all that it considers."[69] The archetypal dwells in the aesthetic presentation of the here and now.

What is archetypal about BDSM? Following Moore's advice "to see every fragment of life . . . as myth and poetry,"[70] the archetypal element runs through the world of BDSM like a major artery. The archetypal brings an exquisite intensity to the patterns of play, it brings meaning and value to suffering, it transforms ordinary rooms into dungeons and ecstatic ritual spaces, it summons the shadowy complexity of love, and it illuminates the mystery of death. There is something mythic at work in the world of BDSM and something of BDSM at work in the world of myth. The archetypal imagination creates similar patterns in both. Let us consider a few illustrative examples of the archetypal convergence in themes and images between modern BDSM and ancient myths.

In Sumerian mythology, Inanna is the goddess of heaven as well as love, beauty, sex, desire, fertility, justice, war, and political power.[71] In one famous legend, she descends into the Underworld of Kur, where she encounters her sister Ereshkigal. Inanna undergoes an arduous journey through the seven gates of the Underworld in which she is required to surrender all her clothing and all her outward expressions of beauty, power, and authority. The rigorous protocol of the Underworld resembles the meticulous ritualized steps a modern-day submissive might follow to strip slowly according to the rules of his or her Dominant. Everything is taken away from Inanna in order for her to meet Ereshkigal, Queen of the Underworld. She stands naked before her sister and gazes into the icy eye of death.[72] Like Inanna, BDSM practitioners journey toward the mythic nether regions of soul, places where ego is surrendered and the borderland between life and death becomes a symbol of initiation. Kaldera[73] has referred to the ritual initiatory aspects of BDSM as the ordeal path. Lest there be any doubt about the element of ruthless sadomasochism in Inanna's story, Ereshkigal proceeds to strike her dead and hang her naked body on a hook in the Underworld for three days until other deities summon spirits to revive and rescue her. Jungian authors such as Sylvia Brinton Perera[74] see in Inanna's tale a parable of feminine initiation into the transgressive unknown aspects of one's own nature. These same aspects are a realm of self-discovery for practitioners of BDSM.

The Underworld is significant in classical Greek mythology as well. The place was synonymous with the God who ruled it, Hades. He was mysterious and foreboding, stern and austere, faceless and unnamable. Hades ruled over the land of the dead, where all souls journey after life, never to return.[75] The similarity between classical underworld imagery and BDSM is noticeable, particularly when it concerns the torture and suffering of wrongdoers in the region of Hades known as Tartarus. Consider the torments of Tantalus, forever stricken with thirst and hunger, teased with the denial of food and water just out of reach. It is a cruel predicament sure to inspire the admiration of even the most sadistic of Doms. In Tartarus, the classical imagination found a mythic location to showcase the soul's sadistic necessities with a numinous theatricality. Ixion, bound to his eternally flaming wheel, is an image of both horror and exuberance that can still elicit a shudder of dread. It is arguably the same mythic sensibility of underworld suffering that brings meaning to a submissive strapped into a modern-day bondage wheel in a BDSM dungeon. In fact, the comparison highlights the connection between the power of myth and the contemporary fascination with bondage and discipline: it is the archetype's ability to captivate and fascinate that imbues BDSM experiences with a numinous quality rarely found in everyday life.

In the Nordic tradition, the mythic ash tree, Yggdrasil, appears as a symbol at the center of the cosmos, providing access to multiple dimensions of life and death.[76] It leads to sources of knowledge, wisdom, and prophecy. The god Odin hangs from Yggdrasil for nine nights. He sacrifices himself to look into the secret depths of the Earth and retrieve the runes, which give him mystic wisdom and great power. Like Inanna, Odin's ordeal becomes an initiation involving a confrontation with death, which results in an augmentation in knowledge, wisdom, and power. The fact that Odin's sacrifice is voluntary and self-inflicted bears particular relevance to contemporary BDSM. The consensual submissive posture of hanging through suspension play is well established and popular with many BDSM groups around the world. What many might overlook is the archetypal presence of the ordeal path. From the mythic perspective, the hanging submissive voluntarily makes an offering of the conscious personality to a process of transformation and growth. The archetypal relation between the hanging Norse god and the modern kinkster suspended at a local play party suggests that there is a deeper psychological significance to the practice. It carries a particular value for soul.

Mythology from around the world provides further examples of these themes of suffering, torment, torture, cruelty, submission, sacrifice, restraint, and physical hardship in the service of transformation and growth. These grim psychic elements form the point of convergence between the presence of the mythic and archetypal in the world of BDSM and the characteristics of BDSM that are present in the mythic and archetypal world of soul. By placing the world of BDSM in dialogue with the logos of soul, both are illuminated and clarified. Hillman was fond of quoting the Greek philosopher Plotinus: "All knowing comes by likeness."[77] So it is the aim of this book to facilitate a kind of psychological knowing that places the psyche as a reflective surface between the obscure regions of soul and the archetypal world of BDSM.

Notes

1 Corbin, H. (1972).
2 Moore, T. (1990/2022).
3 Ibid. (p. 3).
4 Cowan, L. (1982).
5 There are several outstanding books that provide a well-organized and comprehensive introduction to BDSM. The overview in this chapter does not attempt to reproduce what other authors have already accomplished. Readers seeking a detailed primer on BDSM terminology and activities should seek out one of these texts. For example, *The Leather Couch* by Stefani Goerlich (2021), *Becoming a Kink Aware Therapist* by Caroline Shahbaz and Peter Chirinos (2017), *Sexual Outsiders* by David Ortmann and Richard Sprott (2013), and *Ties That Bind* by Guy Baldwin (2003) are four excellent resources.
6 Oxford English Dictionary (n.d.).
7 It is customary practice within the BDSM community to capitalize roles designated as Dominant and to write roles designated as submissive in lower case (e.g., Top/bottom, Master/slave, Dom/sub, etc.). It is an editorial decision to respect the practice in this text.
8 Tupper, P. (2018).
9 Stein, S. K. (2021).
10 Ibid.
11 stein, d. (2016).
12 Stein, S. K. (2021, p. 23).
13 Ibid. (p. 47).

14 Ibid. (p. 41).
15 Ibid. (p. 52).
16 stein, d. (2016, p. 94).
17 Tupper, P. (2018, p. 166).
18 Ibid. (p. 169).
19 Stein, S. K. (2021, p. 62).
20 Ibid. (p. 62).
21 Ibid.
22 Ibid. (p. 130).
23 Tupper, P. (2018, p. 215).
24 Stein, S. K. (2021, p. 82).
25 Ibid. (p. 74).
26 Stein, S. K. (2021).
27 stein, d. (2016).
28 Stein, S. K. (2021, p. 167).
29 www.mast.net
30 National Coalition for Sexual Freedom (2021).
31 Stein, S. K. (2021).
32 Tupper, P. (2018).
33 Stein, D. (2000).
34 Switch, G. (2017).
35 Kaldera, R. (2016, p. vii).
36 James, E. L. (2015).
37 Stedman, A. (2015).
38 Marcus, S. (2015).
39 Shahbaz, C., & Chirinos, P. (2017).
40 Joyal, C. C., & Carpentier, J. (2016).
41 Krafft-Ebing, R. (1886/2011).
42 Freud, S. (1905/2000, p. 23).
43 Barker, M., Iantaffi, A., & Gupta, C. (2007).
44 Barker, M., Iantaffi, A., & Gupta, C. (2007); Kolmes, K., Stock, W., & Moser, C. (2006); Lawrence A. A., & Love-Crowell J. (2008); Shahbaz, C., & Chirinos, P. (2017).
45 Goerlich, S. (2021).
46 Beerschoten, K. V. (2017); Saketopoulou, A. (2014, 2019, 2020).
47 Shahbaz, C., & Chirinos, P. (2017, p. 25).
48 Kleinplatz, P., & Moser, C. (2004); Richters, J., De Visser, R. O., Rissel, C. E., Grulich, A. E., & Smith, A. (2008).
49 Sagarin, B., Cutler, B., Cutler, N., Lawler-Sagarin, K. A., & Matuszewich, L. (2009).
50 Ambler, J. K., Lee, E. M., Klement, K. R., Loewald, T., Comber, E. M., Hanson, S. A., Cutler, B., Cutler, N., & Sagarin, B. J. (2016, September 22).
51 Dietrich, A. (2003).
52 Hillman, J. (2004, p. 28).
53 von Sacher-Masoch, L. (1870/2000).
54 Jung, C. G. (1926/1981, p. 325 [*CW* 8, para. 618]).
55 Hillman, J. (1977).
56 Jung, C. G. (1934/1985, p. 149 [*CW* 16, para. 320]).
57 Jung, C. G. (1926/1981).
58 Hillman, J. (1975/1992, p. xvii, emphasis added).
59 Jung, C. G. (1957/1974, p. x).
60 Edinger, E. (1992, p. 3).
61 Jung, C. G. (1954/1990).
62 The terms *Master* and *slave* will be problematic for many readers in the present historical moment. The pervasive and insidious effects of systemic racism, especially the wide-rang-

ing injustices against Black people in the United States, are increasingly recognized as an extension of the historic atrocities of the transatlantic slave trade and the institution of human chattel slavery on the North American continent. BDSM practitioners who self-identify as Masters and slaves believe that the words have different connotations in the context of voluntary and consensual erotic servitude. However, the BDSM community is presently debating whether such recontextualizing is possible, given the profound multi-generational trauma associated with the words. An in-depth discussion of this complex and inevitably painful question will be part of Chapter 6.

63 Jacobi, J. (1957/1974).
64 Ibid.
65 Ellenberger, H. (1970, p. 724).
66 Corbett, L. (2007, pp. 12–13).
67 As cited in Cobb, N. (1992, p. 136).
68 Moore, T. (1989, p. 15)
69 Ibid. (p. 15).
70 Ibid. (p. 15).
71 Black, J. A., & Green, A. (1992).
72 Wolkstein, D., & Kramer, S. N. (1983).
73 Kaldera, R. (2006).
74 Perera, S. B. (1981).
75 Grimal, P. (1986); March, J. (2003).
76 Crawford, J. (2015).
77 Hillman, J. (1975/1992, p. 99).

References

Ambler, J. K., Lee, E. M., Klement, K. R., Loewald, T., Comber, E. M., Hanson, S. A., Cutler, B., Cutler, N., & Sagarin, B. J. (2016, September 22). Consensual BDSM facilitates role-specific altered states of consciousness: A preliminary study. *Psychology of Consciousness: Theory, Research, and Practice*. Advance online publication. http://doi.org/10.1037/cns0000097

American Psychiatric Association. (2013). *Diagnostic and statistical manual of mental disorders* (5th ed.). American Psychiatric Association.

Baldwin, G. (2003). *Ties that bind* (2nd ed.). Daedalus.

Barker, M., Iantaffi, A., & Gupta, C. (2007). Kinky clients, kinky counselling? The challenges and potentials of BDSM. In L. Moon (Ed.), *Feeling queer or queer feelings: Radical approaches to counselling sex, sexualities and genders* (pp. 106–124). Routledge.

Beerschoten, K. V. (2017). *The meaning of BDSM experiences*. Teneo.

Black, J. A., & Green, A. (1992). *Gods, demons and symbols of ancient Mesopotamia: An illustrated dictionary*. The British Museum Press.

Cobb, N. (1992). *Archetypal imagination: Glimpses of the Gods in life and art*. Lindisfarne Press.

Corbett, L. (2007). *Psyche and the sacred*. Spring Journal Books.

Corbin, H. (1972). Mundus Imaginalis or the imaginary and the imaginal. *Spring Journal*, 1–19.

Cowan, L. (1982). *Masochism a Jungian view*. Spring.

Crawford, J. (Ed.). (2015). Introduction. In *The poetic edda* (pp. ix–xxiv). Hackett.

Dietrich, A. (2003). Functional neuroanatomy of altered states of consciousness: The transient hypofrontality hypothesis. *Consciousness and Cognition*, *12*, 231–256. http://doi.org/10.1016/S1053-8100(02)00046-6

Edinger, E. (1992). *Ego and archetype*. Shambhala.

Ellenberger, H. F. (1970). *The discovery of the unconscious*. Basic Books.

Freud, S. (2000). *Three essays on the theory of sexuality* (J. Strachey, Trans.). Basic Books. (Original work published 1905)

Goerlich, S. (2021). *The leather couch clinical practice with kinky clients*. Routledge.

Grimal, P. (1986). *The dictionary of classical mythology* (A. R. Maxwell-Hyslop, Trans.). Blackwell.

Hillman, J. (1977). An inquiry into image. *Spring*, 1977, 62–88.

Hillman, J. (1992). *Re-visioning psychology*. HarperCollins. (Original work published 1975)

Hillman, J. (2004). *Archetypal psychology*. Spring. (Original work published 1983)

Jacobi, J. (1974). *Complex/archetype/symbol* (R. Manheim, Trans.). Bollingen Foundation. (Original work published 1957)

James, E. L. (2015). *Fifty shades of Grey*. Vintage Books.

Janus, S. S., & Janus, C. L. (1993). *The Janus report on sexual behavior*. John Wiley & Sons.

Joyal, C. C., & Carpentier, J. (2016). The prevalence of paraphilic interests and behaviors in the general population: A provincial survey. *The Journal of Sex Research, 54*(2), 161–171. http://doi.org/10.1080/00224499.2016.1139034

Jung, C. G. (1974). Foreword, by C. G. Jung (R. Manheim, Trans.). In J. Jacobi, *Complex/archetype/symbol* (pp. x–xi). Bollingen Foundation. (Original work published 1957)

Jung, C. G. (1981). Spirit and life (R. F. C. Hull, Trans.). In H. Read et al. (Eds.), *The collected works of C. G. Jung* (Vol. 8, 2nd ed., pp. 319–337). Princeton University. (Original work published 1926)

Jung, C. G. (1985). The practical use of dream-analysis (R. F. C. Hull, Trans.). In H. Read et al. (Eds.), *The collected works of C. G. Jung* (Vol. 16, 2nd ed., pp. 139–161). Princeton University. (Original work published 1934)

Jung, C. G. (1990). Archetypes of the collective unconscious (R. F. C. Hull, Trans.). In H. Read et al. (Eds.), *The collected works of C. G. Jung* (Vol. 9, Part 1, pp. 3–41). Princeton University. (Original work published 1954)

Kaldera, R. (2006). *Dark moon rising: Pagan BDSM and the ordeal path*. Asphodel.

Kaldera, R. (2016). Foreword. In P. Tupper (Ed.), *Our lives our history: Consensual Master/slave relationships from ancient times to the 21st century* (pp. vii–xiii). Perfectbound.

Kleinplatz, P., & Moser, C. (2004). Toward clinical guidelines for working with BDSM clients. *Contemporary Sexuality, 38*(6), 1, 4–5.

Kolmes, K., Stock, W., & Moser, C. (2006). Investigating bias in psychotherapy with BDSM clients. In P. Kleinplatz & C. Moser (Eds.), *Sadomasochism: Powerful pleasures* (pp. 301–324). Binghamton, NY: Haworth Press.

Krafft-Ebing, R. (2011). *Psychopathia sexualis* (F. S. Klaf, Trans.). Arcade Publishing. (Original work published 1886)

Lawrence, A. A., & Love-Crowell, J. (2008). Psychotherapists' experience with clients who engage in consensual sadomasochism: A qualitative study. *Journal of Sex & Marital Therapy, 34*, 67–85.

March, J. (2003). *Cassell's dictionary of classical mythology*. Sterling.

Marcus, S. (2015, February 16). 'Fifty Shades of Grey' isn't a movie about BDSM, and that's a problem. *Huffington Post*. www.huffingtonpost.com

Moore, T. (Ed.). (1989). *A blue fire*. HarperCollins.

Moore, T. (1990). *Dark Eros: The imagination of sadism*. Spring.

National Coalition for Sexual Freedom. (2021). American Law Institute project. https://9xj1d5.a2cdn1.secureserver.net/wp-content/uploads/2021/07/Summary-of-the-ALI-Project.pdf

Ortmann, D. M., & Sprott, R. A. (2013). *Sexual outsiders: Understanding BDSM sexualities and communities*. Rowman & Littlefield.

Oxford English Dictionary. (n.d.). *BDSM*. Retrieved August 5, 2017, from www.oed.com

Perera, S. B. (1981). *Descent to the goddess*. Inner City Books.

Richters, J., De Visser, R. O., Rissel, C. E., Grulich, A. E., & Smith, A. (2008). Demographic and psychosocial features of participants in bondage and discipline, "sadomasochism" or dominance and submission (BDSM): Data from a national survey. *Journal of Sexual Medicine, 5*(7), 1660–1668.

Sagarin, B., Cutler, B., Cutler, N., Lawler-Sagarin, K. A., & Matuszewich, L. (2009). Hormonal changes and couple bonding in consensual sadomasochistic activity. *Archives of Sexual Behavior, 38,* 186–200. http://doi.org/10.1007/s10508-008-9374-5

Saketopoulou, A. (2014). To suffer pleasure: The shattering of the ego as the psychic labor of perverse sexuality. *Studies in Gender and Sexuality, 15*(4), 254–268.

Saketopoulou, A. (2019). Draw to overwhelm: Consent, risk, and the re-translation of enigma. *Journal of the American Psychoanalytic Association, 67*(1), 133–167. http://doi.org/10.1177/0003065119830088

Saketopoulou, A. (2020). Risking sexuality beyond consent: Overwhelm and traumatisms that incite. *The Psychoanalytic Quarterly, 89*(4), 771–811. http://doi.org/10.1080/00332828.2020.1807268

Shahbaz, C., & Chirinos, P. (2017). *Becoming a kink aware therapist.* Routledge.

Stedman, A. (2015, June 10). 'Fifty Shades' spinoff 'Grey' copy reportedly stolen from publisher. *Variety.* http://variety.com

Stein, D. (2000). Safe, sane, consensual. *Leather Leadership Conference Library.* www.leatherleadership.org/library/safesanestein.htm.

stein, d. (2016). From S&M to M/s: How consensual slavery became visible in the gay leather community, 1950 to 1999. In P. Tupper (Ed.), *Our lives, our history consensual master/slave relationships from ancient times to the 21st century* (pp. 75–110). Perfectbound.

Stein, S. K. (2021). *Sadomasochism and the BDSM community in the United States kinky people unite.* Routledge.

Switch, G. (2017). Origin of RACK: RACK vs. SSC. *Ambrosio's BDSM Site.* www.evilmonk.org/a/rack.cfm

Tupper, P. (2018). *A lover's pinch: A cultural history of sadomasochism.* Rowman & Littlefield.

von Sacher-Masoch, L. (2000). *Venus in Furs* (J. Neugroschel, Trans.). Penguin Classics. (Original work published 1870)

Wolkstein, D., & Kramer, S. N. (1983). *Inanna, queen of heaven and earth.* Harper & Row.

2

A JUNGIAN PERSPECTIVE

Introduction

Jungian psychology offers BDSM a perspective oriented predominantly toward personal growth and inclusion, a refreshing contrast to the legacy of Krafft-Ebing's[1] emphasis on pathology. The Jungian perspective is particularly valuable in exploring the meaning and deeper psychological function of BDSM in the lives of its practitioners because his model of the psyche allows the troubling destructive and irrational impulses of the human soul to have a legitimate place in individual development.

The publication in 2009 of Jung's deeply personal manuscript, *The Red Book*, or *Liber Novus*, provided new insights into the origins of Jung's original perspectives. Partially a beautiful illustrated chronicle of dreams and fantasy-images, partially a work of self-analysis, and partially a stream-of-consciousness dialogue with the soul, *The Red Book* became the wellspring of many of his most important ideas. It contains numerous references to sadomasochism, slavery, and underworld ordeals, which he introduces as metaphors for the process of psychological transformation. The inclusion of such details in Jung's personal experiment with the deep psyche suggests that these original images offer an understanding of BDSM as an expression of soul.

There are aspects of Jungian psychology that may be problematic for a twenty-first-century audience. In many regards, Jung's work is solidly anchored in the values and attitudes of elite European society in the early

                    DOI: 10.4324/9781003223597-3

twentieth century. A cultural bias is particularly apparent in his treatment of gender, sexuality, and race as binary constructs. His understanding of gender presupposes that one is either male or female, and healthy normative sexuality is based on heterosexual attraction. Jung frequently compared the civilized (white) to the primitive (Black). In more recent years, the emergence of feminist, queer, and transgender voices and scholarship supporting anti-racism have introduced new more inclusive non-binary constructs of gender, sexuality, and race. These advances have challenged the biases of Western thought that are evident in Jung's thinking. There are aspects of BDSM culture that develop the notion of "queering" mainstream attitudes and beliefs by playing with cultural taboos and notions of self and other, particularly regarding experiences of authority and power. As shall be seen, the conscious othering that takes place in BDSM activities and relationships through the process of negotiation and consent marks a departure from the potentially catastrophic effects of non-consensual othering through social stigma, systemic oppression, and sexual assault. Despite the problematic aspects of Jung's psychology, his vision of psyche yields fresh insights into the deeper significance of BDSM and its psychological value.

The first section of this chapter summarizes the main differences between Freud's and Jung's views of sexuality. Jung developed his own ideas about psychic reality through his work on *The Red Book*, and a closer consideration of its medieval fantasy elements highlights a point of convergence with modern BDSM. Several major concepts from Jung's mature psychology developed from the years spent on his personal project, such as the individuation process, the shadow, and the *syzygy;* their relevance to BDSM will occupy the next part of the chapter. The question of Jung's legacy for our modern era and a discussion of the benefits and limitations of a Jungian approach will conclude the chapter.

Jung Versus Freud: Two Views on Sexuality and Libido

In 1912, Jung experienced one of the great crises of his life, as he and Sigmund Freud agreed to sever their relationship. The break had been developing for some time for both personal and professional reasons. Jung had risen to prominence within Freud's growing psychoanalytic community, serving as the president of the International Psychoanalytic Association in the same year that the two men split. Although Freud had regarded him as his psychological heir apparent, the younger Jung had from early on disagreed with some aspects of Freud's theories. In his late-life autobiography, Jung wrote that the divergence was particularly problematic regarding how the two men regarded the role of sexuality and libido.[2]

Freud's views on sexuality were central to his grand theory of psychological development.[3] In general, Freud described libido as a sexual drive, which is present from early infancy. Our sexuality begins in childhood and its development into adulthood is interwoven with the vicissitudes of our relationships with our early caregivers, particularly our mothers. The longings, fears, and resentments that inevitably arise from the irrevocable separation from our mothers become a lifelong desire to recapture the closeness and physical intimacy of that relationship. What his contemporaries regarded as perversions, Freud characterized as variations in sexual expression—a perspective that was less moralistic than that of his peers. He considered human sexuality to be fundamentally polymorphous (i.e., appearing in many forms), malleable, and divertible well beyond the constrictions of the socially accepted "normative" variation of heterosexual, genital, coital, reproductive intercourse. He held that, regardless of sex or gender, there are both active and passive aspects to human sexuality, such that sadomasochism is a given, a natural psychic force that exists within all of us. Like our sexuality in general, sadomasochism always has an unconscious aspect, which is sometimes lived out and other times manifests only in dreams and fantasies. Finally, Freud's concept of sublimation is particularly relevant to the practice of BDSM and kink. Because we are always open to sexual arousal, we learn to delay, substitute, and sublimate our urges and desires. Our capacity to express sexual longings in diverse ways draws our sexuality into relationship with the poetic and aesthetic functions of the psyche. We can recognize in the transgressive theatricality of kink and BDSM a sublimation of our innate sadomasochistic desires.

Even before he met Freud, Jung was developing a conceptualization of the psyche that envisioned a broader context than the personal narrative of one's developmental history. Jung considered Freud's ideas invaluable so far as they went but incapable of explaining elements of dreams, visions, and fantasy-images that presented psychic material beyond the life events of one individual.[4] Such images bear a resemblance to the symbols and themes in myths and legends around the world throughout history, a fact that Jung found impossible to ignore. Consequently, he formulated his theory of the collective unconscious, which asserts that the deeper layers of the psyche are not of a personal nature but emanate from a collective source of primordial images, the archetypes.[5] For Jung, the sex drive was an expression of an archetypal life force that carried deep symbolic meaning far beyond the particulars of an individual's developmental history.[6]

Libido for Jung is concerned with more than sexual drive: it is psychic energy that can find expression in a variety of ways. When Jung extended Freud's sexual model beyond personal development and biology to include an archetypal dimension, he was elaborating the notion of the sex drive's polymorphous character: libido can manifest through potent fantasy-images, through creativity and works of art, or through passionate convictions and pursuits to name a few possibilities.[7] The Jungian perspective on sexuality and libido extends the Freudian model's compatibility with the range of activities that make up the world of BDSM. Bondage and discipline, domination and submission, and sadism and masochism can be erotic pursuits without necessarily involving sexual gratification. For example, some Master/slave relationships do not involve any sexual contact between the partners—the focus is on other forms of service and control.[8]

In Jung's view, the fundamental problem of the Western attitude "is not sexuality per se, but the domestication of libido, which concerns sexuality only so far as it is one of the most important and most dangerous forms of libidinal expression."[9] Jung regarded sexuality as a creative force that rivals spirituality in its powerful effect on the psyche. In fact, he regarded the role of sex in "procreation, pregnancy, birth and childhood" as a source for early symbolic expressions of spirituality.[10] The origin of the word *fetish* illustrates Jung's insight. Prior to its contemporary association with kink, it originally referred to an object "believed to have magical or spiritual powers, especially . . . associated with animistic or shamanistic religious practices."[11] An ancient relationship between sexuality and spirituality is embedded in the etymology of modern fetishism. In addition, some serious practitioners of BDSM pursue a path of spiritual development through archetypal erotic discipline and suffering known as pagan BDSM.[12] Their practice further illustrates libido's intermediary role between spirituality and sexuality.

The Red Book, BDSM, and the Medieval Imagination

The crisis period that followed Jung's break with Freud lasted several years. It involved a significant reduction in his professional output while he re-examined what he believed to be fundamentally true about the psyche, based on his own lived experience and on observations he made working with patients. He referred to these years as his "confrontation with the unconscious."[13]

Beginning in October of 1913, Jung began having waking visions and dreams of some great calamity on the European continent: oceans of blood, images of murder, savage cruelty, and the deaths of thousands were among the horrific scenes he encountered from the non-physical dimension.[14] At first, Jung feared that these scenes presaged his own cataclysmic psychosis but then the dreams and visions came to an end with the outbreak of World War I. Jung concluded that his psyche had been under the influence of the collective unconscious. In response to a crisis that had developed both internally in his personal psyche and externally across the European continent, Jung began an extensive project of consciously working with the fantasy-images of his imagination and chronicling the results.

Jung meticulously recorded his dreams, and he worked in waking life with dream images as figures of the imagination. He rendered the encounters in highly detailed transcriptions and drawings. Based on these experiences, he developed a formal psychological practice he referred to as "active imagination."[15] As part of his own process, Jung eventually compiled his inner work into a modern illuminated manuscript that he called the *Liber Novus*. It was not until 2009 that it was published for the first time as *The Red Book* thanks to the painstaking archival scholarship of Sonu Shamdasani and his associates.

Of particular interest to an archetypal consideration of BDSM, *The Red Book* draws repeatedly upon themes and images of suffering, torture, domination, submission, and enslavement. For example, in the Liber Primus, Jung wrote:

> I had to recognize that I am only the expression and symbol of the soul. In the sense of the spirit of the depths, I am as I am in this visible world a symbol of my soul, and I am thoroughly a serf, completely subjugated, utterly obedient.[16]

Subjugation and obedience are familiar components of domination and submission. Here, Jung referenced the soul as the superior agent that dominated his conscious life. As an archetypal theme with roots that extend into the collective psyche, Jung found that the dynamic of domination and submission had psychological value for his own process of growth. Granted, that same dynamic practiced between consenting adults is of a different order than subjugating oneself to the necessities of the soul. However, Jung encountered an archetypal agent within the psyche that shapes the contours of both experiences in similar recognizable patterns.

Jung's reference to himself as a serf in the preceding quotation exemplifies the importance he placed on the Middle Ages as a historical era that continues to influence the Western psyche from within. In the Liber Secundus of *The Red Book*, he wrote, "I must catch up with a piece of the Middle Ages—within myself."[17] Perhaps he was responding to the medieval impulse when he adopted the archaic format of an illuminated manuscript to portray his own encounter with the soul. His fascination with the psychological effects of the medieval world went beyond the pages of *The Red Book*. From 1923 to 1955, he designed and constructed a medieval tower and dwelling, an abode without electricity or running water, where he would go for periods of reflection, writing, and self-renewal.[18]

Jung considered the succession of historical and cultural periods in the West from antiquity to the present as having an enduring effect on modern consciousness, although the Middle Ages were a period of particular interest for him. His statement, "I must catch up with a piece of the Middle Ages—within myself," represents his deeply held conviction that each of us carries the collective psychological history of our civilization as part of our inner life. In a rather exalted tone, which characterizes much of Jung's colloquy with the soul in *The Red Book*, he continued:

> I must begin early in that period when the hermits died out. Asceticism, inquisition, torture are close at hand and impose themselves. The barbarian requires barbaric means of education. My I, you are a barbarian. I want to live with you, therefore I will carry you through an utterly medieval Hell, until you are capable of making living with you bearable.[19]

Jung describes his conscious personality, his "I," as a barbarian, placing it in opposition to the potent wisdom and authority of the soul as the greater force of psychological development. Jung frequently critiqued the one-sided attitudes of the conscious personality in the West as a source of psychological imbalance, necessitating an equilibrating correction from the unconscious.[20] In the excerpt earlier, Jung addresses his own ego as if it were a disobedient submissive in need of severe corrective discipline from the Dominant soul.

Interestingly, the Middle Ages appear as a historicized metaphor for the travails of sadomasochism, domination, and submission not only in *The Red Book* but also in the modern world of kink. The imprint of the medieval imagination is readily apparent in the world of BDSM. Some commentators have chronicled the influence of World War II military fashion and post-war biker clubs on the look and style of leather culture,[21] but the Middle Ages seem to exert an even greater effect on the psyche of modern kink. The familiar BDSM elements of the dungeon, executioner's hood, chains, shackles, whips, floggers, racks, Saint Andrew's cross, fire play, knife play, blood play, or other methods of restraint and controlled suffering all find their source in collective fantasies of medieval life. Similar images of medieval castles, torture chambers, and the descent into "an utterly medieval Hell" also populate the pages of *The Red Book*.[22] The value placed on protocol, codes of conduct, and acts of domination and submission during the Middle Ages further demonstrates the medieval imprint on BDSM. For example, the strict adherence to chivalric code is a frequent theme in medieval literature and an archetypal forerunner of the martial discipline and strict rules of conduct in contemporary leather culture. The mysterious seductresses of medieval lore find an archetypal counterpart in the modern dominatrix. Today, an enchantress like Morgan le Fay sports a black leather corset and stiletto boots as she holds her errant knight in thrall and debates whether to lead him to paradise or disaster.

The devices of torture and execution that emerged from the medieval imagination are indeed horrific, as are the depictions of hell and its minions. They conjure images of other-worldly torment and terror: the flames of hell converge with the literal hot coals of the torture chamber; the fires of damnation lick at the feet of apostates tied to the stake in the cathedral square. Centuries before the Marquis de Sade's sexualized visions of controlled suffering, the calculated cruelty of the medieval dungeon, the public humiliation of the pillories and stocks, and the grim entertainment of public executions provided the Western psyche with historic reference points depicting the human impulse to torment, to degrade, and to annihilate other human beings.

The medieval fantasy of hell was also of interest to Jung. In the *Vision Seminars*, he offered an archetypal interpretation of the journey to hell as one version of a mythic descent to the Underworld, a place of origin for the soul. In Jung's analysis, the Christian concept of original sin asserts that man "is bad from the beginning and the place of his origin is hell." He continued:

> A terrible punishment in hell does not appeal to us, but for seventeen or eighteen hundred years our life has been a part of that formula and we naturally suffer from the psychological effect of such an education. There is no escape. We can be quite liberal in our point of view, atheists perhaps, but we cannot get away from it because it is in our blood. In our heads we are liberated from it but go a little farther down and we are right in the Middle Ages.[23]

The degradation fantasy takes us back to our fundament, a homecoming to the psychological origins of our own being at the headwaters of the Western psyche, a place that Christian theology designated as hell. It is an impulse of the soul in its natural rhythm to pull us back periodically into primal images of chaos, the yawning void, the paradoxical place from whence we came but where we do not exist or where we suffer eternally. Beyond its Christian connotations, a journey to hell is a degrading initiation. It is a return to the land of our psychological origins, where, as James Hillman put it, "the ego is a paltry thing."[24] Such an infernal homecoming is familiar to many who have found a sense of fulfillment and completion through the world of BDSM.

What concerned Jung regarding these brutal aspects of our medieval ancestors was that the historical progression of human reason drove their inhumanity into the unconscious. Cultural forces evolved that celebrated the triumph of logic over ignorance, superstition, and evil (think of the influences of Descartes, Bacon, and Locke on the trajectory of Western thought). When society represses ignorance, superstition, and evil as enduring aspects of the personal and collective psyches, the effect is potent and dangerous. For Jung, the great calamities of the twentieth century were the two world wars and the detonation of the atomic bomb.[25] Virtue and reason did not prevent these massive destructive human events.

Jung regarded the return of medieval psychic material as part of the back-and-forth movement of progression and regression that constitutes psychological growth.[26] One instance of the reappearance of the medieval imagination is in the modern world of BDSM and kink. On a personal level, most kinksters would surely laugh at the suggestion that their adoption of medieval tropes signifies a historical regression into the collective unconscious. Yet why not ask if the emergence of medieval material bears some broader psychological significance? The archetypal template hidden behind the images of the Dark Ages has resurfaced in a more adaptive form through the high play of contained, negotiated, and consensual BDSM. Artifacts of the medieval psyche now come forth in a de-literalized and less lethal iteration. Deeper than the physical endorphin rush, there is the necessity of the soul to inhabit and embody its own images. Collective medieval patterns give form to modern play. Beyond conscious awareness, kinksters are catching up with an archetypal piece of the Middle Ages within themselves.

The Red Book: Wellspring of Jungian Theory

The Red Book chronicled a progression from soulless despair to an encounter with vital autonomous forces in the unconscious that are more powerful than the conscious personality. In the end, Jung arrived at a conscious attitude of greater understanding and acceptance. In the decades that followed its creation, Jung developed the inherent meaning of these original images into a more sophisticated and coherent language to describe the psyche and its processes.[27] The fact that these images had a seminal influence on Jung's mature psychology makes their correlation with the images and themes of BDSM especially intriguing.

Shamdasani has identified key elements of Jungian psychology that had their origins in the fantasy writings of *The Red Book*. Specifically, the concepts of individuation, differentiation, and the shadow all evolved from what Jung referred to as "my most difficult experiment."[28] The Jungian concepts of individuation, the shadow, and the *syzygy* contribute to a soul-centered understanding of BDSM.

Individuation and Differentiation

When Jung began the conversation with his soul that ultimately became the *Liber Novus*, he had reached a point of crisis in his own life. He had attained a pinnacle of professional achievement and acclaim, yet he felt himself alienated from his inner world. He could not find a way forward to the next step in his personal psychological development. What emerged in his writing was a discourse between contrasting forces he referred to as "the spirit of this time" and "the spirit of the depths."[29] He made a similar distinction in his autobiography between his No. 1 and No. 2 personalities.[30] Personality 1 was socially adapted to the concerns of modern life, and Personality 2 was more mysterious and timeless in nature. He found that the demands of his soul were in opposition to the ambitions and convictions of his ego. Where the ego wanted progress, the soul insisted on regression; where he sought sense and reason, the soul insisted on nonsense and the irrational; outward distinction and acclaim lay in opposition to the soul's demand for humiliation and submission. Opposition and tension between contrary forces of conscious and unconscious attitudes became a cornerstone of Jung's mature psychology.[31] To move forward in life, he had to face the demands of his unconscious and establish an ongoing dynamic relationship with its contents.

Jung learned to collaborate with the unconscious and to integrate the lessons and perspectives it provided through the process of active imagination, which involved treating fantasy-images as real and interacting with them. He viewed the psyche as traveling a trajectory of growth toward increasing understanding, knowledge, and wholeness—a trajectory (never fully complete) unique to each individual leading toward an authentic amalgam of conscious and unconscious material. Jung called it the individuation process, and the Self, the word that designates the numinosity associated with the wholeness of individuation, was its ultimate aim.[32] Jung believed he had made a discovery that applied to human development in general, and he hoped that his psychology would provide individuals with the guidance they lacked in contemporary life to consciously support their own psychological development.[33]

In one of the first major works Jung published after the years of immersion in the deep unconscious, he presented the concept of individuation: "In general, it is the process by which individual beings are formed and differentiated; in particular, it is the development of the psychological individual as a being distinct from the general collective psychology."[34] He elaborated the concept several years later: "Individuation means becoming an 'in-dividual,' and, in so far as 'individuality' embraces our innermost, last, and incomparable uniqueness, it also implies becoming one's own self. We could therefore translate individuation as 'coming into selfhood' or 'self-realization.'"[35] Individuation involves making the unconscious conscious. Regarding the question of whether one reaches a final destination in the individuation process, Jung tended to assert that the psyche's journey toward wholeness occurred throughout the lifespan.[36]

As his own process of individuation unfolded while he worked on *The Red Book*, Jung discovered that the images of the soul were diverse and distinct in their presentation and perspective. Part of the work of individuation, then, was to differentiate between the images and to distinguish between dynamics linked to the particulars of personal history and those emanating from the deeper archetypal levels of the psyche.[37] Reflecting on his work, Jung wrote, "I took great care to try to understand every single image, every item of my psychic inventory, and to classify them scientifically—so far as this was possible—and, above all, to realize them in actual life."[38] Jung's effort to understand and realize (i.e., integrate into his own life) the unique characteristics of each image became a technique, which Shamdasani has called "the hermeneutic treatment of creative fantasies."[39] In the Jungian lexicon, the technique is related to the task of differentiation.

The concepts of individuation and differentiation are of fundamental importance for all individuals, but they are particularly relevant for understanding how BDSM and kink may contribute to the psychological growth of practitioners. Alternative sexualities are by their nature countercultural and subversive.[40] The history of the psychological profession's pathologizing of sadomasochism for so many years is part of a larger pattern of social stigma marginalizing kinky people. It is not necessarily easy for an individual to embrace the surprising delights of sexual arousal or the emotional thrill of fantasies that transgress what is socially designated as proper or acceptable. In the individuation process, an inner imperative guides us toward that which is unique, perhaps even odd or unconventional within us, to form a more authentic version of ourselves. It is the soul making itself known through its necessities. At some point, a kinky person acknowledges that he or she cannot feel authentic or whole without allowing deeper truths to become a part of life.

The emotional upheaval that accompanies the decision to live one's inner truth is a familiar experience for those who find their identity through kink and BDSM. For some, it is in the authority dynamics of these relationships that they feel most fully who they are meant to be.

Richard Levine, who openly identifies as a slave, described his experience in his autobiography: "the challenges . . . the ways that I am different from the societal norm, have been the very things that have sparked the greatest spiritual growth and soul evolution in this lifetime."[41] However, answering the call to be a more authentic and integrated person can involve working through painful feelings of guilt and shame (a symbolic journey to hell). Jung's conceptualization of the individuation process and the technique of differentiation offer a means of understanding the sometimes-turbulent emotions that occur.

Jung observed that the demand for adaptation in one's life comes in two forms: the necessity to adapt to external social demands and the necessity to adapt to the conditions of the inner life.[42] Jung characterized opposition as the essence of his struggle.[43] He asserted that the individuation process begins with guilt because one can no longer conform to the outer rules and injunctions of society.[44] For BDSM participants who find the discovery of their passion occurs with some measure of guilt and self-questioning, Jung's model offers a compassionate explanation. There is, perhaps for all of us, a split between the external demands of our social lives and the internal demands of the soul, but it may be particularly intense for BDSM practitioners.

The emergence from the depths of the particular image or images that demand an adaptation in one's outer life prompted Jung to develop the technique of differentiation. In the practice of BDSM, differentiation is a relatively novel psychological concept that could help participants distinguish between the psychic factors that make up their personal identity and the deeper archetypal nature of what they are enacting. Here, the importance of a poetic basis of mind discussed in Chapter 1 comes into play. For example, someone who self-identifies as a submissive can easily conflate the particulars of his or her personal identity with the archetype of *the submissive*. A poetic basis of mind allows both to be true: one is both a unique, psychologically complex person and also a true physical embodiment of *the submissive*, the archetypal figure that has forever been a part of the human psyche in the collective unconscious. The archetypal figure emerges from the depths and seizes us, captivates us, and has the potential to guide us along the path of individuation. (Perhaps the way of the archetypal submissive is the catalyst for personal growth and transformation for all of us.) *The Red Book* invokes the attitude of submission in relationship to the soul as a necessity of individuation: "I have had to recognize that I must submit to what I fear; yes, even more, that I must even love what horrifies me."[45] And further on he wrote, "You are a slave of what you need in your soul,"[46] meaning that we are enslaved to those qualities lying dormant or discarded in the soul, whose inclusion could help make us whole. However, archetypal possession and over-identification are risks that accompany one's submission to the soul.

Jung cautioned that over-identification with an archetypal image constitutes a fusion of the personal and collective levels of the psyche, which can induce extreme feelings of superiority or inferiority.[47] The fusion of psychic levels explains the intense feelings that can overtake participants in authority-imbalanced relationships and transform their personalities in exaggerated ways: Masters can become drunk on power and control, which they wield indiscriminately; slaves can sink deep into spirals of shame and worthlessness without some form of internal anchor to modulate the effects. Such is the power of the archetypes that live behind the dynamics of the relationship. They can take over other dimensions of the individual personality, creating a one-sided stereotyped version of one's identity. Ironically, literalization is the danger that occurs with possession: as the psyche grows rigid and inflexible, the archetype circumscribes and dictates one's self-image as a literal fact.

Differentiation, with its poetic basis of mind that can articulate both the personal and the archetypal, facilitates a sophistication of identity through deep, intense encounters with archetypal reality: one embodies the characteristics of the archetype without the loss of psychological perspective that occurs with archetypal possession. It is particularly important in authority-imbalanced relationships because a form of psychic differentiation has already occurred formally and structurally between the two partners. Metaphorically speaking, the psychic voltage of these relationships can be extremely high. Differentiation helps distinguish between personal and collective psychic material, which allows them to coexist peacefully, thereby easing the flow of archetypal energy. Master David Schacter acknowledged Masters and slaves harbor ideals and aspirations gleaned from erotic fiction (a form rich in archetypal figures) but offered a word of caution: "Words and images from fiction tell us who we are and how we should interact with each other. They create an ideal for our relationships, and that's ok if it is tempered by reality."[48] Learning how to differentiate between the reality of everyday life and the reality of the psyche is an essential part of the individuation process.

The Shadow

Jung's concept of the shadow helps explain the power and fascination that BDSM holds for so many. As an archetype that is active on both personal and collective levels, the shadow participates in the fearsome imaginative fantasies of practitioners and in the social taboos that themselves become the source material for various forms of kink. If the conscious personality is unable to work with shadow material and to come to terms with its destructive aspects, its appearance is potentially devastating. Jung encountered the shadow during his personal crisis, and it established for him one of the major principles of his approach to the psyche: that the tension of opposing forces generates psychic growth. In the case of the visions that he came to see as foretelling World War I, the tension was between his conscious personality and the primal bellicose forces of the collective unconscious, which threatened to engulf him. Jung imagined the psyche as heavily populated with binaries in opposition: conscious versus unconscious, inner versus outer, subjective versus objective, order versus chaos, reason versus nonsense, masculine versus feminine, spirit versus matter, etc. Jung posited that the dynamic tension between opposing psychic forces leads to a transcendent synthesis of the polarities, which is a catalyst for psychological growth.[49] One of the most important pairs in opposition is the adaptive personality (the persona) versus the shadow.

The Red Book describes Jung's encounter with the shadow on both the personal and collective levels. Throughout his discourse with the soul, he asserted that all he encountered, even that which was horrific and repugnant, was a disowned part of his inner world. Reflecting on the image of a slain hero, he wrote, "I myself am a murderer and murdered, sacrificer and sacrificed. The upwelling blood streams out of me."[50] However, he went on to connect his inner visions to the collective carnage and bloodshed that was synchronistically occurring across the European continent: "You all have a share in the murder. . . . Your blood will stream forth. The peoples demonstrate this at the present time in unforgettable acts, that will be written with blood in unforgettable books for eternal memory."[51] Jung took on the difficult psychological task of recognizing and taking ethical responsibility for the murderous and barbaric aspects of his own psyche, as well as the insight that the object of his hatred was also a projection of some disowned part of himself. Though banished from consciousness, these disowned parts continued to function in the unconscious, reappearing in visions and nightmare images and through daytime projections onto perceived enemies. Simultaneously, he saw those same forces waging destruction on the European collective, which imagined itself rational, refined, and civilized. The war had unleashed the destructive impulses of the collective unconscious upon a continent turned against itself. *The Red Book* documents the process of psychological growth that occurs with the reclamation and integration of the disowned soul.

Jung converted his insights into the formal concept of the shadow, an image that suggests that the light of consciousness always casts a shadow of unconscious material. The person we imagine ourselves to be is only part of who we really are. The values espoused by a society are only part of how it actually operates. Jung described the shadow as connecting the hidden and inferior aspects of the personal unconscious to our collective evolutionary origins, but he also asserted that the shadow holds potentially beneficial qualities that a person has not yet developed.[52] The integration of shadow material is one of the primary and most arduous tasks of the individuation process.[53]

The inherently transgressive nature of BDSM and kink suggests a vital connection to the Jungian shadow. On a meta-level, BDSM has always been about the recuperation and synthesis of what the collective has disowned and discarded. Leopold von Sacher-Masoch published *Venus in Furs* in 1870, recounting the protagonist's sublime obsession to be humiliated and enslaved by a powerful, beautiful woman.[54] In novels like *Justine*, Sade created fictions showcasing libertine pleasures of extravagant cruelty, sexual abuse, and torture.[55] The countercultural elements in the works of both authors are overt: societal values such as human dignity, benevolence, innocence, fairness, reason, and compassion are turned on their heads. The shadow side of the collective psyche appears in their place through the salacious and wicked misadventures of their protagonists.

Although the modern BDSM movement draws inspiration from these iconic fictions, practitioners today differentiate contemporary play from such works. The emphasis on safety and well-being through negotiation and consent underscores the importance of personal responsibility and self-determination, values that are generally affirmed by the collective.

Unlike her modern counterparts, Justine never had the option of a safe word. Despite these differences, the tension between the conscious personality and its shadow activates an archetypal taproot that travels through these fictions and into their realization in modern-day play spaces and relationships.

In many cases, it is the shadow that compels a person to start experimenting with bondage, sadomasochism, or authority transfer. Sometimes people are not able to say why they are drawn to these activities and dynamics other than to say that it brings them happiness, pleasure, and excitement. Some might say that they had felt incomplete until they found themselves in a BDSM dungeon. Others say that they felt a need to explore their destructive side, which comes closer to acknowledging the shadow: what attracted them was some hidden part of themselves that was not easily expressed or casually revealed. In a 2009 interview, Levine described his experience of shadow integration: "Going into those dark, shadowy places and integrating them is how I achieve wholeness. When parts of me are not experienced, when they're pushed away or pushed down, there's not an experience of wholeness."[56] BDSM provides a structured container to begin to explore hidden and neglected aspects of the personal psyche.

The presence of the shadow in the world of BDSM extends beyond the personal dimension. Beyond the disowned parts of the personality that people refer to as "my shadow," there is the objective archetypal Shadow. It is appropriate to designate the Shadow of the depths with a capital "S" because it is a primordial autonomous figure, urging the imagination into its own obscurity, inspiring somber fantasies, and giving form to what emerges as a reflection of itself. The shadowlands of the soul give rise to collective forms and images that guide the imagination back toward a homeland for the hidden and the unknown. The world of BDSM incorporates elements of the collective Shadow through the unconscious medieval elements previously discussed: the play space for the scene is a dimly lit dungeon, hoods and masks conceal and transform daytime identities, the instruments of pleasure resemble instruments of torture, and black is the preferred color for one's wardrobe. But in kink, the image par excellence of the Shadow is unquestionably the full-body latex bondage suit (more popularly referred to as a gimp suit).[57]

A submissive concealed in a hooded full-body black latex suit is among the most iconic images from the world of BDSM. It is not unusual to see it appear as a meme in pop culture that is instantly recognizable and disconcerting. All distinguishing characteristics that make up a personal identity have been erased. The suit effaces the personal by covering over the physical—it is a rigorous exercise in objectification taken to its extreme. The person of the submissive transformed into a property object belonging to the Dom is the Shadow's response to Western culture's privileging of self-reliance, personal responsibility, independence, individuality, and ability. As an exercise in negation and erasure, the image poses the unthinkable questions: What remains of "you" when you are no longer a person? When you let go of the vestiges of identity, where do "you" go? What happens to a personal relationship when the construct of the person disappears? What happens to the psyche when it is unshackled from the stories you tell yourself and others about the person you think you are? In a personal communication, a self-identified slave familiar with the experience of being in a bondage suit offered the following:

> Nothing is more sublime or divine connecting to the Self than erasing the ego and its sense of self. What happens from an interior perspective when the [submissive] is led around on a chain is that all senses are heightened beyond the egoic mind, you are left with an aesthetic orientation. If you think you have to be in control in order to orient to the world, you've had it. But if you're in a state of deep submission and you trust the person pulling you along then all of your senses are focused on them, which takes you out of yourself and leaves you in a place that's beyond the ego mind. You're kind of in your limbic system. And it heightens a sense of selflessness in a really deep state of submission, which can spiral you into this sense of Self oneness-connection with the senses that are left. It's connection at least to the person leading you if not to a state of being bigger than the encased body.

From the perspective of the soul, such an experience has value because it exposes the unexamined shadow of egoic consciousness as well as the biases of our collective thinking. The passage earlier illustrates the pleasure of surrender that can accompany submission. In his autobiography, Jung described the resolve it required for his own act of submission in letting his mind "drop" into the depths of the unconscious, an act that represented his initiation into the individuation process.[58] Such submission requires courage and strength—it is not to be construed as weakness.

For the submissives who find the truest expression of their nature in the negation of identity that comes with the skintight containment of the latex suit, the gesture of submission is an immersive descent into the collective Shadow. For the Dom or Master, it is no less an act of psychological value to claim ownership of the gimp and face the collective Shadow, which challenges social injunctions against degrading, objectifying, or owning another human being. In the *Vision Seminars*, Jung mentioned the ancient Greek image of the *synopados*, "the one that comes with me and is behind me."[59] One could not hope to find a better embodiment of the *synopados* than the modern-day skintight silhouette of the submissive following behind on the leash of his Master or Mistress, or chained up in the dungeon like an undiscovered self, a human shadow both connected and concealed.

The current popularity of BDSM, which has brought enthusiasts together to create communities, a shared culture, and a movement, demonstrates the collective aspect of what is occurring. On a larger social level, the Shadow is using BDSM to bring forth the difficult truths of our collective nature: despite what we would like to believe about ourselves and our society, at times, we are cruel, we are destructive, we enjoy inflicting suffering, we find pleasure in inequality and feeling superior, some of us enjoy seizing control and others enjoy relinquishing it, sometimes we seek out abuse and enjoy it, sometimes we wish somebody else would just take control, or we imagine sinking into nonexistence to find something beyond ourselves.

BDSM practitioners explore the truth of the Shadow within a structured system that protects personal safety and well-being and affirms personal responsibility and self-determination. In other cultures and in other historical periods, such truths were the subject of spiritual practices and rituals, and in other instances, these same energies emerged unstructured and uncontained in the gross inhumanity and violence of one social group against another. These psychological forces are clearly at work in injurious ways on an unconscious level in society today. BDSM is a social movement that acknowledges the reality of these forces and has the capacity to metabolize them on a conscious level. In the negotiated and consensual relationships of BDSM, the Shadow emerges like a dimly lit reflecting pool whose surface mirrors the collective figures of the hidden, the repugnant, and the unspeakable.

The archetype of the Shadow is capable of terrible chaos, violence, and destruction when it is not given proper recognition as a part of psychic reality. For Jung, the challenge of facing and integrating the reality of the shadow was not only a psychological concern; it was also an ethical concern. It became a matter of social health and well-being that each person takes responsibility for the unfinished work with the aspects of the psyche that the conscious personality repressed and denied.

Syzygy

In the epilogue to *The Red Book*, Jung wrote that he discontinued working on it, as he grew increasingly interested in the psychological significance of alchemy.[60] In the images of medieval and Renaissance alchemical treatises, Jung now found a visual language that described the very psychological concepts he was formulating through his own inner work. Whereas others saw a failed science in alchemy's pursuit of turning base metals into gold, Jung saw a forerunner of modern psychology. A theme of particular importance shared between alchemy and Jung's model of the individuation process is that the tension held between opposites serves as the primary agent of transformation and growth.[61] Alchemists frequently represented the principle through the heterosexual pairing of male and female, often depicted as king and queen, or the *syzygy*, the primordial opposition of sun and moon.[62]

The field of alchemy developed over time along divergent paths, one pursuing the scientific inquiry into the nature of physical matter and the other an esoteric pursuit of spiritual transformation.[63] The image of a divine marriage between king and queen could simultaneously represent the synthesis of two physical substances and the union of opposing forces in the soul of the alchemist. In the image of the *syzygy*, Jung believed he had found an early symbol for psychological integration of the opposites.

Hillman built on Jung's understanding of the *syzygy* by arguing that opposition is only one possible expression or mode of the psyche's innate binary patterns.[64] What Jung had characterized as the tension between opposites, Hillman represented as a tandem or dialectical pairing that placed two elements in perpetual relationship, one clarifying the nature of the other. The notion of the *syzygy* as a tandem provides a means to reflect on the nature of BDSM relationships and the potential psychological value found there. There is no Dominant without a submissive, no Sir without a boy, no Master without a slave. As tandems, they do not occur so much in opposition as in dialectical tension. They operate as counterparts rather than opposites. One cannot exist without the other, and the loss of one negates the functional identity of the other.[65]

As a *syzygy*, these pairs pass through various modes of expression with a range of attitudes and affects: the Mistress and her slave can be connected in attitudes of base degradation, submissive tenderness, domestic servitude, fearsome possession, or the stillness of deep mental and physical control; but in each instance, it is their connection as counterparts forming a unit that defines and clarifies who and what each one is. The relationship itself becomes the transcendent synthesis of the two roles, which Jung described as the engine of psychological transformation.[66] Due to the emphasis placed on negotiation and consent, *BDSM activities involve a conscious othering of the partner*. The explicit agreement to form a tandem between self and other is a unique feature that distinguishes alternative sexualities from other social situations that turn the Other into a problem. The specter of the Other may bedevil race relations, encounters with diverse genders, sexual politics, socioeconomic injustice, or other examples of power inequality in society; but in the world of BDSM, the Other is a source of pleasure and a necessity for the scene to take place.

In voluntary, consensual submission to a Dominant partner, a *syzygy* is formed that transforms the dynamics of injustice and oppression that normally occur within non-consensual othering. The element of conscious consent is the psychological pivot point that distinguishes BDSM authority transfer from unconscious and non-consensual enactments of oppression and sociopathy. In fact, kink pushes its own limits by venturing into the most provocative and taboo issues of collective oppression in the form of race play, age play, and financial domination to name three examples. Here, the conscious consensual othering of the BDSM *syzygy* draws energy from collective social tensions. For many, these tensions generate discomfort and controversy, which is part of the thrill for kinksters. The world of kink draws upon the raw material of the collective shadow and reconstitutes it in a conscious, consensual container, where it can be held with intention to explore otherness in a new way that is not tainted by projection, exploitation, unconscious prejudice, or overt malice. Referencing BDSM's novel approach to power, Kaldera wrote about Master/slave relationships: "After thousands—perhaps tens of thousands—of years of human beings doing power-over in personal relationships astoundingly badly, here we are at least trying to do it well, something that has never been done before."[67] The intentional relationship with the Other as a counterpart in tandem to the partner creates a container for the difficult necessities of the soul to emerge, to reveal themselves, and to play themselves out in the scene and in negotiated life situations.

Jung's psychology invites a further nuanced consideration of the psychological dynamics behind domination and submission in BDSM relationships. Within Jungian psychology, the concept of the *syzygy* is principally seen as an inside job, as an intrapsychic reality. It refers to a union of the disparate elements, conscious and unconscious, of one's own soul. In an authority transfer, the psyche of the Dominant partner shelters an inner submissive, and within the submissive, there is a corresponding inner Dominant. For Jungian psychotherapists, the concept is not novel. Jung illustrated the paradigm in his essay *The Psychology of the Transference*, in which the alchemical king and queen are related to each other both consciously and unconsciously.[68] The royal union served as a metaphor for the human psyche, in which each of us implicitly carries a contrasexual figure in the unconscious that corresponds dialectically to the conscious personality. Jung referred to these gendered figures of the psyche as *anima* for men and *animus* for women.[69] In the clinical setting, Jungians are also familiar with the notion that the healing agent in the therapeutic relationship is not the therapist per se but the newly awakened *inner healer* in the unconscious of the patient.[70] Practitioners of BDSM who identify as Dominant or as submissive might assert that the truest expression of their nature occurs in the negotiated transfer of power and authority with their partner. The identity they cherish is associated with the conscious personality. Yet Jung's psychology considers the unconscious nature of the relationship.

For Doms to be effective in relationship with a sub, there needs to be an empathic connection that allows them to calibrate the stress and strain imposed on the partner to an optimal degree so that the submissive is challenged in endurance and dedication but not to the point of extinguishing the ardent desire to submit and please. For submissives to be effective in relationship with a Dom, there needs to be an empathic connection that enables them to anticipate the needs and desires of the partner so that an exquisite symbiosis occurs between the submissive's service and the Dom's will. Drawing directly from Jung's concept of the anima and animus as the complementary contrasexual figures of the unconscious, kink expert Master Patrick Califia addressed the internal representation of the Other:

> I believe the Master needs more than a dominant ideal or role model to guide him in developing his craft. I believe it is essential for an intuitive Master to have an internalized archetype of the slave, just as the anima is essential to the well-balanced male psyche, and the animus protects and nurtures women. This Slave Consultant is the source of my compassion, the compass that guides my [apparent] cruelty, the pressure that drives me into my possession and allows me to savor their surrender. It is the bridge between us, and when a slave has displeased me, it is that internalized notion of ultimate servitude that intercedes for them and mediates on their behalf.[71]

In the Master/slave *syzygy*, both partners need to establish a connection with an inner archetypal representation of the other to function in tandem as a unit. Califia indicates that the scene is psychologically significant for both the Master and the slave by virtue of coming to know the inner representation of each person's archetypal counterpart. It is not that one person functions as the Dominant and the other as the submissive. As a *syzygy*, both people are inhabiting both roles (and archetypally, both roles are inhabiting both people).

Conclusion: Jung's Legacy

Jung's analytical psychology offers a multi-dimensional vision of the psyche that provides what Stein has called a "map of the soul."[72] Jung's map imagines a complex protean system of images, emotions, ideas, and dreams that are continually interacting between dimensions of the conscious and unconscious minds. Through his own personal crisis and subsequent work on *The Red Book*, Jung formulated an approach to the psyche that respects the mystery of the human mind in its irrational, chaotic aspects by recognizing the role played by disorganization in psychological growth. Consistent with his formulation of the psyche as an expression of nature,[73] Jung regarded sexuality as part of his broader conceptualization of libido: a life-affirming instinctual energy that can stimulate the individuation process.[74] Our sexual lives bridge the divide between the unconscious and conscious dimensions of the psyche.

The recognition of sexuality as a bridge between biological instincts and psychological symbol formation has remained a part of Jung's legacy that subsequent generations of analysts have done little to develop.[75] Back in 1960, Hillman noted:

> The step that Jung took has still to be taken by many even now. Jung saw that instinct has an imaginal aspect, a mythic factor, and that therefore the sexual is also an activity of the imagination, a psychological expression; the sexual is a way the soul speaks.[76]

When the soul speaks, it is the logos of psyche that comes forth to create psychology. The world of BDSM provides the soul with the opportunity to speak freely in its twisted erotic richness, and Jung's psychology provides a framework and a vocabulary to articulate the value found there. The value in question concerns the vitality and meaning that comes from living as a whole person. Along with potential benefits, there are risks that can occur in BDSM relationships, most notably when partners fail to properly negotiate scenes or when limits are violated.[77] From a Jungian perspective, such cases signal the absence of psychological work on shadow integration and differentiation.

The individuation process is a journey toward wholeness. In the modern era, the sense of apathy, fatigue, and emptiness that so many feel corresponds to Jung's understanding of what catalyzes the individuation process: there is a realization that too much of one's soul has been sacrificed to accommodate the demands of social conventions.[78] Jung said, "If one only lives a half or a third of life, what is the use of living? What is its meaning? Life only has meaning when it is really lived."[79] BDSM presents an opportunity for individuals to reclaim discarded parts of the inner life that are countercultural in nature yet psychologically necessary for them to gain self-knowledge and move toward becoming a whole person. In the Jungian paradigm, wholeness is a greater ethical mandate than goodness. Jung's student Erich Neumann developed a clear articulation of the ethical dimension of depth psychology in the aftermath of World War II and the horrors of the Holocaust.[80] In seeking to make psychological sense out of a seemingly civilized world gone mad, he argued that an ethics based on moral goodness and reason had not held back the ferocious primitive brutality of national socialism in Germany or the corresponding acts of annihilation by

Allied forces. The call to be psychologically whole requires a reclamation and integration of one's projected shadow to own the destructive potential of one's own nature. Part of Jung's legacy is to recognize shadow integration as an ethical call to engage responsibly and seriously with the unconscious.

The work of shadow integration involves a struggle Jung characterized as holding the tension of the opposites. In so doing, conscious and unconscious aspects of the psyche are held together, and a living symbol is generated, which promotes the individual's maturation and sophistication.[81] The alchemical image of the king and queen united in holy union, historically known as the *hieros gamos*, or *syzygy*, has been one of the privileged symbols of the process.[82] However, in the new millennium, challenges to conventional thinking about binary constructs such as gender and sexuality call into question the use of difference to designate opposition (e.g., we speak of the *opposite* sex despite evidence that both biology and gender identity occur along a spectrum). Jung's reliance upon a binary model to explain the dynamism of the psyche merits scrutiny from more recent trends in thinking about gender, sexuality, and race in the twenty-first century.

BDSM has evolved in tandem with larger postmodern trends in queer culture, which celebrate the interrogation of normativity, particularly regarding gender and sexuality).[83] Kink finds pleasure in what could be described as *queering the conventional*, which can sometimes include thwarting assumptions about identity, gender, sexuality, eroticism, power, and authority. Even the adoption of traditional patriarchal structures in some BDSM relationships, such as heterosexual pairs in which the woman is submissive and the man is Dominant, allows for an element of personal agency and choice that is more often missing in so-called conventional patriarchal relationships: both people make a conscious decision to participate in the exchange of authority as a path of pleasure, self-realization, and fulfillment (in some cases, couples in more normative patriarchal structures exercise a similar degree of personal agency and choice, so the distinction here does not designate exclusivity). Power and authority in such a situation are less susceptible to unconscious shadow forces, which can indulge hostile destructive impulses. In negotiated relationships, authority that has been surrendered is authority that can be reclaimed. A hetero-normative Dom/sub couple enjoys the theatricality of enacting a patriarchal mythology. In effect, they are queering the patriarchy. Is Jung's estimation of opposition as an engine of psychological development still relevant in such an instance? What if one member of the couple identifies as non-binary and the other as a gay trans man? A theory of contrasexual figures situated in the personal unconscious founders against the subjectivity of such queer identities.

Kink, with its penchant for queering the conventional, resists the temptation to simplify or generalize itself and what it represents. For a kinkster, almost anything and everything is fair game as an opportunity to turn an unconscious habit of mind upside down to expose the germ of a new fetish underneath. Ropes, feet, shoes, uniforms, business suits, fantasy costumes, superheroes, robots, furries, monsters, vampires, and human dolls all find a niche of specialization in the fetishes of kink. With a poetic basis of mind, a fetish offers the opportunity to play with social conventions in unconventional ways (the caveat is, of course, that the pursuit of pleasure remains supple and not grow into a rigid, joyless compulsion—one of the warning signs of an archetypal possession). On a meta-level, kink calls into question how we collectively address the specter of the Other, which raises one further concluding thought.

Jungian scholar Renos Papadopoulos has argued that, although Jung never developed a systematic theory of the Other per se, his entire opus can be regarded as articulating a "problematic of the Other."[84] Coming to terms with the potent psychological figure of the Other was a recurring theme for Jung. Throughout his work, Jung addresses the presence of the Other as a psychological force that contributes both to conflict and growth in the individual. His concept of the Self could be regarded as the archetype of all archetypes, the psyche's ultimate symbol of wholeness, capable of holding together all aspects of the soul, illuminated and obscure, known and unknown. Papadopoulos pointed out that its diversity makes the Self paradoxically "the ultimate Other."[85] It anticipates a wholeness of a higher order as a future possibility "to transcend all existing oppositions."[86] The archetype of the Self presents a dialectic between opposition as difference and opposition as completion. The capacity of the ultimate Other both to affirm and to transcend opposites provides a partial answer to the question of Jung's relevance regarding BDSM's penchant for queering and de-literalizing cultural constructs.

The queering of authority and power in BDSM suggests an alternative paradigm for engaging these potent archetypes. Authority-transfer relationships occur in a liminal de-literalized zone in which the couple experiences power and authority as both real and unreal—a living symbol not of a binary based on power-over or power-against but of mutual consent and a gifting of domination and submission as offerings freely given to satisfy the desire of the Other. *There is both an affirmation of difference and a potential for completion that transcends it*, similar to Jung's archetype of the Self, which expresses wholeness through paradox. To be clear: the paradigm of de-literalized power and authority is not generalizable to every couple practicing BDSM. The queering tendencies of kink are not equally present in every relationship. As a movement, BDSM resists generalization and simplification. The argument here is that the relationship between the world of BDSM and the soul creates the possibility for new ways to imagine power and authority as archetypes present in every human relationship.

Often, the archetype of love is also active in the lived experience of these negotiated, consensual exchanges. Acknowledging an individual's right to choose submission to another person as a path of fulfillment, love, and transcendence makes the critical difference in understanding how these relationships subvert historical systems of oppression. True, there are individuals who overstep the ethical dividing line between love and abuse in their practice of alternative sexualities, and BDSM groups and organizations regularly seek methods to hold such people accountable. The argument cannot be made at the level of every practitioner. The focus here is on the potential of the imagination: instead of a binary paradigm of antagonistic opposites, in BDSM, the dialectical tandem means that one cannot exist without the Other, that the Other exists simultaneously as an embodiment of both difference and completion, and that the Other has the potential to become a beloved.

Notes

1 Krafft-Ebing, R. (1886/2011).
2 Jung, C. G. (1961/1989).
3 Freud, S. (1905/2000).
4 Jung, C. G. (1946/1985, p. 185, n. 34 [*CW* 16, n. 34]).
5 Jung, C. G. (1954/1969b), pp. 4–5 [*CW* 9i, para. 5]).
6 Jung, C. G. (1946/1985, p. 179, n. 22 [*CW* 16, n. 22]).
7 Jung, C. G. (1928/1969c, p. 17 [*CW* 8, para. 32]).
8 Stein, D., & Schachter, D. (2009).
9 Jung, C. G. (1921/1971, p. 220 [*CW* 6, para. 372]).
10 Jung, C. G. (1921/1971, p. 57 [*CW* 6, para. 107]).
11 American Heritage (2011, p. 652).
12 Kaldera, R. (2006).
13 Jung, C. G. (1961/1989, p. 170).
14 Shamdasani, S. (2009).

15 Jung, C. G. (1958/1981, p. 68).
16 Jung, C. G. (2009, p. 134).
17 Jung, C. G. (2009, p. 457).
18 Jung, C. G. (1961/1989).
19 Jung, C. G. (2009, pp. 457–458).
20 Jung, C. G. (1958/1981, 1961/1989, 1976b).
21 Andrews, V. L. (2012); Baldwin, G. (2003); Thompson, M. (2004).
22 Jung, C. G. (2009, p. 458).
23 Jung, C. G. (1976b, vol. 1, pp. 30–31).
24 Hillman, J. (1975/1992, p. xxii).
25 Jung, C. G. (1945/1970a).
26 Jung, C. G. (1976b, vol. 1, p. 148).
27 Shamdasani, S. (2009).
28 As cited in Shamdasani, S. (2009, p. 24).
29 Jung, C. G. (2009, p. 119).
30 Jung, C. G. (1961/1989, pp. 44–45).
31 Shamdasani, S. (2009).
32 Jung, C. G. (1921/1971).
33 Shamdasani, S. (2009, pp. 80–81).
34 Jung, C. G. (1921/1971, p. 448 [*CW* 6, para. 10]).
35 Jung, C. G. (1916/1966a, p. 173 [*CW* 7, para. 266]).
36 Jung, C. G. (1916/1966a, p. 177 [*CW* 7, para. 274]; 1957/1969d, p. 73 [*CW* 8, para. 143]).
37 In practice, images are amenable to interpretation on both levels (Jung, 1966a).
38 Jung, C. G. (1961/1989, p. 192).
39 Shamdasani, S. (2009, p. 51).
40 Kaldera, R. (2016); Tupper, P. (2016).
41 Levine, R. (2016, p. i).
42 Jung, C. G. (1970/1976a, p. 452 [*CW 18*, para. 1098]).
43 Jung, C. G. (2009).
44 Jung, C. G. (1970/1976a, p. 451 [*CW 18*, para. 1094]).
45 Jung, C. G. (2009, p. 139).
46 Ibid. (p. 228).
47 Jung, C. G. (1916/1966b, p. 282 [*CW* 7, para. 467]).
48 Stein, D., & Schacter, D. (2009, p. 12).
49 Jung, C. G. (1958/1981).
50 Jung, C. G. (2009, p. 153).
51 Ibid. (p. 153).
52 Jung, C. G. (1951/1969a, p. 266 [*CW* 9ii, para. 423]).
53 Ibid. (p. 8 [para. 14]).
54 Sacher-Masoch, L. V. (1870/2018).
55 Sade, M. D. (1791/2012).
56 As cited in Stein & Schacter (2009, p. 64).
57 The full-body latex bondage suit is commonly referred to as a "gimp suit." The origins
    of the term "gimp" are unclear. Apparently because the suit is so restrictive in limiting
    mobility, kinksters originally appropriated the derogatory term for a disabled person
    to describe the submissive in the suit (yet another example of how the transgressive
    shadow element appears even in the language of kink). Over time, the term "gimp suit"
    came to refer to the latex apparel without any intent to disparage people with disabil-
    ities.
58 Jung, C. G. (1961/1989, p. 179).
59 Jung, C. G. (1976b, vol. 1, p. 11).
60 Jung, C. G. (2009).
61 Jung, C. G. (1946/1985).

62 Jung, C. G. (1951/1969a).
63 Schwartz-Salant, N. (1998).
64 Hillman, J. (1985).
65 Leather Master Jess, whose interview appears in Chapter 6, disagreed with this assertion. He believed that the subjectivity of one's identity as Master or slave remains regardless of whether one is paired with the other role.
66 Jung, C. G. (1958/1981).
67 Kaldera, R. (2016, p. viii).
68 Jung, C. G. (1946/1985).
69 Jung, C. G. (1961/1989, p. 186).
70 Groesbeck, C. J. (1975); Jung, C. G. (1946/1985); Perry, C. (1997); Samuels, A. (1984).
71 Califia, P. (2002, p. 169).
72 Stein, M. (1998, p. 2).
73 Jung, C. G. (1912/1967, p. 23 [CW 5, para. 26]; 1927/1970b [CW 10]; 1977).
74 Santana, E. (2017).
75 Ibid.
76 Hillman, J. (1960, p. 141).
77 Stefani Goerlich (2021) has provided helpful guidelines to help clinicians distinguish BDSM play from physical abuse and intimate partner violence.
78 Jung, C. G. (1916/1966a, p. 173 [CW 7, para. 267]; 1976b, p. 34; Jung, 1977; Jung, 2012, p. 74).
79 Jung, C. G. (1976b, vol. 1, p. 91).
80 Neumann, E. (1990).
81 Jung, C. G. (1958/1981, p. 90 [CW 8, para. 189]).
82 Jacoby, J. (1984); Jung, C. G. (1946/1985); Perry, C. (1997); Schwartz-Salant, N. (1998); Spiegelman, M. (1996).
83 Jagose, A. (1996).
84 Papadopoulos, R. (1991, p. 54).
85 Ibid. (p. 80).
86 Ibid. (p. 84).

References

American Heritage. (2011). Fetish. In J. P. Pickett (Ed.), *The American heritage dictionary of the English language* (5th ed., p. 652). Houghton Mifflin Harcourt.

Andrews, V. L. (2012). *The complete leatherboy handbook*. Adynaton.

Baldwin, G. (2003). *Ties that bind*. Daedalus.

Califia, P. (2002). Afterword. In G. Baldwin (Author), *Slavecraft* (2nd ed., pp. 143–178). Daedalus.

Freud, S. (2000). *Three essays on the theory of sexuality* (J. Strachey, Trans.). Basic Books. (Original work published 1905)

Goerlich, S. (2021). *The leather couch*. Routledge.

Groesbeck, C. J. (1975). The archetypal image of the wounded healer. *Journal of Analytical Psychology, 20*(2), 122–145.

Hillman, J. (1960). *The myth of analysis*. Northwestern University Press.

Hillman, J. (1985). *Anima: An anatomy of a personified notion*. Spring.

Hillman, J. (1992). *Re-visioning psychology*. HarperCollins. (Original work published 1975)

Jacoby, M. (1984). *The analytic encounter: Transference and human relationship*. Inner City Books.

Jagose, A. (1996). *Queer theory, an introduction*. New York University Press.

Jung, C. G. (1966a). The relations between the ego and the unconscious (R. F. C. Hull, Trans.). In H. Read et al. (Eds.), *The collected works of C. G. Jung* (Vol. 7, 2nd ed., pp. 123–244). Princeton University Press. (Original work published 1916)

Jung, C. G. (1966b). The structure of the unconscious (R. F. C. Hull, Trans.). In H. Read et al. (Eds.), *The collected works of C. G. Jung* (Vol. 7, 2nd ed., pp. 269–304). Princeton University Press. (Original work published 1916)

Jung, C. G. (1967). Symbols of transformation (R. F. C. Hull, Trans.). In H. Read et al. (Eds.), *The collected works of C. G. Jung* (Vol. 5, 2nd ed.). Princeton University Press. (Original work published 1912)

Jung, C. G. (1969a). *Aion* (R. F. C. Hull, Trans.). In H. Read et al. (Eds.), *The collected works of C. G. Jung* (Vol. 9ii, 2nd ed.). Princeton University Press. (Original work published 1959)

Jung, C. G. (1969b). Archetypes of the collective unconscious (R. F. C. Hull, Trans.). In H. Read et al. (Eds.), *The collected works of C. G. Jung* (Vol. 9i, 2nd ed., pp. 3–41). Princeton University Press. (Original work published 1954)

Jung, C. G. (1969c). On psychic energy (R. F. C. Hull, Trans.). In H. Read et al. (Eds.), *The collected works of C. G. Jung* (Vol. 8, 2nd ed., pp. 3–66). Princeton University Press. (Original work published 1928)

Jung, C. G. (1970a). After the catastrophe (R. F. C. Hull, Trans.). In H. Read et al. (Eds.), *The collected works of C. G. Jung* (Vol. 10, 2nd ed., pp. 194–217). Princeton University Press. (Original work published 1945)

Jung, C. G. (1970b). Mind and earth (R. F. C. Hull, Trans.). In H. Read et al. (Eds.), *The collected works of C. G. Jung* (Vol. 10, 2nd ed., pp. 29–49). Princeton University Press. (Original work published 1927)

Jung, C. G. (1971). *Psychological types* (R. F. C. Hull, Trans.). In H. Read et al. (Eds.), *The collected works of C. G. Jung* (Vol. 6). Princeton University Press. (Original work published 1921)

Jung, C. G. (1976a). Adaptation, individuation, collectivity (R. F. C. Hull, Trans.). In H. Read et al. (Eds.), *The collected works of C. G. Jung* (Vol. 18, pp. 449–454). Princeton University Press. (Original work published 1970)

Jung, C. G. (1976b). *Vision Seminars* (Vols. 1–2). Spring.

Jung, C. G. (1977). A talk with students at the institute. In W. McGuire & R. F. C. Hull (Eds.), *C. G. Jung speaking* (pp. 359–364). Princeton University Press.

Jung, C. G. (1981). The transcendent function (R. F. C. Hull, Trans.). In H. Read et al. (Eds.), *The collected works of C. G. Jung* (Vol. 8, 2nd ed., pp. 67–91). Princeton University Press. (Original work published 1958)

Jung, C. G. (1985). The psychology of the transference (R. F. C. Hull, Trans.). In H. Read et al. (Eds.), *The collected works of C. G. Jung* (Vol. 16, 2nd ed., pp. 163–326). Princeton University Press. (Original work published 1946)

Jung, C. G. (1989). *Memories, dreams, reflections* (R. Winston & C. Winston, Trans.; A. Jaffé, Ed.). Vintage Books. (Original work published 1961)

Jung, C. G. (2009). *The red book, Liber Novus: A reader's edition* (M. Kyburz, J. Peck, & S. Shamdasani, Trans.; S. Shamdasani, Ed.). W. W. Norton.

Jung, C. G. (2012). *Introduction to Jungian psychology: Notes on the seminar in analytical psychology given in 1925* (S. Shamdasani, Ed., revised ed.). Princeton University Press.

Kaldera, R. (2006). *Dark moon rising: Pagan BDSM and the ordeal path.* Asphodel.

Kaldera, R. (2016). Foreword. In P. Tupper (Ed.), *Our lives, our history: Consensual Master/slave relationships from ancient times to the 21st century* (pp. vii–xiii). Perfectbound.

Krafft-Ebing, R. (2011). *Psychopathia sexualis* (F. S. Klaf, Trans.). Arcade Publishing. (Original work published 1886)

Levine, R. (2016). *Jolted awake.* Alfred.

Neumann, E. (1990). *Depth psychology and a new ethic.* Shambhala.

Papadopoulos, R. K. (1991). Jung and the concept of the other. In R. K. Papadopoulos & G. S. Saayman (Eds.), *Jung in modern perspective* (pp. 54–88). Avery Publishing Group.

Perry, C. (1997). Transference and countertransference. In P. Young-Eisendrath & T. Dawson (Eds.), *The Cambridge companion to Jung* (2nd ed., pp. 147–170). Cambridge University Press.

Sacher-Masoch, L. V. (2018). *Venus in furs* (J. McNeil, Trans.). Gray Rabbit. (Original work published 1870)

Sade, M. D. (2012). *Justine or the misfortunes of virtue* (J. Phillips, Trans.). Oxford University Press. (Original work published 1791)

Samuels, A. (1984). Transference/countertransference. In R. K. Papadopoulos (Ed.), *The handbook of Jungian psychology* (pp. 177–195). Routledge.

Santana, E. (2017). *Jung and sex*. Routledge.

Schwartz-Salant, N. (1998). *The mystery of human relationship*. Routledge.

Shamdasani, S. (2009). Introduction. In S. Shamdasani (Ed.), *The red book, Liber Novus: A reader's edition* (pp. 1–96). W. W. Norton.

Spiegelman, M. (1996). *Psychotherapy as mutual process*. New Falcon.

Stein, D., & Schachter, D. (2009). *Ask the man who owns him*. Perfectbound.

Stein, M. (1998). *Jung's map of the soul*. Open Court.

Thompson, M. (Ed.). (2004). *Leather folk*. Daedalus.

Tupper, P. (2016). Introduction: The first word on the subject. In Peter Tupper *Our lives, our history: Consensual Master/slave relationships from ancient times to the 21st century* (pp. 1–6). Perfectbound.

3

AN ARCHETYPAL PERSPECTIVE

James Hillman and Archetypal Psychology

James Hillman, one of the leaders of the post-Jungian generation, had the ability to synthesize complex ideas and build one surprising insight upon another. His conclusions are dazzling and at times overwhelming. For those unfamiliar with the velocity and inquisitive range of Hillman's mind, it can be challenging to encounter his work for the first time. It may be helpful to remember that Hillman's psychological compass was always pointed not toward north—not toward healing, not toward happiness—but toward soul, metaphorical south. He found soul in neglected places: suffering and disease, the deformed and the distorted, nature and cityscapes, betrayal, war, masturbation, pornography, and the hidden images of language itself through etymology.[1]

Jung's theory of the archetypes became the focus of his interest in advancing the frontiers of Jungian thought. In creating what came to be known as archetypal psychology, Hillman was unafraid to craft original ideas based on Jung's model, often departing from established concepts in radical directions. Although Hillman was an innovator, he was also careful to trace the origins of his own ideas back to their source in Jung's psychology and even further back to classical philosophers such as Heraclitus and Plotinus and those of the Renaissance such as Vico and Ficino.

Hillman[2] made a vital distinction between *the archetype* as a concept and *archetypal* as a formal descriptor of lived psychic experience. With

DOI: 10.4324/9781003223597-4

characteristic precision, he articulated what he saw as the advantages and weaknesses of conceptualizing *the archetype* as a fixed concept. Hillman affirmed Jung's[3] commitment to metaphorical language to describe archetypes, and he developed the idea as a central feature of his approach. Archetypes "tend to be metaphors rather than things," he said.[4] They elude our attempts to define them in literal, or concrete, terms. Instead, we are more inclined to use metaphorical and imaginative language to say what they are like. Archetypes are real but not physical, which leads to problems employing concretistic language to describe them. By contrast, *archetypal* infers the reality of archetypes by studying their appearance as images. The concept intentionally avoids the metaphysical questions that bedeviled Jung, such as where exactly archetypes come from or how they differ from biological instincts. Hillman's distinction suggests that, perhaps, the noun is not the best part of speech to describe what grabs us or fascinates us; perhaps instead it is the adjective.

Hillman's designation of *archetypal* is a more serviceable descriptor of psychic reality, and it has profound implications. Whereas the concept of *the archetype* risks being overly abstract, the *archetypal* is always immanent, phenomenal, and rooted in lived experience.[5] At the same time as it adheres to the phenomenology of the image, the designation of *archetypal* also directs attention to the psychological value of the experience, a value that manifests in the "subliminal richness" and "invisible depth" of immediate phenomena.[6]

For example, in the world of BDSM, the *archetype* of bondage is an idea one could discuss in the abstract, noting the similar patterns between bondage in dreams, mythology, historical events, literature, and the actual practices in the modern dungeon. The conversation could be an interesting intellectual exercise. But such an abstract discussion does not introduce us to the *archetypal* experience of bondage. We miss a sense of its psychological value. To imagine archetypally, we must ask the question: *What is bondage like?* Hillman would direct attention to the precise lived experience of restraint—in chains, for example. One is invited to imaginally experience the sensual qualities and emergent value of what presents itself: cool metal, naked skin, futile struggle, straining muscles, primal vulnerability, ultimate surrender, oceanic calm. These are images of subliminal richness, at once visceral, metaphorical, circular, interconnected, and imbued with soul. The fundament of existence emerges here in its raw necessity. We are reminded that we are all creatures of limitation, eternally vulnerable, destined to struggle and ultimately surrender to the great forces beyond our control. To be human is to be restricted. To choose submission is to choose the mystery of life. As we feel more deeply into the inevitability of our existential bondage, if we were to scream, who would hear us? The beautiful, terrifying angel from Rilke's first *Duino Elegy* comes to mind.[7] The archetypal dimension of bondage has led to a reverie on angelic beauty and terror. It is through *archetypal* experience that visceral phenomena find their way back to the poetry of the soul.

Developing Jung's[8] concept of archetypes as primordial images, Hillman focused on the fundamental role played by image as an irreducible element that brings form and substance to psychic reality. Much of Hillman's work was an impassioned tribute to image as the basis for encountering and experiencing the psyche. The connection between Jung and Hillman is clear in the following two passages. The first is Jung's assessment of psychic reality based on fantasy-images:

> The psyche creates reality every day. The only expression I can use for this activity is *fantasy*. Fantasy is just as much feeling as thinking; as much intuition as sensation. There is no psychic function that, through fantasy, is not inextricably bound up with the other psychic functions. . . . *Fantasy, therefore, seems to me the clearest expression of the specific activity of the psyche.*[9]

Hillman advanced Jung's original premise:

> Following Jung I use the word fantasy-image in the poetic sense, considering images to be the basic givens of psychic life, self-originating, inventive, spontaneous, complete, and organized in archetypal patterns. Fantasy-images are both the raw materials and finished products of psyche, and they are the privileged mode of access to knowledge of soul. Nothing is more primary. Every notion in our minds, each perception of the world and sensation in ourselves must go through a psychic organization in order to "happen" at all. Every single feeling or observation occurs as a psychic event by first forming a fantasy-image.[10]

For both Jung and Hillman, image is the essence of psyche, and psyche connotes soul. Their formulation suggests that what we typically call material reality is in fact an apperception of fantasy-images. In other words, our interpretation of reality is an operation of the *imagination* (a term Hillman used interchangeably with *fantasy*) such that reality is only available to us through fantasy. Psychic life organizes itself according to the operations of "imaginal realities."[11] The concept is radical, but it is clearly anchored in Jung's original thoughts about the nature of the psyche. Hillman emphasized the integral relationship between image, imagination, and soul, anchoring all three in the concept of the archetypal. This anchoring facilitates the transit between corporeal existence and subtle body (i.e., the body of the imagination, a non-material basis of consciousness). It is a transit into the non-literal (*poetic*) reality of the image, what anthropologist Henri Corbin referred to as the *imaginal* dimension, or *mundus imaginalis*.[12]

Cobb offered the following description of what is meant by *image* in archetypal psychology:

> We must remember that image is not just some object or other out there; it is not the same as a picture, not the same as an optical, visual thing, not at all the same as what modern psychology refers to as "sense data." Nor is it an optical event, an afterimage, or even the same as memory. *It is neither inside us nor outside us, but somewhere in between.* What I am reaching for is that sense of the image we can find among the ancient Greeks and again in the Florentine circles of the Renaissance—the image considered as the way in which the heart perceives.[13]

By Cobb's account, an image involves a co-creative process between the world and one who is touched by the world. As with all creativity, it implies the necessity of an aesthetic response "in the original Greek sense of *aithesis*, which at root is a gasp and 'Ahh!' of wonder and recognition, a sniffing, a breathing in of the world."[14] Without the aesthetic gasp, the heart does not awaken to the image. It is not sufficient to imagine psyche only as image in the conventional sense of the word: "*psyche is the life of our aesthetic responses*, that sense of taste in relation with things, that thrill or pain, disgust or expansion of breast: those primordial aesthetic reactions of the heart are soul itself speaking."[15]

Image is a point of fascination for archetypal psychology because images are sourced by the soul and bring soul into the world.[16] The emergence of soul through image is why the admonition to *stick with the image* has become a mantra of the archetypal approach.[17] Just as Freud and Jung developed theories to explain human suffering, archetypal psychology proposes that the suffering of Western culture is due to a loss of sensitivity toward images and an imaginal sense, which translates into a loss of soul.[18]

The beauty that Hillman had in mind was the beauty of the soul. The aesthetic response to the soul's imaginal presentation may be a spontaneous reaction of wonder and delight, but it can also express shock, horror, disgust, or confusion. To look at the world of BDSM by focusing not on the lives of the participants but on the aesthetic experience of fantasy-images is a novel approach. A new language of soul becomes available to describe BDSM's erotic aesthetic value. It leads to an appreciation of the craftsmanship that goes into the minutiae of fetish wear and gear that is often handmade and exquisite. Finely tailored bespoke leather clothing, creative designs in latex and neoprene including the iconic pup mask, the form-fitting attire of the modern dominatrix conjuring fear and arousal, superbly crafted floggers, whips, head harnesses, hoods, and ball gags are all examples. At the same time, they are images that already insinuate a deeper aesthetic of the odd, the disturbing, and the morbid before they are put to use in the dungeon.

Hillman's regard for the soul's unconventional beauty recognizes an aesthetic of the depths. In BDSM, there is an aesthetic gasp that is also related to suffering and surrender: the stinging blows of impact play such as caning, the agony of genital torture, the convulsive torments of electric play, cutting and blood-letting, choking, gagging, fisting, and scat play. All are familiar activities under the rubric of alternative sexualities. By conventional standards, there is nothing beautiful about such ordeals, yet they elicit the primordial aesthetic reactions that Hillman referenced in relation to the soul speaking through us.

A visit to almost any European art gallery would support the notion that torment, violence, suffering, and surrender have all along been aesthetically linked to soul in the Western psyche. One thinks of the voluptuous depictions of naked Saint Sebastian, bound and pierced with arrows; the popular subject of Judith severing the head of Holofernes; Orpheus dismembered by the Maenads; Prometheus bound and eviscerated; and, of course, the omnipresent image of the bloodied Christ pierced and dying on the cross. These are some of the more obvious examples from the Western art tradition, which provides countless grotesque depictions of torture, murder, martyrdom, betrayal, and damnation. These are the images that shock, excite, and impress themselves indelibly upon the memory. The bulging eyes and distorted mouths of the victims confront us from their frames hanging on the museum walls, and we gaze back with uneasy smiles of polite restraint, unsure what we feel beneath the surface, less sure still what is being asked of us as witnesses. What we encounter constitutes an aesthetic of violence, horror, and agony. The exploration of these same themes in the world of BDSM and kink provides a place within modern culture, a place where the soul continues to speak through "those primordial aesthetic reactions of the heart."[19]

Hillman admired the raw potency of images to explode any allegorical meanings that we creatures of consciousness try to impose on them. In his view, images are the true iconoclasts because the capacity of dreams and fantasies to distress and disgust us through distortion and perversion can break apart our constructed notions of ourselves and others. "The 'worst' images are thus the best," he said, "for they are the ones that restore a figure to its pristine power as a numinous person at work in the soul."[20] From the archetypal perspective, BDSM liberates the pristine power of the "worst" images by blowing apart our conventional ideas about sexuality, pleasure, and intimacy. BDSM restores a sense of value to the disgusting, the distorted, and the perverse as numinous persons (i.e., living images) of the soul. Perhaps the potency of the image is the deeper energy source for getting into sub headspace or Dom headspace. What we think we know about ourselves is exploded by the primal energy of the image that we inhabit during a scene, and the "worst" images are the best.

By following the archetypal path, experience takes on a life of its own, *depersonalized* and *dehumanized*, to use two of Hillman's[21] deliberately challenging terms. From this perspective, experience is not primarily a personal matter—it belongs to soul, which turns events into experiences and makes meaning possible.[22] Benjamin Sells concurred: "Recognizing and respecting the impersonal and autonomous nature of the image is basic to archetypal psychology and points to a numinous value assumed inherent in every image as a direct expression of soul."[23] Archetypal images precede and supersede human egoic experience as a taxonomic set of the first order. As will be seen, recognizing the impersonal reality of the image affords a new psychological perspective that paradoxically finds value in the countercultural enthusiasm of BDSM to degrade and humiliate human worth because the image of degradation itself is "a direct expression of soul."

Based on the primacy of the image and the centrality of the soul, arche-typal psychology developed in the 1970s as one of the major post-Jungian schools.[24] For Hillman, archetypal psychology's "exposition must be rhe-torical and poetic, its reasoning not logical, and its therapeutic aim nei-ther social adaptation nor personalistic individualizing but rather a work in service of restoration of the patient to imaginal realities."[25] In contrast to Jung's emphasis on individuation as the aim of therapy, archetypal psychol-ogy seeks "a development of a sense of soul" through the cultivation of the imagination.[26]

Personifying

In 1975, Hillman published what is arguably his most important work, *Re-Visioning Psychology*. In it, he described the key themes of archetypal psychology as *personifying, pathologizing, psychologizing*, and *dehumanizing*. *Personifying* refers to the tendency of the psyche to present its own subjec-tivity and intentionality in the guise of imaginal characters. For example, the soul is personifying when a tightly sealed jar is "stubborn" or a storm is "ferocious." Through personifying, the metaphorical power of the world reveals itself, the heart returns as an organ of emotion and intention, and loving becomes a way of knowing, a way of understanding. Master Patrick Califia's remarks included in the previous chapter reveal how he instinctive-ly recognized the value for the Master of personifying the slave archetype as an inner image:

> I believe the Master needs more than a dominant ideal or role model to guide him in developing his craft. I believe it is essential for an intuitive Master to have an internalized archetype of the slave, just as the anima is essential to the well-balanced male psyche, and the animus protects and nurtures women. This Slave Consultant is the source of my compassion, the compass that guides my [apparent] cruelty, the pressure that drives me into my possession and allows me to savor their surrender. It is the bridge between us, and when a slave has displeased me, it is that internalized notion of ultimate servitude that intercedes for them and mediates on their behalf.[27]

For Califia, the slave archetype is no abstract concept—it is a living *per-sonified* entity, a Slave Consultant, presenting its own subjectivity and

intentionality to help guide the development of the Master's craft. Personification animates the abstract concept of empathic attunement and brings
it to life in the image of a numinous advisor, a fantasy-image that can share
valuable insights with the Master, separate from the observations and judgments of the conscious personality.

Psychologizing refers to the soul's root activity of reflecting on its own
reality, inviting us to see beyond surface appearances into the depths.[28] Psychologizing is present in the world of BDSM when practitioners allow time
for deeper reflection on a scene or on their relationships, looking for their
deeper psychological value. Examples include the process of negotiation
before a scene when partners develop a more nuanced understanding of
what combinations of domination and submission will release each other's
pleasure, or the highly ethical practice of "aftercare" following a scene's conclusion. Aftercare refers to the practice of allowing a period of decompres-
sion following an encounter that involves taking stock of what occurred and
how it was experienced for both people. The intent is to facilitate a mindful
transition out of the headspace of the submissive and Dominant roles and
to attend to any unintended harm that might have occurred during the
scene. The particulars of what constitutes aftercare will vary from couple
to couple, and not every instance constitutes an example of psychologizing. However, when the process involves deeper reflection on the meaning
of what transpired individually and together, it is likely that the layered,
multi-dimensional vision of the soul is seeing through the experience.

Pathologizing

Any exploration of images from dreams and myths, two of the great reser-
voirs of imaginal reality, soon bumps up against personified figures that express distortion, disorder, suffering, disease, decay, and collapse. When such
figures are literalized as aspects of human experience, psychologists have
traditionally assessed them as pathological. Hillman[29] noted that pathology was the first point of contact between early psychologists and the soul.
Patients originally came to Freud and to Jung because they were suffering
from baffling disorders of thought and behavior, such as hysterical conver-
sions, catatonic states, and psychosis. Hillman, looking past the personal
details of their case histories, believed that the pathos of the patients (i.e.,
their pathology) was an expression of a timeless necessity of the soul to describe itself in primordial images of suffering, breakdown, and destruction.

What is odd, cruel, ugly, or degraded is now recognized as an expression of the soul itself, a mode of being in archetypal reality, imbued with a particular innate value.

For Hillman,[30] the unrelenting campaign of the psychological profession to cure and to heal overlooks the need of the soul itself to speak through modes of distortion and affliction. The archetypal approach finds a common source for the images of myth, the images of nightmares, and the terrible afflictions of our personal lives: they all emanate from the necessity of the soul to express itself in a profoundly distressed fashion. The impulse to redeem and repair that which is broken in the human condition is only one of many possible responses to the images themselves. It is a response that forecloses on any curiosity about what suffering "might be saying about the soul and what the soul might be saying by means of it."[31] Hillman asserted that pathologizing was a "valid, authentic, and necessary" mode of psychological expression and a fundamental part of our very being.[32] It asks practitioners to listen and to understand the soul's somber native tongue before they attempt to alleviate suffering.

The relevance of pathologizing to the activities and relationships of BDSM is immediately apparent. Morbidity, disorder, abnormality, and suffering are all woven into the fabric of BDSM as fundamental elements. Hillman's perspective shifts the location of these elements from the personal psychology of individuals (the perverse fetishists and sadomasochists of Krafft-Ebing's[33] catalog) to the creative life of the soul. BDSM has created a space to experience and reflect on these expressions of suffering, breakdown, and destruction.

Hillman recognized that pathologizing is intimately connected to our sense of individuality. He suggested that we fear being truly ourselves because we fear the psychopathological aspect of who we really are. Each of us is peculiar, and we must contend with our unique disappointments and failures. Despite our best efforts, those who love us often don't understand us. "Destruction seeps out of us autonomously," Hillman wrote, and sometimes our broken lives cannot be redeemed or repaired.[34] But our failures are not entirely the result of our personal defects. Our flaws and fiascos, our brokenness, and our suffering are part of archetypal reality. The fantasy that I am a person obstructs my understanding that the failures that make me unique are not really mine—they are the pathologizing expressions of the soul. The contemporary pursuits of BDSM provide a bridge between the problematic aspects of our individuality and the necessity of the soul to tell its own tales of pathos, cruelty, ugliness, and destruction through us. The reorientation of perspective from person-centered to soul-centered supports what Hillman referred to as "the individuation of imaginal reality."[35] The shift in orientation may be challenging for BDSM practitioners. Sadomasochism customarily refers to the marriage of personal pain and personal pleasure. The concept of pathologizing, however, suggests that pleasure and pain, rather than being personal, are innate to the particular soul-images that inspire sadomasochistic pursuits.

One of the other aspects of pathologizing particularly relevant to the world of BDSM is connected to Hillman's[36] assertion that the fantasy of death is the inevitable terminus of every imaginal process of disease, decay, and breakdown. In his writing, Hillman repeatedly pointed out death's essential relationship to the life of the soul.[37] Death as a soul-image is not to be confused with the literal deaths that bring an end to mortal biological lives. The distinction once again marks the difference between imaginal reality and physical reality. It is the significance of death to the soul that interested Hillman. He wrote, "Pathologizing forces the soul to a consciousness of itself as different from the ego and its life—a consciousness that obeys its own laws of metaphorical enactment in intimate relation with death."[38] As a fundamental operation of the psyche, pathologizing activates metaphorical imagining and arouses the soul's consciousness of its existence separate from the world of the ego and daytime physical concerns. In its imaginal world, pathologizing leads every fantasy of disease and destruction down to death as the ultimate inevitable conclusion.

Hillman's conviction that death is an archetypal given that permeates the life of the soul is radically at odds with modern culture's valorization of life at all costs. Yet despite mainstream culture's aversion, death is an indispensable element in every major myth, every great story, and almost every major motion picture. (Can one imagine an epic saga or tragic love story without somebody dying?) Death as an archetypal image works its way deeply into the imagination and operates metaphorically in the background of every experience of loss, every sexual release (the French call the orgasm *la petite mort*), every ending, every sorrow, every breakdown, every breakup, and every failure. Unlike a scene in BDSM, death is non-negotiable and non-consensual, dominating our psychological lives, forcing us into submission to its authority and demanding a personal individual response from each of us. Hillman wrote:

> It is not upon life that our ultimate individuality centers, but upon death. Its kingdom, Greek myths of Hades and Tartarus say, is the world under and within all life, and there souls go home. There, psychic existence is without the natural perspective of flesh and blood, so that pathologizing by taking events to death takes them into their ultimate meaning for soul. . . . Symptoms are death's ambassadors, deserving honor for their place, and life mirrored in its symptoms sees there its death and remembers soul.[39]

Here, we can see that Hillman is building upon Jung's association between the unconscious and the Underworld. He finds both the source and the destination of all fantasy-images in the image of death. To deny the significance and even the necessity of death to the psyche is to rob the pathologized images of the soul of a homecoming to their native territory, the Underworld, "the mythic land of the dead."[40]

To see the relevance of pathologizing and its intimate relation with death to the world of BDSM, it is necessary to liberate the images of BDSM from the personal stories of its practitioners and, once free, to allow them to operate as agents of metaphorical imagination. The experience of humiliation provides one example. With this shift in perspective, every image of humiliation is now more clearly an instance of the soul's pathologizing tendencies. Humiliation takes us out of hubris and into humus, our psychic earth. It involves a loss of status for the ego and a movement downward toward soul. Similarly, images of degradation are a familiar part of pathologizing's lexicon. The Dominant who casually rests a well-polished boot on the back of a prostrate submissive's hooded head and the submissive who is placed below the lowest spot of the Master's physical domain are participating in the same archetypal fantasy: both are touched by the soul's pathologizing impulse. Kidnapping role-plays provide another example: behind every kinky kidnapping fantasy is the fantasy-image of the mythic abduction into the Underworld. Complicit in that abduction down into the unknown, the shadowy specter of death adds to the sense of dread (it was Hades who abducted Persephone into his mysterious kingdom). The ultimate thrill of the kidnapping role-play is the captive's momentary thought, "Holy shit!

I wonder if I'm going to die here." Pathologizing leads every fantasy of calamity toward death as the ultimate conclusion of the journey.

As pathologizing finds its destination in death, other images constellate around the process: there are images of the extreme (*in extremis* can mean the point of death), images of limit, and the loss of life as the ultimate loss of control, to name the most obvious. From the imaginal perspective, these archetypal characters also appear in BDSM's fascination with pushing and testing limits, playing with intensity, and exploring the pivot point between control and chaos. They all constitute metaphorical enactments, unfolding at various depths in imaginal space between pathologizing and death. But by no means should these imaginal experiences be taken literally. BDSM practitioners are not seeking to fulfill a death wish through their activities. The archetypal pattern in question emerges only when the soul moves to the foreground of thought and finds a mirror of itself in the de-literalized and poetically reimagined images of BDSM and kink.

The physical risks associated with edgeplay also reflect the soul's fondness for pathologizing: pain can surpass the limits of pleasure and endurance, fire can burn too hot, a knife's incision can cut too deeply, skin breaks down, blood flows. Play partners may have negotiated safe limits and obtained enthusiastic consent, but the soul recognizes the scene as a mythic enactment of transgression, human frailty, surrender, torture, suffering, and ego death. Such is the archetypal experience that occurs through the activities and relationships of BDSM, lending them a numinous power and intensity that is uncommon in tamer daytime pursuits. In fact, the world of BDSM is one of the few places in modern life where the soul's pathologized images can enter de-literalized into human consciousness while retaining their potency as expressions of imaginal reality. Distorted images are held within the sexual imagination just as they are held in the designated play space, where they have a chance to develop "subliminal richness" and "invisible depth."[41]

Dehumanizing

One of the more extraordinary developments from Jung's conceptualization of the pluralistic psyche is Hillman's move of *dehumanizing*. Although Jung often described the aim of the individuation process as psychic wholeness, he acknowledged that such a state "has never yet been reached."[42] Instead, he considered psychic life to be an age-old paradox: "a plurality of souls in one and the same individual."[43] Due to the autonomous nature of archetypes, they cannot be integrated into the ego-personality per se; they can only be made conscious.[44] Based on this limitation, Hillman concluded that the psychological effect of something that is universal is that it "amplifies and de-personalizes experience."[45] *The effect of archetypal experience is to move consciousness away from the personal and toward the universal.* Following Jung's suggestion that personality is essentially pluralistic, archetypal psychology understands personality not in terms of individual characteristics but rather in terms of the many-faceted images of the soul:

> Personality is imaginatively conceived as a living and peopled drama in which the subject "I" takes part but is neither the sole author, nor director, nor always the main character. Sometimes he or she is not even on the stage.[46]

The conventional idea of an individual personality undergoes a revision in Hillman's psychology so that it becomes a dynamic concatenation of various archetypal figures. The ego is not in charge of the show.

Hillman's[47] concept of *dehumanizing* as a fundamental operation of the soul is intentionally provocative. It challenges large-scale cultural commitments to the inherent supremacy of human beings and the associated postulates of humanism as it developed during the Protestant Reformation and the Enlightenment.[48] It is not so much that human beings lack value in Hillman's view but rather that human value originates in the autonomous images of the soul. He offered a thoughtful and cutting critique of the historical development of Western thought, noting how the image of a human as a concretized person emerged during the European Reformation: "The self as a reflexive intensive pronoun, expressed a new reflective style, a new interiority and intensification of the person."[49] Hillman believed that the Reformation contributed to the West's growing tendency to conflate the ideas of self, person, and human into a homogenized concept of the individual at the soul's expense.

Hillman found the trend of Western thought to increasingly imagine soul as contextually dependent on the human being psychologically dubious.[50] Clearly, if one compares human to soul, soul is the more embracing, the more enduring, and the more encompassing notion. In his view, soul contains, affects, influences, and defines everything that comprises the human domain. It is an error to imagine that the psyche exists within us as an internal process. It is the other way around: we exist "in the midst of psyche."[51] The soul surrounds us and operates within the deep subjectivity of the world itself.

By privileging soul as the originator of the human imagination and, therefore, the architect of all human experience, Hillman reached a startling conclusion. What we think of as our unique individual personality is actually an amalgam of attitudes and characteristics bestowed upon us as a gift from an archetypal daimon or spirit who in turn demands our service.[52] Hillman proposed that a person's psychological imperative is not to individuate, as Jung had asserted, but to care for those figures of the psyche (Hillman called them numinous persons) entrusted to one's stewardship. If we consider the fantasy persons of the soul who inhabit the world of BDSM, one is not born a Master or a slave—rather, one has been called and entrusted to care for that numinous living image.

Dehumanizing challenges us to remember that what matters most in life is how we use our lives to care for the soul.[53] It is important to bear in mind that "the realities that take place in the soul" govern our human reality.[54] Because the psyche precedes and determines our perception of what is real, Hillman concluded that fantasy-images are the only entities that are irreducible: they appear precisely as they exist. "Only fantasies are utterly, incontrovertibly real."[55] Morality, too, is then subject to the realities of the soul before it is an operation of human reason.

Hillman[56] postulated an archetypal morality as part of his attempt to "de-moralize" the psyche from a personal humanistic center. He proposed that any morality can only be evaluated according to the structure and principles of each particular image that governs it or, adopting the language of the classical imagination, according to the values associated with one god or another. Hillman argued that when the human becomes a literalization of the archetypal person, the result is a bifurcated morality. Moral choices fall into binaries of right versus wrong and good versus bad. "What does not fit in becomes inhuman, psychopathic or evil," and the rejected Other is the problematic result.[57] So rather than endorsing a classical Jungian integration of projected shadow material, Hillman proposed a new vision of morality based on the presentation of the image. In place of imposing a moral human-centered judgment on the image as right/wrong or good/bad, archetypal morality concerns itself with the integrity of the image: *How is one to remain faithful in word and deed to the archetypal character of the image that structures one's reality?*

Such a dehumanized perspective on morality provides a fresh insight into aspects of BDSM that are at odds with conventional mores. The immorality of BDSM is part of its excitement as well as a factor in its disapproval by the mainstream. Eroticizing the immoral dates back to the writings of the Marquis de Sade and Leopold von Sacher-Masoch (it likely predates them in the mythic imagination), and it has remained a feature of sadomasochism up to the present day. Morality changes according to the archetype that presides over an experience. For example, bondage has a particular (non-literal) moral character determined by the archetypal image that governs its activities. The principles and structure of bondage-as-image demand control, restriction, confinement, and immobilization. The imagination moves along various pathways that follow the moral structure of the archetypal image: there can be a paradoxical experience of being overpowered and diminished on the one hand and of being contained and embraced on the other; a denial of external freedom on the one hand and a liberation into the possibilities of inner realities on the other. Bondage-as-image forms a moral system that holds these dichotomies in peaceful coexistence. Here is another example: the morality of domination and submission emerges from fantasies of over and under. There is the imposition of control and authority from above, the fantasy of the superior and the inferior, and the gestures of surrender, obedience, and devotion in moving beneath. There is a collaborative giving up and taking over, a looking down upon and looking up toward. The D/s relationship as moral system holds the attitudes of idealization and devaluation within the same intimate context. The archetypal morality of D/s evaluates how well we adhere to the imaginal characteristics that structure the relationship.

How might sadomasochism reflect archetypal morality? The sadist follows imaginal principles of calculating cruelty and the augmentation of pleasure through libertine exploitation. Masochistic morality obeys the imaginal necessities of self-debasement/humiliation and the conflation of pain and pleasure. Each type of experience has a distinct character that places a claim on the practitioner, guiding the integrity of one's thoughts, feelings, and actions according to the nature of the fantasy-image. When morality is liberated from the human sphere, it serves soul by adhering to the integrity of the image. Morality becomes a derivative of imaginal necessities.

Consider a sadomasochistic couple involved in a scene that combines one partner's fierce brutality and cruelty with the other's ecstatic surrender. There is an inhuman aspect to the encounter that can arouse fascination and pleasure for the couple: the impulse to inflict pain and suffering on a person paired with the desire to feel one's own human worth degraded. When attention shifts from the personal to the archetypal, then *dehumanizing* is at work. So long as each person's voluntary consent remains intact and no serious harm has occurred, the question is no longer whether the dynamic is healthy or unhealthy, right or wrong, good or bad. Instead, the moral question concerns how fully the couple embodies the archetypal character of the fantasy. It is an active shift in attention in which there occurs a restoration of the inhuman to imaginal possibilities. Such a return liberates the impulses and desires from the personal sphere. The couple's personal pleasure finds itself situated in the larger primordial field of images that source the sadomasochistic fantasy. *Archetypal* reality dominates the experience, and the play space becomes a mythic space of inhumanity—personal pleasure becomes a byproduct rather than an end. Through *dehumanizing*, sadist and masochist alike become servants of the soul by caring for the details of the fantasy-images and adhering to their necessities.

Hillman's Legacy

Hillman died in 2011. His life ended during a period in which the psychobiological facts of neuroscience and the quantifiable certainty of evidence-based research were guiding the larger trends in psychology. Throughout his career, Hillman challenged the presumption that the rigors of quantitative science and the disease-based model of medicine would improve psychology as a helping profession. Most clinicians would argue that the profession has an ethical duty to patients and clients to prove that psychotherapy is effective at alleviating human suffering.

Neuroscience and evidence-based research have made invaluable contributions to the profession despite Hillman's critique. But what has become of psychology as a field that concerns itself with the mysteries of psyche as soul? Hillman concluded *Re-Visioning Psychology* by declaring modern psychology impotent regarding its ability to keep soul in mind.[58] Hillman's critique sought a therapy that exposes the inhumanity of civilization's shadow and articulates the longings of the soul. Perhaps archetypal psychology has found an unwitting proponent in modern BDSM—its eroticized enactments both reveal and contain our collective inhumanity, beauty emerges through the weird and the ugly, and the mysterious longings of the depths have a voice.

The commitment to imaginal realities is a central tenet of Hillman's work that remains on the periphery of the field in the present day. Yet these same realities of the soul enter and take center stage in the scenes and relationships of BDSM. Until recently, psychology has had little favorable to say about alternative sexualities, and many clinicians remain at a loss as to how to be of genuine service to practitioners of BDSM. Hillman's legacy, which privileges archetypal reality, offers a way of seeing through BDSM experiences to the animating forces of the Underworld, where psychological life originates.

Hillman's approach to psychological experience leads to new insights regarding the value and meaning of BDSM and kink not as individual personal preferences but as emanations of the soul's transgressive necessities. Archetypal psychology moves the conversation away from endless deliberations over whether kink is psychologically unhealthy or morally perverse to a deeper reflection on what is "just so" in its lived experience. The core concepts of archetypal psychology invite a new way of seeing alternative sexualities as a poetics of the psychosexual.

The core principles of archetypal psychology, *personifying*, *psychologizing*, *pathologizing*, and *dehumanizing*, provide a point of departure for exploring the world of BDSM as a world of living images. Rather than focusing on the fetishes of a particular person who dons a harness, a collar, or a hood, the archetypal psychologist turns to the figures that animate the imagination as these accoutrements gain vitality and intensity. The fantasy-images become the point of focus. It is not the person in the role but the role itself and the image behind it that draw the players into an experience of soul.

Notes

1 Hillman's talent for finding soul through the anomalous was one of the inspirations for Thomas Moore's (2022/1990) treatise on the Marquis de Sade, in which Moore recast the Marquis as a mythographer of the perverse. The present work builds on the same archetypal premise.
2 Hillman, J. (1975/1992).
3 Jung, C. G. (1951/1990b, p. 160).

4 Hillman, J. (1975/1992, p. xix).
5 Ibid. (p. 14).
6 Hillman, J. (1977, p. 80).
7 Rilke, R. M. (1923/1999, p. 77).
8 Jung, C. G. (1934/1990a).
9 Jung, C. G. (1921/19971, p. 52 [*CW* 6, para. 78], emphasis added).
10 Hillman, J. (1975/1992, p. xvii).
11 Hillman, J. (1983/2004, p. 15).
12 Henri Corbin (1972) also coined the neologism *imaginal* to describe the perception of images as real yet non-literal. He developed the notion that the images are autonomous from our experience of them. "It is their individuation, not ours," he said (as cited in Hillman, 1983/2004, p. 39), from which Hillman deduced that soul-making is "the individuation of imaginal reality" (p. 39).
13 Cobb, N. (1992, p. 30, emphasis in original).
14 Ibid. (p. 30).
15 Hillman, J. (2007, p. 39, emphasis in original).
16 Hillman, J. (1983/2004, p. 21).
17 Hillman, J. (1977); Hillman, J. (1983/2004); Sells, B. (2000).
18 Hillman, J. (1983/2004, p. 33).
19 Hillman, J. (2007, p. 39).
20 Hillman, J. (1975/1992, p. 8).
21 Hillman, J. (1975/1992).
22 Hillman, J. (1983/2004, p. 28).
23 Sells, B. (2000, p. 6).
24 Samuels, A. (2004).
25 Hillman, J. (1983/2004, p. 15).
26 Ibid.
27 Califia, P. (2002, p. 169).
28 Hillman, J. (1975/1992).
29 Hillman, J. (1975/1992).
30 Ibid.
31 Ibid. (p. 57).
32 Ibid. (p. 58).
33 Krafft-Ebing (1886/2011).
34 Ibid. (p. 55).
35 Hillman, J. (1983/2004, p. 39).
36 Hillman, J. (1975/1992).
37 Hillman, J. (1960/1972); Hillman, J. (1975/1992); Hillman, J. (1979); Hillman, J. (1983); Hillman, J. (1997).
38 Hillman, J. (1975/1992, p. 89).
39 Ibid. (p. 110).
40 Jung, C. G. (1961/1989, p. 191).
41 Hillman, J. (1977, p. 80).
42 Jung, C. G. (1954/1981, p. 175 [*CW* 8, para. 366]).
43 Ibid. (p. 174 [para. 365]).
44 Jung (1953/1975, pp. 342–343).
45 Hillman, J. (1983/2004, p. 23).
46 Hillman, J. (1983/2004, p. 63).
47 Hillman, J. (1975/1992).
48 By contrast, Hillman was a great admirer of the humanistic commitments of the classical age and of the Renaissance, which were tempered by a polytheistic cosmology.
49 Hillman, J. (1975/1992, p. 172).
50 Ibid. (pp. 172–173).

51 Ibid. (p. 173).
52 Ibid. (p. 175, emphasis in original).
53 Ibid. (p. 175).
54 Ibid. (p. 209).
55 Ibid. (p. 209)
56 Ibid.
57 Ibid. (p. 178).
58 Ibid. (p. 220).

References

Califia, P. (2002). Afterword. In G. Baldwin (Author), *Slavecraft* (2nd ed., pp. 143–178). Daedalus.

Cobb, N. (1992). *Archetypal imagination*. Lindesfarne.

Corbin, H. (1972). Mundus imaginalis or the imaginary and the imaginal. *Spring*, 1972, 1–19.

Hillman, J. (1972). *The myth of analysis*. Northwestern University Press. (Original work published 1960)

Hillman, J. (1977). An inquiry into image. *Spring*, 1977, 62–88.

Hillman, J. (1979). *The dream and the underworld*. HarperCollins.

Hillman, J. (1983). *Healing fiction*. Spring.

Hillman, J. (1992). *Re-Visioning psychology*. HarperPerennial. (Original work published 1975)

Hillman, J. (1997). *Suicide and the soul* (2nd ed.). Spring.

Hillman, J. (2004). Archetypal psychology: A brief account. In *The uniform edition of the writings of James Hillman* (Vol. 1, pp. 13–94). Spring. (Original work published 1983)

Hillman, J. (2007). *The thought of the heart and the soul of the world*. Spring.

Jung, C. G. (1971). Psychological types (R. F. C. Hull, Trans.). In H. Read et al. (Eds.), *The collected works of C. G. Jung* (Vol. 6). Princeton University Press. (Original work published 1921)

Jung, C. G. (1975). Letter to Anonymous, 2 January 1957 (R. F. C. Hull, Trans.). In G. Adler & A. Jaffé (Eds.), *C. G. Jung letters* (Vol. 2, pp. 341–343). Princeton University Press. (Original work published 1953)

Jung, C. G. (1981). On the nature of the psyche (R. F. C. Hull, Trans.). In H. Read et al. (Eds.), *The collected works of C. G. Jung* (Vol. 8, 2nd ed., pp. 159–236). Princeton University Press. (Original work published 1954)

Jung, C. G. (1989). *Memories, dreams, reflections* (R. Winston & C. Winston, Trans.; A. Jaffe, Ed.). Vintage Books. (Original work published 1961)

Jung, C. G. (1990a). Archetypes of the collective unconscious (R. F. C. Hull, Trans.). In H. Read et al. (Eds.), *The collected works of C. G. Jung* (Vol. 9i, 2nd ed., pp. 3–41). Princeton University Press. (Original work published 1934)

Jung, C. G. (1990b). The psychology of the child archetype (R. F. C. Hull, Trans.). In H. Read et al. (Eds.), *The collected works of C. G. Jung* (Vol. 9i, 2nd ed., pp. 151–181). Princeton University Press. (Original work published 1951)

Krafft-Ebing, R. (2011). *Psychopathia sexualis* (F. S. Klaf, Trans.). Arcade Publishing. (Original work published 1886)

Moore, T. (2022). *Dark eros* (3rd revised ed.). Spring. (Original work published 1990)

Rilke, R. M. (1999). Duino Elegies. In *The essential Rilke* (G. Kinnell & H. Liebmann, Trans., pp. 77–148). HarperCollins. (Original work published 1923)

Samuels, A. (2004). *Jung and the post-Jungians*. Brunner-Routledge.

Sells, B. (Ed.). (2000). *Working with images: The theoretical base of archetypal psychology*. Spring.

PART TWO
PSYCHOLOGICAL LESSONS

4

PLAY

Introduction

Part One of this study focused on theories about the psyche that provide constructive psychological approaches for considering BDSM and kink as expressions of soul. The psychology of C. G. Jung offers a system for understanding the irrational and eccentric tendencies of the psyche as normal and potentially beneficial for becoming a well-integrated person. In contrast to the legacy of Richard von Krafft-Ebing,[1] which supported a psychology that conflates normal and abnormal with healthy and unhealthy, Jung's psychology encourages a more open attitude of curiosity about alternative sexualities. A Jungian approach recognizes potential pathways to the invigorating forces of the deep psyche through BDSM and kink. James Hillman's emphasis on image as an irreducible given of psychological reality liberates the fantasy operations of the soul from the limitations of the personal. From the archetypal perspective, practitioners of BDSM can be viewed as creating a space in the modern world for the transgressive necessities of the soul to present themselves as living images engaged on peculiar journeys of their own. It is not a question of whether we can understand or endorse the impulses behind BDSM and kink. Archetypal psychology invites us to imagine the fantasy-images that bring the world of BDSM to life as autonomous, numinous persons with something to say on their own behalf.[2] Hillman's approach to the psyche inspires a poetic reading of

DOI: 10.4324/9781003223597-6

BDSM as a twisted but strangely beautiful pageant of the soul. To participate in it is to be changed by it.

The present chapter initiates a series of psychological reflections on topics that illuminate the relationship between BDSM and soul. The subject here is play. The discussion will acknowledge the difficulty of defining play and the ambivalence surrounding the word within the BDSM community. The central portion of the chapter is devoted to the work of three twentieth-century thinkers: D. W. Winnicott, Johan Huizinga, and Hans-Georg Gadamer. The concluding discussion integrates their ideas into a deeper psychological understanding of play as a form of soul-making.

Play—You Don't Say?

To explore how play relates to the world of BDSM, it helps to begin by defining what play is. Arriving at a definition, however, appears to be more difficult than one might think, even though play is virtually omnipresent in childhood fantasies, games, and sports. Since psychologists, social scientists, scholars, critics, and philosophers have all been unable to reach consensus on a working definition of play as a topic for more in-depth consideration, psychologist Shachaf Bitan[3] has suggested that the impulse to create a definition for play is itself problematic. Definitions tend to restrict phenomena and render them static, a tendency inherently antithetical to the nature of play.

As an alternative, Bitan proposed, first, that rather than examining play as a thing, we view it as a process that requires movement through time in order to exist. Second, he brought attention to play's paradoxical nature: it oscillates between "real and unreal, inside and outside, present and absent, et cetera [sic]."[4] And finally, in play, dichotomies peacefully coexist. In other areas of life, dichotomies usually depend on binarism, which posits opposites as contradictory or complementary. Bitan suggested that in play, dichotomies are allowed a peaceful coexistence without a resolution of the paradox.

For an exploration of the world of BDSM, Bitan's working definition is both useful and problematic. It is useful because it offers a framework for understanding the paradoxical experiences that often emerge from a scene. Imagine two people who meet at a local play party and negotiate a scene involving sadomasochism, one tying the other up and flogging the other. When they finish, they both smile and say that it was great, and perhaps there is a bit of aftercare. They put on their street clothes and go their separate ways. The person in the submissive role (also referred to as "the bottom") goes home and looks at the red traces across the skin where the flogger landed sharp and hard. The person feels a sudden rush of excitement and emotion while looking at the marks. What do they mean? What is that complex feeling that is so vivid yet so hard to describe? Is what just happened real, or is it unreal? "Was that physical abuse?" the person might ask. "Or was that just play?" The person in the Dominant role (also referred to as "the Top") might reflect on the experience with a similar combination of excitement and confusion: "Did I really just enjoy inflicting pain on a stranger? Did that really happen? Was it really okay?" These are all important psychological questions. The play element in BDSM allows for the experience and the marks to be both real and unreal.

What transpired was real: the red welts do not lie. The Top really tied the person's limbs to a Saint Andrew's cross in a darkened room and flogged the bottom with swift, sharp strokes. The emotions were real: they were exciting, fierce, and passionate. Maybe the experience was even transcendent for both partners, creating a sense of merger and intimacy between them, a trancelike blurring between who holds the flogger and who receives the blows. The experience was also unreal: the players did not know each other before the scene. What occurred was the enactment of a fantasy. It was different from "real" abuse because the couple negotiated and agreed about what was to happen before they started, and at one point, the bottom had even taunted the Top to strike harder. The bottom held the ultimate control over the scene because the safe word would make everything stop. The conventional idea that intimacy comes from sharing personal information with another through the expression of inner thoughts and feelings did not occur. In the absence of personal knowledge, the space between them was filled with assumptions about each other (assumptions based on fantasy-images). And yet there might also be a lingering conviction that together, they had dipped into the shadowy waters of the soul and touched upon something profoundly true (a soul-centered orientation asserts that the archetypal dimension of an experience is just as real, perhaps even more real, than the material facts that comprise it). Play is the element that allows all these contrasting impressions to coexist peacefully in the same moment.

Understanding the psychological aspect of play as a process can be useful for exploring the paradoxical experiences of BDSM and kink. At the same time, it can be problematic. Some practitioners object to the casual use of the word *play* to describe scenes and activities in the kink community. For individuals who find a deeper truth about their own identity through the activities and relationships of BDSM, the word can seem to trivialize what for them is an essential part of who they are and how they experience intimacy. The following passage from the memoir of self-identified slave Richard Levine describes his sense of the significance of SM practices with his Master. It expresses the depths of meaning that a committed Master/slave relationship can attain:

> Master Skip used and enjoyed SM (sado-masochism) practices. They were the sacraments he offered as a Priest in Black Leather. He found them erotic, but he also felt they were tools for what he called slave development, which would support greater trust, obedience and surrender in the slave. Ultimately, it was about surrendering the ego and aligning the slave's will with the Master's will. If the Master was spiritually awake and in touch with a greater Divine Will, then both ultimately became similarly aligned, leading to a spiritually directed life of service. Master Skip believed that many SM practices were modern-day evolutions of primitive shamanic practices, all of which had a specific intention for growth and ego transcendence.[5]

Levine describes a relationship oriented toward transformation and growth in service to a higher life purpose that has an overtly spiritual quality. The Master needs to possess a high level of maturity and expertise because he assumes responsibility for guiding and developing the slave. It is understandable that someone invested in BDSM's potential for expanded consciousness would object to describing their practices as play. The popular connotation of the word suggests a lighthearted, frivolous activity. Some practitioners might prefer to describe their pursuits as a personal craft, a life practice, or a spiritual discipline.

Although this perceived incompatibility indicates that the term "play" may be problematic for gaining insight into BDSM, the word often appears in descriptions of BDSM activities. It is frequently employed to describe niche interests such as role-play, rope play, impact play, fire play, knife play, pup play, age play, edgeplay, and water sports (which infers play) among many others. In addition, the practice of referring to an encounter as "a scene" and referring to the place of the encounter as a "play space" further emphasize the play element in BDSM. In the language of soul, play is a welcome and necessary ingredient to stimulate the metaphorical imagination and to generate the living symbols of what Jung[6] called the transcendent function.

In the twentieth century, three major thinkers about the deeper significance of play were Winnicott, Huizinga, and Gadamer. Winnicott was an English leader in the object relations school of psychoanalysis, Huizinga was a Dutch cultural historian, and Gadamer was a leading German philosopher in the generation after Martin Heidegger. Each was a prominent figure in his field, and all devoted a significant part of their work to writing about the importance of play for the individual and for society. Although none of them directly addressed the phenomenon of alternative sexualities, they each offer a unique perspective that helps explain the psychological meaning of play in the context of BDSM activities and relationships.

Winnicott: The Space Between

Winnicott was a preeminent figure in the object relations school of psychoanalysis in the mid-twentieth century. Although the psychoanalytic tradition largely viewed sadomasochism as pathological, he had surprisingly little to say about the subject. However, his ideas about play can illuminate the psychological mechanisms at work in contemporary BDSM. There is also a correlation between Winnicott's insights and the concept of imaginal reality fundamental to depth psychology. An exploration of the similarities between what Hillman called imaginal space and what he called potential space opens new possibilities to consider BDSM play as a healing activity that connects with the archetypal energy of the psyche.

Winnicott proposed that throughout our lives, we face the fundamental psychological challenge of "relating inner and outer reality."[7] The object relations model views the inner subjective world as filled with largely unconscious, emotionally turbulent fantasies, whereas the external objective world limits our ability to gratify our desires and meet our needs. The inner and outer worlds would feel more congruent if we were omnipotent and could truly control our surroundings, but external reality thwarts those expectations. The psychological strain of mediating these divergent realities is with us from infancy onward, but, Winnicott said, if a mother or caregiver can establish what he called a holding environment that mitigates the stress of incongruence between inner and outer, the child will learn how to play and develop symbolic thought.

What Winnicott meant here by play is consistent with Bitan's working definition: play is a process, a doing, or possibly, a way of being that allows the divergent aspects of inner and outer to coexist peacefully in the same space. The paradox is held and not resolved. Because the division between inner and outer is not rigid, there exists, Winnicott believed, an in-between region in which *transitional phenomena* can occur.[8] Play occurs in this region of transition from internal psychic reality to an external objectively real world. Winnicott called the zone of the in-between *potential space*.[9] The term *potential* communicates the *potency* of playing in the area between inner and outer to create multiple meanings and thereby holding the paradox of that which is and at the same time is not. Playful paradox is the origin of symbolic representation and the basis of poetic thought.

Winnicott brought attention to play as a vital source of healing in psychotherapy and also as an essential agent in creativity and societal well-being. By refining the idea that we relate to people through our internal representations of others and the world around us, his model provides invaluable insights into the vicissitudes and the delights of human relationships across the lifespan. His description of our inner lives presents a powerful de-literalization of our encounters with others by foregrounding the role played by the unconscious. How do his ideas correlate with those of Jung and Hillman? And how does his perspective on play relate to BDSM? The present discussion proposes a playful response to these questions, in which paradoxical contrasts and incompatibilities find a peaceful coexistence.

There is a clear and significant contrast between Winnicott's conceptualization of the psyche and that of the Jungian and post-Jungian schools. As a result, there are fundamental differences in how they imagine the location and the agency of the play element. Winnicott's model is based on a person-centered psyche: inner and outer exist in a Cartesian cosmos in which a person at the epicenter struggles between chaotic internal subjective states of omnipotent madness and an external objectively real world that requires adaptation. Play occurs either between persons or between person and world. In contrast, Jung imagined what might be called a gnostic cosmos, meaning that we come to know the nature of the world through our participation in it. The objective psyche surrounds and subsumes subjective personal reality.

In Jung's model, psyche is not within us; it is we who are within psyche.[10] In Hillman's[11] re-visioning of psychology, the displacement and relativizing of the personal ego became even more explicit. His concept of *dehumanizing* makes the radical assertion that the images of the soul are more enduring and ontologically more real than the fantasy of the person. In the archetypal model, it would appear either that the imaginal world is located outside the fantasy of the person or that the two are, at a minimum, so intertwined that the notion of a transitional space between them collapses. Faced with such a contrast in the location of inner and outer, what happens to Winnicott's concept of potential space, which is where play occurs?

If a correlate exists for Winnicott's potential space in the archetypal model, it might be present in the work of French anthropologist Henri Corbin. Corbin was a pioneer in the Western study of ecstatic Islam and Sufism. He identified the need to craft a new term to accommodate a dimension of Islamic thought that describes a world of images (the *mundus imaginalis*) that is as ontologically real as the material world.[12] He introduced the term *imaginal* to designate this dimension in distinction to the Western term "imaginary," which connotes something unreal. Corbin's imaginal world can be viewed as an archetypal correlate to Winnicott's potential space. For Corbin, the intermediate zone is not between the internal psychic reality of the person and an objective external reality. Instead, the intermediate region occurs between the autonomous reality of the image (the *mundus imaginalis*) and the material reality of the physical world. The paradox of an incompatible dichotomy has shifted from the zone between people and their surround to the zone between the world of image and the world of physical matter. Corbin challenges us to play with the notion that the imaginal is at once both real on its own terms and unreal because it lacks material substance.

Here, we come back to the kinky couple who met at the play party. Was their encounter real or unreal? Winnicott's conceptualization that play occurs in potential space allows the dichotomy of real and unreal to coexist without a need to resolve the paradox. In fact, Winnicott[13] maintained that it was important not to resolve the paradox. Play, in Winnicott's sense of the word, did not end when the scene ended between the kinksters. The potential space in which play occurs actually expanded after the scene, as both partners separately reflected more seriously on what took place. To be clear, potential space is different from physical space. It does not come into being because two people are together, although it can coincide with the space between people and their fantasies. The point is that potential space is an operation of the mind, not a physical location.

As the submissive bottom looks in the mirror at the red marks on the flesh and wonders what they mean, contrasting emotions rise to the surface, and contradictory evaluations are formed (e.g., "they show my strength, but they show my weakness; they are beautiful, but they are terrible; I love them, but I'm ashamed of them," etc.) The person is playing in potential space as long as the paradox of the contradictions is held without resolution and the contrasting thoughts and feelings are allowed peaceful coexistence. The submissive partner plays with multiple meanings and contemplates what is and at the same time is not. The person has discovered a "poetic basis of mind,"[14] and the flogging and the resulting marks become symbols of something transformational but only partially understood. As Winnicott and Jung would agree, symbol formation contributes to psychological growth and healing.

The bottom's experience can also illustrate an encounter with the imaginal world posited by Corbin. The red marks and the bare flesh now exist in the reality of two worlds: the physical consequences of the flogging as a material fact and the archetypal world of image in which the ageless fantasies of wounding, sacrifice, submission, and initiation all find their home. The gaze into the mirror is also both literal and imaginal because gazing into mirrors always has a non-literal visionary aspect. The bottom looks into the reflection and sees what lives beyond it through the image that is looking back. Play is occurring in the space between the two dimensions of personal experience and archetypal image. Both are allowed a peaceful coexistence in the same space, and the paradox of what is and at the same time is not can be held between the bottom and the reflection without resolution. The red marks on the flesh emerge as a symbol that holds the two worlds together without being fully understood.

By now, it might be apparent that there is a further correspondence between Winnicott's concept of play and a soul-centered approach. In Chapter 1, a definition of what it means to be soul-centered proposed a non-literal, image-focused approach to lived experience. To be soul-centered is to engage in a metaphorical style of imagining and "a poetic basis of mind."[15] To favor metaphorical and symbolic modes of thought is to play with multiple layers of meaning. Metaphor is a figure of speech that says what something is and at the same time what it is not. Similarly, Winnicott's potential space allows the synchronous presence of the "is" and the "is not." Such a poetic attitude is the genesis of creativity, as Winnicott himself said: "the reason why playing is essential is that it is in playing that the patient is being creative."[16] Play, through its connection to metaphor and to creativity, brings soul into the world.

Is a kinkster's play space inevitably coextensive with potential space? That is unlikely. Sometimes the pleasure of playing in BDSM scenes involves shutting off the mind and enjoying an immersion into another world far from workaday concerns. For some, kink is a decidedly anti-intellectual activity devoid of the self-reflection and mentalization that Winnicott's model seems to imply. However, Winnicott formulated his ideas about play by working with both children and adults. If a child immersed in play with a set of dolls can have a healing emotional experience, it follows that kinksters playing inside a modern dungeon also could. Winnicott asserted that play is a given of the human condition and a form of therapy in and of itself.[17]

Designating BDSM activities as *play* lifts them out of the literal and emphasizes their performative aspect. To create a scene involving torture is not the same thing as interrogating a political prisoner using waterboarding. Not only does the element of mutual consent distinguish one from the other, but in the case of BDSM, the notion that the activity is play implies that there is also a fantasy element at work in which layers of meaning are present and open to exploration. It is an enactment, a performance, a play of torture, that is and is not real. The play that occurs in BDSM is like an improvised drama (or sometimes a comedy) in a theater of the erotic imagination. As with any form of theater, the play of BDSM takes place between the physical reality of the everyday and the imaginal fantasy reality of what is being enacted. Behind every scene of domination and submission there are archetypal fantasy-images guiding the action and the narrative. The scene remains a paradox in which practitioners are players, held in the potential space between the mundane and the archetypal, between what is and at the same time is not.

Huizinga and Play as Social Agent

In his landmark work, *Homo Ludens*, the Dutch cultural historian Huizinga[18] developed the concept of play in the context of social evolution. In his analysis, play is the vital agent that promotes cultural progress. He found evidence of play as an element in some of society's most earnest and sacred activities, including law, politics, warfare, and religious rituals and festivals. He regarded play as the motor of social development, a view that transcends play's popular associations with frivolity and caprice, although play characteristics are also undeniably present in our lighter moments. He associated play with the mythopoetic function of the psyche—that deep impulse to bring order and meaning to the rhythms of nature within us and around us through story, metaphor, and ritual.

Through his analysis of cultural history, Huizinga distilled his findings into a phenomenological reduction of play to its essential characteristics: it is voluntary and free; it occurs outside of so-called "ordinary" or "real" life; its locality and duration are secluded and limited; it creates order ("into an imperfect world and into the confusion of life it brings a temporary, a limited perfection"); it involves tension; it has rules that are clear and binding; and it enjoys an air of secrecy.[19] This list of essential characteristics is surprisingly relevant for describing how the play element appears in the world of BDSM.

Play is voluntary and free. The element of negotiation and consent is one of the cornerstones of the modern BDSM movement. If individuals are not participating voluntarily and exercising free will in what they are doing, then there is a risk that personal limits will be crossed and that coercion or abuse might occur. The concept of free will is also evident in the use of safe words that give participants the option of voluntarily calling an end to a scene when personal limits are reached. What may be less obvious but psychologically very important is that, according to Huizinga, without voluntary consent and personal freedom, the play element is absent from BDSM activities.

The characteristic of volition might appear at odds with some of the more extreme forms of domination and submission, such as the iconic Master/slave (M/s) relationship. Is not the very notion of slavery anathema to the idea of free will? In fact, an individual today who identifies as a slave within a BDSM context *must* have the freedom to choose a life of voluntary servitude to a Master. Freedom to choose is a hallmark of the modern M/s relationship. Many M/s couples sign a contract agreeing to the details of servitude, which makes the element of free will explicit. The authority-transfer relationship is voluntary.

Huizinga also posited that play occurs outside of so-called "ordinary" or "real" life. It is readily apparent that the world of BDSM is a world outside the everyday. Its capacity to transgress conventional social norms is part of its erotic allure. As previously stated, in order for eroticism to be kinky, it has to be outside the norm. When kinksters describe their activities as "doing a scene," it is a clear statement that what transpires is set apart and outside the banality of daily life. Huizinga also reintroduces the dichotomy of real versus unreal discussed in the previous section. Real life is associated with the ordinary and the literal. The play element sets BDSM apart from "real" life.

Play's locality and duration are secluded and limited. Usually, a kinkster's departure from the ordinary and the real includes a movement into a play space specifically designated for the scene. The seclusion of the dungeon or the private club is part of what evokes the mystique. Seclusion has an archetypal fantasy quality that lends itself to any space in which BDSM play occurs. What happens here is not for open public display. The secluded location brings with it a quality of secrecy (another one of Huizinga's essential characteristics), as well as intimacy and interiority. The other essential characteristic here involves the limited duration of play. Like Bitan and Winnicott, Huizinga held that play is a mode of doing or being that moves through time. But there is a limit. Not everything is play. Just as it is spatially limited by the secluded locale, it is temporally limited by a clearly defined beginning, middle, and end. Getting whipped by a single tail at a play party may last a matter of minutes, or doing a scene in a Master's private dungeon may last an entire weekend, but in either case, the period of time in which the scene occurs is limited and agreed upon. Seclusion and the demarcation of time are familiar elements of BDSM and an essential part of what characterizes the activities as play.

Does the temporal characteristic of play apply to those BDSM relationships that involve long-term commitments enduring over a period of years? As with a conventional marital relationship, it would be more accurate to identify the play element as it appears in the rituals and ceremonies that designate the special status of the coupling rather than characterizing the relationship itself as play. A committed long-term relationship may have discrete periods of time in which the play element is present, but it would be inaccurate to characterize the daily life of the couple as play. For example, a Master/slave couple might engage in a scene in the home dungeon for a limited period of time, which could be considered play. But if the couple talks over who will take the car to the mechanic for a tune-up, the frame has shifted to everyday life.

For Huizinga, another essential characteristic of play is that it creates order ("into an imperfect world and into the confusion of life it brings a temporary, a limited perfection").[20] Order and perfection are frequent themes in the world of BDSM. In his ethnographic study of SM, psychoanalyst Robert J. Stoller[21] characterized the primal forces underlying the desires of his interview subjects as an ambivalent struggle between control and freedom. The author made a compelling case that much of what occurs in professional dungeons involves flirting with loss of control as an erotic pivot point. After describing in detail a visit with a professional dominatrix at her private club, Stoller summarized what he learned:

> Important in all this is that the customer experiences a genuine lack of control within the overall control (safety) of this being a club. The lack of control of the gadgetry is contained by the women's skill in letting the man . . . know he is safe. Though he really feels out of control, the situation is not beyond what he wants.[22]

The fear of losing control is itself a response to the specter of chaos familiar to all of us. Very little seems to be within our frail grasp. BDSM offers a kind of order that temporarily contains the fear and plays with it in that potential space where control and the loss of control both exist without negation. Such containment is perhaps what Huizinga had in mind when he asserted that play creates "a limited perfection."[23]

The rigorous protocols that are a hallmark of Dom/sub (D/s) relationships also play with a similar exquisite attention to order and perfection in the context of the submissive's behavior. The Dom may express authority over the sub by controlling multiple aspects of the person's life down to minute details, such as specifying where and when to stand, kneel, or sit and what posture to assume for different ritualized moments. Stoller's observation regarding the desire for a loss of control squares with a comment made by kink scholar, Caroline Shahbaz:

> When I think of people who are intelligent people who choose to be submissive, part of what they are seeking is the reassurance and

stability that comes from living within structured boundaries. That is what authority creates. If you're in a constant soup of autonomy, every single decision has to be renegotiated, reprosecuted every single time, which is extremely taxing on the psyche because we're living in a constant stream of unpredictability and chaos.[24]

The unpredictability and instability of modern life leads to uncertainty and anxiety. Shahbaz powerfully describes the pleasure of submission as an antidote to such pressures. Back in the 1980s, Roy Baumeister expressed a similar opinion regarding the capacity of masochism to relieve "the burdensome pressure of selfhood."[25] Knowing that someone else is in charge and knowing that the daily demands for achievement have been radically circumscribed bring a sense of order and perfection to a chaotic life. For the Dom who is the architect of the submissive's highly structured world, the satisfaction can be equally intense for having created a temporary order and limited perfection in a chaotic world. According to Huizinga, it is the play element at work in these activities and relationships that facilitates such pleasure.

The next essential characteristic in Huizinga's inventory is that play involves tension. There is a temptation to literalize the idea of tension by thinking of the experience of bondage. Clearly, tension and struggle are common, if not essential, elements in the erotic excitement of being restrained or immobilized. Rope, chain, tape, or plastic wrap require tension to be effective. But beyond the literal physical presence of tension, how is bondage at play with the soul? In addition to physical suspension, there is also emotional suspense. Stoller's[26] description brings into view the suspense that comes with not knowing how much one can take or what will happen if control is lost.

As discussed earlier, to be soul-centered is to be image-centered, and it is interesting to discover that there is an image at the root of the word *tension*, which derives from the Latin word *tendere*, meaning to stretch.[27] Stretching can imply going beyond ordinary limits, one of the hallmarks of BDSM. The verb "to tend" shares the same root. Stretching is also linguistically related to reaching and touching. In BDSM, there is a tending of the craft, a stretching, a reaching, and an invitation to touch and to be touched, to be sensuously and aesthetically engaged not only with the partner who joins in the play but also with the archetypal images that come to us from beyond us and participate in shaping the scene. Play involves tension.

Play also has rules that are clear and binding. Rules are common in BDSM activities and relationships. The modern practice of kink and BDSM is characterized by a sustained commitment to protect that first characteristic of play, the voluntary and free practice of alternative sexuality, by establishing and enforcing rules for how to negotiate a scene, how to give and receive real, credible consent, how to end a scene in mid-session if something goes wrong, and how to engage in aftercare to avoid negative consequences once the scene is completed. Such rules regularly appear in clubs and public play spaces, which are staffed by individuals known as dungeon monitors (DMs). Most often serving on a volunteer basis, DMs circulate throughout the play space to enforce the rules of the club and ensure the safety of practitioners. In addition to rules that structure play spaces for group scenes, most experienced practitioners have their own personal rules that allow them to play with confidence and a sense of personal security. When rules are violated, the conventional wisdom is to end the scene and address the infraction. The presence and enforcement of rules is part of how the play element manifests in the world of BDSM.

Huizinga's final postulate is that play enjoys being enveloped by an air of secrecy. When partners meet for a scene and journey into the unknown by testing and pushing limits through sadomasochistic play, secrecy hangs in the ether around them like a micro-climate. On one level, secrecy may emanate from a sense of internalized shame that one or both players experience. There can be a fear that others must never find out about what is happening here. Psychotherapist and expert on gay leather culture Guy Baldwin[28] has written extensively about the connection between shame and secrecy that has characterized much of the leather scene. However, the secrecy that fills the play space transcends the painful emotions of personal shame. There is also the element of surprise that can both delight and terrify a kinky partner during a scene. In a personal communication, Baldwin[29] recalled that BDSM play can be enhanced when the Top intentionally keeps planned details of the scene secret from the bottom to thwart expectations and intensify the erotic uncertainty.

Of course, playing with uncertainty raises questions about the nature of consent and how much detail should be included in negotiations before play begins. Overly detailed planning ensures solid consent for what will happen, but it does not allow for surprises. So while novice practitioners would do best to err on the side of caution, more experienced players familiar with their partners may have established enough trust and security to enjoy a greater element of surprise. Regardless of how one addresses the question of consent, secrets are inherent to the spirit of play.

The mythic archetypal perspective of depth psychology agrees. Russell Lockhart has written about Psyche's fondness for concealment as part of her archetypal nature. He illustrated Psyche's connection to secrecy by describing a statue of Angerona, the Roman goddess of silence:

> Her mouth is bound so there are no words from her. Her uplifted finger points to her sealed lips as if to let us know there is some point to this silence. How do we learn from her if there are no words?[30]

Angerona's posture is the embodiment of secrecy (and a nod to the symbolic power of bondage through her bound mouth). It is a stroke of psychological insight that Lockhart continued with a comment that confirms Huizinga's association between secrecy and play:

> What can we learn of silence from the name of its Goddess? Every name carries with it a kind of secret. Angerona is a shell covering a hidden image that was once a living experience. When we speak now of Angerona, or any other God or Goddess, or even of ourselves, we do not know or remember that hidden image. We know only the shell of the name. The secret mystery hidden in every name—even in every word—requires a seeking after. We must search for the hidden image. It is looking for psyche. She hides, we seek. It is hide-and-seek. It is a game, a kind of play.[31]

Here, Lockhart uncovered the rather surprising relationship between secrecy, play, and the logos of the soul. The game of hide-and-seek is played between the conscious mind and the secret images of the soul. Practitioners of BDSM have the opportunity to explore the deeper truths hidden in their own nature and, perhaps, to discover greater, more difficult truths about human nature in general. The air of secrecy during a scene affirms that the play space is also soul-space.

Gadamer and the Game of Understanding

A discussion of the work of Gadamer, arguably the most important post-Heidegger contributor to the field of philosophical hermeneutics, concludes this survey of influential thinkers regarding the significance of play. Historically, hermeneutics had addressed the challenges involved in interpreting texts, particularly biblical texts. With Heidegger and then Gadamer, hermeneutics came to be associated with the larger philosophical question of how people exist as beings called to understand the world. Understanding is now viewed as a primary aspect of our human being in the world.[32] In his major work, *Truth and Method*, Gadamer[33] designated play as what makes understanding possible. It is through play that we come into existence as understanding beings.[34]

Gadamer's philosophical hermeneutics in general and his insights into the importance of play in particular can initially appear esoteric and removed from the visceral pleasures of BDSM. Yet one of Gadamer's primary objectives was to return the focus of philosophy and the human sciences more generally to the spontaneity and freshness of immediate lived experience. There is a beauty to Gadamer's ideas that can lead to a deeper appreciation of why play is such a vital aspect of BDSM.

Gadamer[35] posited that the process of understanding involves a dialogical encounter with a dynamic Other who has something to say. The Other may be a work of art, a text, or a human being. Understanding does not occur by treating the Other as a lifeless object possessing some hidden truth to be known through dispassionate observation, extraction, and analysis. For Gadamer, the call to understanding is an ethical call to meet the Other as a Thou rather than as an It, terms from Martin Buber.[36] When one encounters the Other as a Thou, it is a holistic experience based on relationship rather than on utility. The truth of understanding emerges between an engaged participatory subject and the Other as a Thou in the intermediate space of back-and-forth exchange. As in Winnicott's[37] formulation of potential space, truth—for Gadamer—lies in the liminal (derived from the Latin word for *threshold*). Understanding as an ontological event is an essentially relational process that requires one's full commitment, engagement, participation, and most importantly, openness to what the Other has to say. There is a to-and-fro movement as the Other presents its claim on truth and one opens oneself to what is presented with all of one's being. The exchange of presentation and recognition is what

Gadamer formulated as play, the essential mechanism that makes under-standing possible.

In order to appreciate the relevance of Gadamer's philosophy to play as it occurs in BDSM, there needs to be some reconsideration of the three ways that the Other manifests in alternative sexualities. First, there is the literal physical presence of the play partner as the Other in the intentional imbal-ance and polarization of authority between a Dominant Top and a submis-sive bottom. Second, as the Jungian model would emphasize, the Other is also present within oneself as part of the personal shadow. "People hate to accept their own other," Jung wrote in *The Red Book*.[38] It is difficult to make peace with the otherness that dwells within. Third, a soul-centered approach recognizes that, in addition to the Other, there is also the presence of *the oth-ers*, the archetypal figures that live as images in imaginal space, which shape the contents of the personal imagination in play and introduce the players to the reality of the soul and its transgressive necessities. When a scene goes deep, practitioners might have difficulty putting into words what happens for them. Words fail because the encounter with the archetypal Other can lead one to a primal level of the soul beyond conventional language, a place where the images are more real than we are. Gadamer believed that such encounters with something so completely foreign to one's view of self and world impose an ethical calling to meet the Other as a Thou. The challenge is to not reject the unfamiliar as irrelevant, worthless, or innately inferior to oneself but to recognize its autonomy and status as an equal presenting its claim on truth and knowledge separate and different from our own.

To return to Gadamer's[39] conceptualization of play, when we engage with the Other as a Thou, our presuppositions and prejudices are placed at risk. The Other presents a claim that is recognized in part as true, depending on what our personal history and tradition have prepared us to be able to recognize. Partial recognition leads to an incomplete response, which reveals that the Other is presenting something outside our current claims on knowl-edge and truth. The Other is presenting something unknown yet potentially knowable. An open and engaged response requires us to risk the prejudices and presuppositions of previously held knowledge claims in order to under-stand what the Other is presenting. The scope and sophistication of our identity and what we know are refined and transformed by the to-and-fro exchange of presentation and recognition. We gain an understanding of the truth that was previously unknown, and now it becomes a part of our being.

The importance of the game in relation to playing is one final element of Gadamer's philosophy that is relevant to the present discussion, particularly his recognition of how the game takes control over the players:

> Gadamer emphasizes the *"primacy of play over the consciousness of the player"* (*Truth and Method*, p. 104). He describes play as having an active life of its own, of absorbing the players into itself, of holding the players in its spell, and of drawing them into the game. As Gadamer describes it, play is less of a thing a person does, and more of a thing done to him—or, better, an event in which one becomes caught-up. Gadamer declares that "all playing is a being-played . . . the game masters the players." (*Truth and Method*, p. 106)[40]

Gadamer privileged the game as play's true subject. Play is not about the players. It is about the game. Understanding is not something that is done to a BDSM scene, a work of art, or a person. It is a process, an event, in which the players are subsumed. The play partners and the multi-dimensional presence of the Other are caught up in the play of the game.

If play, as in Gadamer's model, is indeed the vital activity that leads to our existence as beings of understanding, what are the implications for play in the context of BDSM? The notion of what play is changes from its being an activity to its being a process. Play as recreation or entertainment changes to play as a way of relating that leads to deeper understanding of self and others and a fuller experience of being part of the world. When one reimagines play as a process of relating, one sees how play can lead to a multi-dimensional experience of the Other.

A passage from the book *Slavecraft* illustrates how play may involve the multi-dimensionality of the Other.[41] A slave describes his experience of learning to submit to his Master during long, intense scenes. The slave moves through a process of self-discovery that involves an internal negotiation with areas of resistance to the challenges of submission. He is attuned and responsive to the Master's demands but also experiences an encounter with a realm beyond the personal. An immersion in imaginal reality occurs: the slave descends in the Sea of Surrender, rests in the Great Deep, and hears the Roaring Void. These are places that are just as real as the street with cars parked on it just outside the Master's dungeon, but they exist in the non-physical dimension of the *mundus imaginalis.* The individual experiences a personal transformation that comes from encountering the otherness of these imaginal spaces.

As the slave discovers the depths of the Sea of Surrender, the conventional sense of play as a recreational activity cedes its place to Gadamer's version of play as a process of relating that leads to a deeper understanding of self and others. What occurs is a powerful and deeply transformative experience—an encounter with *the Other as imaginal space.* The presence of the Master as the Other is paradoxically rather limited. The greater part of the slave's experience is an inner journey that leads to transcendent destinations beyond the ego. The play occurs less between two individuals and more as a numinous encounter with a multi-dimensional Other. The slave's account further illustrates Gadamer's privileging the *"primacy of play over the consciousness of the player."*[42] It is an example of how the game of understanding can absorb the players into itself and hold them in its spell.

In the previous example, the dynamic of domination and submission occurs as an ontological event. The author descends into the otherness of the experience and allows himself to risk his presuppositions about who he is and what should happen. Gadamer might say that the player encounters the Other at the horizon of understanding and that he grows in complexity and sophistication from having incorporated some new information about himself and the world because of the experience. Having visited the bottom of the Sea of Surrender and listened to the Roaring Void, one is surely a changed person. The deeper potential of play to facilitate growth through understanding becomes available through BDSM domination and submission as a relational process. Externally, the relationship is with the Master; internally, the relationship is with the images of the soul.

When BDSM activities involve degradation, objectification, or violence, the submissive partner often functions more like an It than a Thou. In such instances, the relational dynamic appears to contradict Gadamer's assertion that in play the Other is encountered as a Thou with a unique claim on the truth. The question touches on a point of controversy in the BDSM community: How far should play involving degradation and violence go? Is the intent of degradation play to effect a literal devaluation and objectification of the person, which reduces the status of the individual to a sub-human *it*? Is it only by inflicting literal physical and emotional hurt that certain desires find consummation? Some practitioners believe that the intensity of "real" degradation is necessary to break the submissive's will as an autonomous person. On the other hand, even in the midst of the most extreme ordeals, is there a well-concealed knowing "wink" between Dom and sub that recognizes the best play is the most serious? The most extreme does not have to be the most literal. Perhaps the unresolved coexistence of valuing and devaluing is what makes a scene transformational (the submissive is simultaneously an It and a Thou). The paradox lies in finding value in devaluing. From the perspective of depth psychology, the "game of degradation" takes over the players and constellates the archetypal *It*, an autonomous soul-image that speaks of the primordial value of objectification on its own behalf.

Conclusion

Collectively, the work of Winnicott, Huizinga, and Gadamer elevates the role of play from being something trivial and entertaining to recognizing it as a generator of growth and transformation for the individual and for the world.

By recognizing a liminal zone between the internal fantasy world of the individual and the limitations of external reality, Winnicott[43] designated potential space as the region where play occurs. In the space between inner and outer, there is a peaceful ambiguity in which multiple meanings can coexist. Winnicott's model permits a comfortable transition to the imaginal reality of Corbin, Jung, and Hillman in which the construct of inner and outer yields to the dichotomy of physical versus imaginal. It is a mistake to suppose that the presence of play in BDSM renders the activities and their potential meaning less substantial to practitioners, just as it is an error to think that invoking play lessens the risks of what can take place in potential space. Calling BDSM play does not make it less complex or less psychologically hazardous. Players can be surprised in the middle of a scene by unexpected feelings of fear, shame, or rage that spontaneously arise from the depths and enter the transitional space. Whether the transition is from inner to outer, or from imaginal reality to material reality, the potential space of play is serious business. It fosters resiliency by building psychological muscles that can tolerate what Jungian analyst Nathan Schwartz-Salant has called "the mad parts of sane people."[44] Play is the agent that facilitates an opening in the fabric of the literal and the mundane for the soul to break through, not as a psychotic break or a dissociative episode but as a way of being open, engaged, and participatory in the liminal.

The designation of the liminal as an imaginal space in which play occurs is part of Huizinga's and Gadamer's framework as well. Huizinga's list of essential characteristics is less overt in its inclusion of an imaginal threshold, yet it is implicit in his assertion that the space of play is set apart from the ordinary and the so-called "real." Despite our sometimes-strenuous objections, we humans are creatures of the ordinary. It is by stepping outside the routine of the everyday through play that we encounter the extraordinary. Play activities are set apart yet inserted in between the course of life's more mundane activities. Huizinga's observation that tension and secrecy are also characteristics of play introduces another aspect of the liminal. In tension, there is a stretching toward the Other across the space that separates the familiar from the unknown, similar to Gadamer's idea that the horizon of understanding is the meeting place between our familiar assumptions about the world and the unfamiliar perspectives introduced by the Other. Because play involves secrecy, it evokes a space between speech and silence, between manifest and latent, between shared content and secrets (which include the secrets of the soul).

In some cases, overt and in others, implicit, the notion of liminality as an element of play is shared by Winnicott, Huizinga, and Gadamer. It also appears in the work of Jung and Hillman as a valuable and potentially generative dimension of psychological experience. Jung's[45] technique of active imagination is a form of psychological play, a game of understanding with the soul as the Other. It is a game that takes place in the imaginal realm of the in-between.

Similar to Huizinga's insight that play involves an air of secrecy, Hillman wrote, "The soul draws us through the labyrinth of literalisms ever inward, realizing itself through retreat."[46] The poetic image of the soul's retreat through the darkened labyrinth of the mind's literalisms has something in common with the somber spirit of BDSM play in dungeon spaces today. There, one finds a similar air of interiority, secrecy, and withdrawal, all essential components of the play element. *Play is a form of soul-making*, as Hillman intended the term. We encounter numinous persons of the soul in the imaginal space of the liminal, where play reigns supreme.

In BDSM, play occurs in a zone between a host of ambiguities that include the space between pleasure and pain, control and chaos, annihilation and ecstasy, strength and weakness, love and shame, and the knowable and the ineffable. Play occurs in the liminal borderland between these dichotomies, and it is the agent that facilitates the tension and secrecy between oneself and the Other. Play is also the agent that transforms the players through the game of understanding. A psychological understanding of BDSM asks more of practitioners than learning how to handle a leather paddle or how to hogtie a partner. Understanding involves a willingness to risk one's self-image as a particular kind of person and to allow the play to change one's presumptions and perceptions through the game with the Other. Understanding also asks practitioners to risk their presumptions about the very nature of the Other, which is an archetypal figure that can emerge simultaneously as an It and a Thou. Just as easily, it can manifest as an imaginal figure (a fantasy-image that appears in a moment of erotic reverie) or as a landscape of the soul (e.g., the Sea of Surrender and the Great Deep). In the world of BDSM, play has the capacity to lead us into a deeper relationship with soul. Play has the capacity to change our lives.

Notes

1 Krafft-Ebing, R. (1886/2011).
2 Hillman, J. (1975/1992, p. 8).
3 Bitan, S. (2012).
4 Ibid. (p. 30).
5 Levine, R. (2017, p. 90).
6 Jung, C. G. (1958/1981).
7 Winnicott, D. W. (1971, p. 18).
8 Ibid. (p. 2).
9 Ibid. (p. 71).
10 C. G. (Jung, 1973, p. 433).
11 Hillman, J. (1975/1992).
12 Corbin, H. (1972).
13 Winnicott, D. W. (1971).
14 Hillman, J. (1975/1992, p. xvii).
15 Ibid.
16 Winnicott, D. W. (1971, p. 72).
17 Ibid. (p. 73).
18 Huizinga, J. (1938/2014).
19 Ibid. (pp. 8–12).
20 Ibid. (p. 10).
21 Stoller, R. J. (1991).
22 Ibid. (p. 135).
23 Huizinga, J. (1938/2014, p. 10).
24 Shahbaz, C. (2019, personal communication).
25 Baumeister, R. (1988, p. 28).
26 Stoller, R. (1991).

27 American Heritage (2011, p. 1794).
28 Baldwin, G. (1993, p. 48).
29 Baldwin, G. (personal communication, 2019).
30 Lockhart, R. (1980, p. 99).
31 Ibid. (p. 100).
32 Vilhauer, M. (2010).
33 Gadamer, H. G. (1975/2013).
34 Vilhauer, M. (2010).
35 Gadamer, H. G. (1975/2013).
36 Buber, M. (1958/1987).
37 Winnicott, D. W. (1971).
38 Jung, C. G. (2009, p. 228).
39 Gadamer, H. G. (1975/2013).
40 Vilhauer, M. (2010, p. 35, emphasis in original).
41 Baldwin, G. (2004).
42 Gadamer, H. G. (1975/2013, p. 104, emphasis in original).
43 Winnicott, D. W. (1971).
44 Schwartz-Salant, N. (1998, p. ix).
45 Jung, C. G. (1958/1969).
46 Hillman, J. (1975/1992, p. 174).

References

American Heritage. (2011). Tension. In J. P. Pickett (Ed.), *The American heritage dictionary of the English language* (5th ed., p. 1794). Houghton Mifflin Harcourt.

Baldwin, G. (1993). *Ties that bind* (2nd ed.). Daedalus.

Baldwin, G. (2004). *SlaveCraft: Roadmaps for erotic servitude*. Daedalus.

Baumeister, R. F. (1988). Masochism as escape from self. *The Journal of Sex Research, 25*(1), 28–59.

Bitan, S. (2012). Winnicott and Derrida: Development of logic-of-play. *International Journal of Psycho-Analysis, 93*(1), 29–51.

Buber, M. (1987). *I and thou* (R. G. Smith, Trans.). Collier Books. (Original work published 1958)

Corbin, H. (1972). *Mundus imaginalis* or the imaginary and the imaginal. *Spring*, 1972, 1–19.

Gadamer, H. G. (2013). *Truth and method* (J. Weinsheimer & D. G. Marshall, Trans., revised 2nd ed.). Bloomsbury. (Original work published 1975)

Hillman, J. (1992). *Re-Visioning psychology*. HarperPerennial. (Original work published 1975)

Huizinga, J. (2014). *Homo ludens*. Roy. (Original work published 1938)

Jung, C. G. (1969). The transcendent function (R. F. C. Hull, Trans.). In H. Read et al. (Eds.), *The collected works of C. G. Jung* (Vol. 8, 2nd ed., pp. 67–91). Princeton University Press. (Original work published 1958)

Jung, C. G. (1973). Letter to Max Frischknecht, February 1946 (R. F. C. Hull, Trans.). In G. Adler (Ed.), *C. G. Jung Letters, 1906–1950* (Vol. 1, pp. 408–412). Princeton University Press.

Jung, C. G. (1981). The transcendent function (R. F. C. Hull, Trans.). In H. Read et al. (Eds.), *The collected works of C. G. Jung* (Vol. 8, 2nd ed., pp. 67–91). Princeton University Press. (Original work published 1958)

Jung, C. G. (2009). *The red book, Liber Novus: A reader's edition* (M. Kyburz, J. Peck, & S. Shamdasani, Trans.; S. Shamdasani, Ed.). W. W. Norton.

Krafft-Ebing, R. (2011). *Psychopathia sexualis* (F. S. Klaf, Trans.). Arcade Publishing. (Original work published in 1886)

Levine, R. (2017). *Jolted awake*. Alfred.

Lockhart, R. (1980). Psyche in hiding. *Quadrant, 13*, 76–105.

Schwartz-Salant, N. (1998). The mystery of human relationship: Alchemy and the transformation of the self. Routledge.

Stoller, R. J. (1991). *Pain and passion*. Plenum.

Vilhauer, M. (2010). *Gadamer's ethics of play*. Lexington Books.

Winnicott, D. W. (1971). *Playing and reality*. Routledge.

5

SUFFERING AND DEGRADATION

Introduction

For those outside the world of BDSM, it may be puzzling and possibly disturbing to realize that people can derive erotic pleasure from experiences of suffering and degradation. Some might argue that the world is full of enough human misery without our having to seek it out or manufacture it. What place does pleasure have in such ordeals? The dominant belief in the West for thousands of years has been that suffering is to be avoided, alleviated, or justified only if it serves some greater redemptive purpose. The idea that suffering and degradation are potentially pleasurable and psychologically valuable challenges a strong cultural bias. And yet, as shall be seen, kinksters are not the only individuals to find value hidden in the suffering that people endure (and inflict) and in the experiences that lay them low. The proposition here is that the valuation of suffering and degradation in the world of BDSM offers a unique psychological perspective containing generative and beneficent possibilities pertinent to all of us.

Why situate suffering and degradation together in the same discussion? They do not necessarily form an obvious or inevitable nexus. However, when suffering and degradation are paired as an archetypal *syzygy*, they can work together to destabilize the ego's privileged perspective. There is merit to considering the two topics together. They lead to similar ideas in the work of C. G. Jung and James Hillman regarding psychological growth and

DOI: 10.4324/9781003223597-7

the care of soul. By destabilizing the ego, both can catalyze a reorganization of the conscious personality.[1]

The devastating consequences of suffering and degradation in the world are serious and they need to be acknowledged. People suffer horrible ordeals in life every day. The ravages of disease, violence, injustice, systemic racism, sexism, homophobia and transphobia, poverty, crime, warfare, and death devastate individuals, families, and communities, and there is little that is noble, generative, or beneficent in the broken lives that are either pieced together or extinguished under such extreme conditions. Degradation occurs in the world with its own corrosive effect: individuals are stripped of livelihood, status, dignity, life necessities, and worth through preju- dice, oppression, abuse, and stigma. In some parts of the world, rigorously enforced caste systems lead to atrocities enacted by the privileged against the outcasts, who are sometimes designated as subhuman. The long, trou- bling history of literal non-consensual slavery casts a shadow that cannot be ignored in any thoughtful discussion of contemporary consensual Master/ slave relationships.

The socially dominant forces of science and medicine, social policy, and mainstream religion all illustrate how pervasively the fantasies of resolv- ing and redeeming suffering operate in the West's collective psyche. These social institutions appear to agree on the same bottom line: suffering and degradation should not be part of a healthy society. For example, a statute in the United Kingdom specifically defines sexual behaviors as "acceptable only on the basis that sexual desire is recognizably pleasurable and appears 'civilised' enough . . . that it will not cause, condone, or promote suffer- ing."[2] The attempt to legislate acceptable sexual behavior by driving a wedge between suffering and pleasure indicates the difficult cultural position in which practitioners of BDSM find themselves. And yet despite the progress of scientific research and medical treatment, despite the legislative efforts of politicians, the commitments of social policy engineers, and the efforts of charity relief organizations, suffering and degradation persist. But beyond the literal material facts of their occurrence, it is also true that suffering and degradation are psychological givens, essential archetypal features of the soul's landscape, which weave meaning into the ordeals and calamities of our physical lives.

There are, of course, notable exceptions to the prevailing Western atti- tude. In specific settings, suffering and degradation are consciously enlisted to facilitate growth through adversity, social cohesion, group identity, and spiritual transcendence.[3] Examples include athletic training and competition, initiation rituals such as fraternity hazing, some religious rituals across multiple theologies (e.g., the Lakota Sun Dance and the Hindu Kavandi ceremony), and military training (which incidentally is the source of many elements of gay leather culture, a cornerstone of the modern BDSM movement).[4]

As the previous chapter made clear, the suggestion that there are places within Western society where people play with suffering and degradation neither trivializes nor negates the seriousness, the complexity, and the importance of these activities. By the same token, the suggestion that play is a legitimate psychological response to suffering and degradation does not minimize or dismiss the terrible consequences when these forces arrive unexpectedly and involuntarily in people's lives. Like other socially sanctioned exceptions to the prevailing Western attitude, the modern practice of BDSM is an intriguing instance of individuals who intentionally and consensually expose themselves to suffering and degradation for a greater purpose. How that purpose involves soul is the topic here.

C. G. Jung and James Hillman both affirmed the value and even the necessity of suffering and degradation as part of the trajectory of psychological growth. From early in Jung's career, he developed the idea that the individuation process follows a mythic structure that is patterned by archetypal forces. "If you accept the lowest in you, suffering is unavoidable," he wrote in *The Red Book*.[5] Degradation and suffering are a part of psychological life that enables the conscious personality to mature and grow in complexity. Coming to terms with the less flattering aspects of our identity can be a degrading experience for the ego. Hillman wrote, "The study of lives and the care of souls means above all a prolonged encounter with what destroys and is destroyed, with what is broken and hurts."[6] To be clear, the archetypal approach does not endorse degradation per se—degradation is not inherently beneficial. The key question is how psychic resources mobilize in the face of such destructive events. The psyche's response becomes an expression of our unique character and the archetypal figures that *personify* our survival instincts. Hillman's dedication to the realities of fantasy-images led him to consider suffering and degradation as necessary archetypal experiences that bring soul into the world.

How do Hillman's[7] four central concepts connect suffering and degradation to soul? *Personifying* operates as a descriptive reflex: whenever suffering or degradation occurs in our lives, someone or something must be responsible. The agent of our suffering becomes a personification of injustice, bad luck, or cruel fate acting against us (e.g., killer tornadoes, evil viruses, treacherous mountain roads, and ideas that stink). *Pathologizing* places that which is unbearable, broken, or downtrodden in intimate relationship with soul. *Psychologizing* explains how we seek some meaning or purpose behind the terrible ordeals we suffer and the cruel indignities that degrade us. Soul is present as we try to see through the surface details of events for some deeper understanding. *Dehumanizing* calls upon us to shift the focus away from a personal humanistic center. Suffering and degradation are examples of *dehumanizing* because they thwart and subvert the designs and intentions of the anthropocentric world. As archetypal figures, suffering and degradation originate among the numinous persons of the soul rather than the personal problems of human beings.

Suffering and Degradation: Definitions and Etymology

How does one define *suffering* and *degradation* in the context of fantasy-images, and what do the words mean in the world of BDSM and kink? A standard dictionary offers a starting place. Suffer: "transitive verb 1a: to submit to or be forced to endure //*suffer* martyrdom b: to feel keenly: labor under //*suffer* thirst 2: Undergo, experience. . . . intransitive verb 1: to endure death, pain, or distress."[8] Several of these terms stand out as particularly relevant to the relationship between BDSM and soul: submit, endure, feel, undergo, experience. At the risk of overgeneralizing, BDSM has less to do with suffering as torment or agony and more to do with undergoing an ordeal that tests and pushes the limits of what is tolerable. The suffering that occurs through the activities of BDSM involves voluntarily undergoing and enduring the pathologized fantasies of soul.

It is important to distinguish between suffering and pain. The definition of pain focuses on bodily sensations. It is the mild to severe discomfort of noxious physical stimuli (to be sure, mental and emotional pain are also very real).[9] In his medical treatise on the nature of suffering, physician Eric J. Cassell proposed the following:

Suffering occurs when an impending destruction of the person is perceived; it continues until the threat of disintegration has passed or until the integrity of the person can be restored in some other manner. It follows, then, that although it often occurs in the presence of acute pain, shortness of breath, or other bodily symptoms, *suffering extends beyond the physical*. Most generally, suffering can be defined as the state of severe distress associated with events that threaten the intactness of the person.[10]

Cassell's definition emphasizes the existential threat that suffering entails. It is compatible with the more general definition under development here, which emphasizes undergoing and enduring a distressing ordeal. In an insight that may be familiar to practitioners of BDSM, Cassell found that bodily pain resulted in suffering under certain conditions, namely, "when [people] feel out of control, when the pain is overwhelming, when the source of the pain is unknown, when the meaning of the pain is dire, or when the pain is apparently without end."[11] When pain is perceived as an existential threat to one's personhood, suffering follows. In other words, suffering emerges as a psychological interpretation of pain.

The world of BDSM regards pain and suffering as distinct concepts as well. There is clearly more happening in BDSM than the manipulation of physical pain for erotic pleasure. Were it a question purely of pain, there would be no need for the elaborate protocols that reinforce a relational imbalance. For example, there are often strict rules around how and when the sub is to address the Dom, specific requirements regarding posture, body position, where the eyes are allowed to gaze, the choice or absence of clothing, and adherence to a daily schedule of service activities. None of these requirements are inherently painful, but it's possible to see the ordeal of submission as a kind of suffering (a kind of destiny perhaps) as well as a kind of pleasure. The distinction here is between, on the one hand, the suffering (and paradoxical pleasure) of the ego's submission to an external authority versus, on the other, physical pain. The distinction should not suggest, however, that pain and suffering are unrelated. When pain is introduced into BDSM activities, the fantasy aspect of the deep imagination makes it meaningful and purposive. "My Mistress controls my pain; I love my Mistress, therefore, I love this pain because it tells me she is happy and in control." Suffering emerges when pain comes into relationship with soul.

Hermann Hesse offered a philosophical testament to suffering as a necessary part of life:

> Action and suffering, which together make up our lives, are a whole; they are one. A child suffers its begetting, it suffers its birth, its weaning; it suffers here and suffers there until in the end it suffers death. But all the good in a man, for which he is praised or loved, is merely good suffering, the right kind, the living kind of suffering, a suffering to the full. The ability to suffer well is more than half of life—indeed, it is all life. Birth is suffering, growth is suffering, the seed suffers the earth, the root suffers the rain, the bud suffers its flowering.
>
> In the same way, my friends, man suffers destiny. Destiny is earth, it is rain and growth. Destiny hurts.[12]

Hesse's understanding of suffering recognizes that it is a fundamental part of all existence. He also sees the inherent relationship between suffering and destiny, another pathway of soul.

True, for some BDSM practitioners, the craft of learning how to push the limits of pain tolerance and endurance is the primary source of fascination and pleasure. But for others, the objective is to experience the pain as meaningful and purposive, which suggests that the fascination is connected to suffering as a form of relating. The suffering might be meaningful because it pleases the Dom, but there are other meanings as well. Perhaps the gradual escalation of pain facilitates an emotional catharsis or leads to a desired altered state of consciousness (a way of relating to the soul). Good suffering, as Hesse called it, can induce transformation. The emphasis on the challenge to suffer the limits of physical and emotional stamina illustrates Robert Stoller's[13] point that BDSM is fascinated with the exquisite, orchestrated loss of control. Raven Kaldera,[14] who has written extensively about the manipulation of pain as a magical ritual technique, acknowledged the legacy of indigenous and ancient cultures, which understood the transformative potential of pain. Such highly controlled and negotiated encounters create a poetics of suffering in which pain is suffused with multiple layers of meaning. Given the proper preparation and attitude, creating a BDSM scene creates a world with its own reality in which suffering intensifies and deepens the thrill and the intimacy between the partners. The scene has the potential to bring soul into the world through the voluntarily imbalanced relationship and the psychophysical effects of pain as a transformative agent. In BDSM, suffering has to do with undergoing and going under.

The image of "going under" appears in the etymology of the word *suffer*, which comes from Latin: *sufferer*—to bear from below (*sub + ferre*, meaning to carry). We suffer that which we bear from below. The root of the word *suffer* leads further to a web of unexpected relationships with other words. The Indo-European root, *bher*, also underlies the words birth, fertility, fortune, and euphoria.[15] In contrast to the prevailing view of suffering as something undesirable to be avoided and alleviated, the word itself is connected to birth and fertility. Suffering has the potential to bring forth something new and generate unimagined possibilities. For practitioners of BDSM, it will come as no surprise that suffering and euphoria are etymologically related. As many would testify, the suffering that comes from bearing and undergoing can also lead to ecstatic experiences.

The meaning of *degrade* in the present context is fairly clear. As the dictionary informs us, to degrade is the following:

1a. To lower in grade, rank, or status 1b. To strip of rank or honors 1c. To lower to an inferior or less effective level 1d. To scale down in desirability or salability. 2a. To bring to low esteem or disrepute 2b. To drag down in moral or intellectual character. 3a. To impair in respect to some physical property.[16]

The word emphasizes the notion of rank and its loss, always with a sense of lowering or being taken down. It is not simply loss, however; a brutal, aggressive spirit animates the definition: to strip, to bring low, to drag down. The connotation is forceful, primal, and erotic. Given the word's etymological connotations, it is small wonder that degradation is so popular in the world of BDSM. It may be important to distinguish between degradation and humiliation. Kinksters often use the two words together when they describe their fetishes. Both ideas involve the experience of lowering or bringing down the rank or status of an individual, but humiliation has more to do with the feelings engendered by the loss of status than with the downgrading itself. Hence, humiliation can involve painful embarrassment, shame, and anxiety. The word also directs attention to the social dimension of how one is seen by a witnessing community (sometimes a community of only one), which can intensify feelings of inadequacy and otherness.[17] Degradation emphasizes the acts and the events that bring us low, and humiliation emphasizes the painful emotions engendered by such experiences.

The process of developing working definitions of suffering and degradation in the context of BDSM's relationship with soul has opened the words to layers of meaning as we search among their roots for insights and possibilities. Suffering and degradation, pain and humiliation, are all present and fundamental to the operations of alternative sexualities. They form a nexus of intensification, which fascinates practitioners.

Suffering, Degradation, and the Contra-psychological

In his seminal work, *Re-Visioning Psychology*, Hillman asserted that everything we perceive and interpret as reality begins first as fantasy. He wrote:

> In the beginning is the image; first imagination, then perception; first fantasy then reality. Or as Jung puts it: "The psyche creates reality every day. The only expression I can use for this activity is fantasy." Man is primarily an imagemaker and our psychic substance consists of images; our being is imaginal being, an existence in imagination. We are indeed such stuff as dreams are made on.[18]

According to Hillman and the depth tradition, the conscious mind is not in charge of the show. We do not make up our fantasies. It is the other way around. Our fantasies (which in fact are not even truly ours) make up who we think we are and what we imagine to be real about ourselves and the world around us. To be psychologically minded is to seek out the vital fantasy-images that generate our lived experience. By contrast, to be literal minded (rejecting the poetic and the imaginal) is to be *contra-psychological*. It is to imagine the life of the mind as soulless. The tendency of literalism to negate and exclude the soul from the operations of the mind is why Hillman spent much of his career critiquing its harmful effects on the Western imagination.[19] A curious consequence of Hillman's assertion is that literalism is in fact one possible mode of fantasy-thinking that negates the validity of fantasy-thinking itself. *Literalism is a dead zone of the soul in which the poetic imagination imagines its own unreality and nonexistence.* It is a mode of psychological thought in which the imagination has turned against itself: the fantasy is one of certainty, surface appearances, non-dimensionality, materialism, concretism, objective truth, and inert, rigid boundaries that separate ideas, things, and persons.

Literalism is a subcategory of thought with its own presumptions about truth and its tendency is to take over and reject other modes of psychological expression. Literalism has a totalitarian flair. From a literalist perspective, suffering and degradation are real only when they occur as concrete events of misfortune and inhumanity (play as an agent of soul is not welcome here because play *de-literalizes* and brings suppleness to imaginative thinking). But there are other forms of reality besides the literal: psychological, imaginal, and poetic among others. Yet for many, the idea of multiple realities is inconceivable: non-literal means unreal. Hence, a psychological discussion about the pleasures of suffering and degradation can be risky.

Literal thinking tends to flatten the multiple dimensions of the imagination into a one-dimensional narrative of factual events. Hillman said that soul is what turns events into experiences.[20] And Jung offered a helpful insight when he wrote, "Taking [the unconscious] seriously does not mean taking it literally."[21] The present discussion seeks a balance between the ethical call to acknowledge properly the human consequences of suffering and degradation while also guarding against the effects of the contrapsychological. Psychologically speaking, the topic asks to be taken seriously but not literally.

Archetypal Versus Literal

Hillman helps us see that suffering and degradation are archetypal presences at work in the human psyche. These two forces have operated psychologically in cultures all over the world throughout history. They are present as thematic patterns in mythology, literature, and other forms of cultural expression. As archetypal presences, suffering and degradation have also always been part of human behavior as ordering patterns of thought, emotion, and action.

There are examples throughout history of cultures that have developed ritual practices that incorporate the ordeal of physical pain as a transformational form of suffering and physical degradation:

> The Lakota tribe of the western plains of America pioneered the Sun Dance, where people suspend themselves from piercings behind their pectoral muscles, or pulled against piercings through the skin of their chests, until they saw visions. In the Hindu Kavandi ceremony, worshipers carry huge shrines in parades borne by masses of large steel needles through their flesh, and others dance in the street with fruit and bells attached to their skin with sharp hooks. In parts of Indonesia and Malaysia, spirit-possessed folk put spikes through the skin of their cheeks as part of inducing a trance deep enough to allow the spirits to enter. The technique of applied pain is probably older than that of psychoactive substances.[22]

Religious scholar Ariel Glucklich[23] concurred that the sacralization of pain as a transformative agent is present as a cross-cultural and transhistorical phenomenon, but he didn't go so far as to suggest that such ritual practices are evidence of an archetypal pattern. However, the present discussion proposes that undergoing any ordeal imbued with psychological meaning, such as an encounter with one's destiny, religious or other, is a form of archetypal suffering. Similarly, the loss of integrity to the physical body through piercing and laceration can be regarded as a form of archetypal degradation in service to spiritual transcendence.

Suffering and degradation often occur together as an aspect of how societies negotiate issues of status and rank. The most extreme examples of human degradation occur within caste systems, such as in India, where a segment of the population was traditionally literally labeled "outcastes."[24] A *National Geographic* article from 2003 detailed the plight of the untouchables, or Dalits, in the twentieth century:

> Despite the fact that untouchability was officially banned when India adopted its constitution in 1950, discrimination against Dalits remained so pervasive that in 1989 the government passed legislation known as The Prevention of Atrocities Act. The act specifically made it illegal to parade people naked through the streets,

force them to eat feces, take away their land, foul their water, inter-fere with their right to vote, and burn down their homes.[25]

There are analogues to India's untouchable class in other parts of the world, such as the burakumin of Japan,[26] the baekjeong of Korea,[27] and the osu of Nigeria.[28] Another example of this archetypal pattern is the institution of involuntary slavery, which continues to be an instrument of dehumaniza-tion and social death throughout the world.[29] There appears to be strong evidence for an archetypal dimension to the suffering, degradation, and de-valuation of human beings by other human beings. The preceding examples illustrate the destructive consequences of subjecting archetypal reality to the contra-psychological force of literalizing.

In clinical and scholarly research, the topic of suffering appears most frequently in the fields of medicine, religious studies, and political-social sciences. Medicine and religion coincidentally provide rich source mate-rial for BDSM and fetish scenes. The areas of convergence highlight the distinction between literal facts and deeper archetypal patterns. They also provide clues to better understand why and how BDSM privileges these psychic elements.

A Taste of Medicine

In medical research, suffering consistently appears as a factor to be mit-igated or as a complication that reduces the effectiveness of treatment.[30] Cassell's treatise *The Nature of Suffering and the Goals of Medicine* specu-lates that researchers have historically struggled with the topic because of its inherently subjective nature: "The only way to learn whether suffering is present is to ask the sufferer."[31] The scientific virtues of objectivity and reductionism have resulted in skepticism toward the vagaries of subjective evaluations. How does one clinically diagnose and treat suffering as a med-ical condition? "The central assumptions on which twentieth-century med-icine is founded provide no basis for an understanding of suffering," wrote Cassell.[32] Western medicine finds itself in a quandary: the alleviation of suffering is an underlying presumption of patients and families who seek care, yet doctors are not trained to meet such a need. Western medicine has evolved to treat bodies, not persons, and "suffering is an affliction of the *person*, not the body."[33] Consequently, patients suffer regularly while under the care of their medical providers.

Not surprisingly, medical play is one of the recurring tropes in the lexicon of BDSM role-play fantasies. The sterile dispassion and objectifying ambience of the examination room, the helplessness of the patient as victim and the sadistic reserve of the doctor or medical researcher, who is at once invasive and withholding, or the saccharine cruelty of an overbearing nurse all provide rich source material for the juxtaposition of control and chaos that thrills the sadomasochistic imagination. It is not uncommon for kinksters to fetishize lab coats, hospital gowns, medical equipment, and the simulation of invasive procedures, such as injections, taking lab specimens, and performing everything from actual enemas to fake lobotomies.

Loss of one's personhood is a form of degradation especially well-known and feared by those who have undergone extensive medical treatment for any serious condition or illness. The recent collective devastation of the global COVID pandemic is a harsh reminder of how crushing the degradation of illness can be. Sometimes with sudden onset, sometimes with achingly slow deterioration, the progression of illness in the body combined with the stoic objectivity of the medical establishment can degrade us until we are a shadow of the person we once were. Forty years before COVID, the AIDS crisis decimated the gay community, and it hit the world of gay leather especially hard. For gay men who lived through the ravages of the eighties and nineties, it is all too easy to recall the horror: the haunted sunken gaze of young men robbed of their vibrancy, the skeletal bodies, the skin lesions, the diapers, the paper-thin translucent skin, and the impotence of not being able to offer anything effective against the progression of illness and death. Such memories reveal how much suffering and degradation have to do with existential pain and subjective feeling. Degradation is about the brutality of loss: loss of status, loss of efficacy, loss of control, loss of personhood. To be degraded is to be stripped, dragged down, brought low. It is serious business.

The medical paradox—a profession charged with the alleviation of suffering but untrained in caring for the subjective integrity of the person—reveals the dual nature of suffering and degradation as both universal (archetypal) and subjective (personal). The physical overwhelm that accompanies progressive degenerative illness and debilitating hospital stays can encumber access to the poetic imagination, which might otherwise provide solace and resiliency. The creative impulse to write, paint, photograph, or dramatize the experience of illness and medical treatment is a testament to the therapeutic potential of the deep imagination (and the power of play) to thwart the withering effects of literalism. Creative expression—not only in the medical setting but in BDSM scenes as well—can confer some measure of archetypal dignity on the experience.

In the medical role-plays of BDSM, the operations of archetypal fantasy work creatively with the images of woundedness, suffering, and degradation. The archetypal pattern might appear obscure. Given the terrible ordeals of literal disease, literal invasive medical procedures, and literal death, it may be difficult to imagine how some people find erotic pleasure in playing with the fantasy-images that inhabit such experiences. But if we consider BDSM as erotic archetypal theater, then we can become curious about the cast of characters performing a scene of suffering and degradation. The doctor who is clinically aloof treating the patient as a specimen; the deceptively maternal nurse eagerly approaching with latex gloves; the technician who immobilizes, pierces, and penetrates during routine procedures ("lie still, don't move, this might hurt"); and the helpless patient whose subjective status as a person is threatened and who is degraded into an objectified set of symptoms and stats for analysis and treatment—they all have a place in the erotic medical scene of the sadistic imagination.

Medical Play: A Firsthand Account

Moth Meadows identifies as a 27-year-old white non-binary lesbian who lives in Montreal, Canada, and they describe themself as a person living with disabilities (preferred pronouns "they/them"). Regarding their kink identity, they describe themself as a switch. They have a degree in Illustration, they are developing a career in food sovereignty, and they do "a bit of sex work." Moth lives with their partner, who identifies as a trans woman and prefers the pronouns "it/them." In 2017, Moth was hit by a car but "wasn't too badly damaged." However, the ambulance ride to the hospital and the subsequent treatment proved to be a more traumatic experience for them than the original accident:

> I was strapped to a spine board for about four hours. I had a really gruesome thing happen where the EMT tried to put an IV needle in my arm in the ambulance and then we went

over train tracks right as he put it in and the needle shot out of my arm. So, that was like one of the worst things that's ever happened to me it was so unpleasant. None of my friends knew that I had gone to the hospital. And I was basically there without anyone in my support circle around. So, I was really isolated in the emergency room. And nurses kept kind of leaving me without telling me what was going on. And suddenly, I'd be alone strapped to a spine board for what felt like a really long time. And the nurses weren't super thrilled with me because I was intoxicated when this happened. And there was just all these very unpleasant things that happened. I had to get a CAT scan and a CRT [laughs] while intoxicated, and having suffered a traumatic injury, and also, I'm very claustrophobic. So those were again, two of like the worst things that have ever happened to me.

So, I had all of these bad things that were deeply traumatic on these very deep levels, and I just didn't really have the space to process it at the time. And since then, I've been very wary of hospitals and doctors and I avoid going to doctors at all costs. I find everything around the medical world uncomfortable and invasive. And I really hate the lack of autonomy that exists when you're a patient, it makes me feel very powerless in a way I don't like and I had kind of the worst experience with powerlessness in my entire life in one night. So, medical play was not really something I had any inclination towards. And I sort of felt like I'm not ready to touch that in any context, when I started getting back into kink, because it just felt like there's some very real wounds here that I'm not super ready to explore yet.

Then I was listening to a podcast that covered the history of lobotomies. And it's a really gruesome history. And there were descriptions with how lobotomies were performed, how it works and everything. And after listening to it, I was just like, wow, I sure could go for a lobotomy right now. I was really into the idea I was feeling so bad that I was just, I wish somebody could just cut a piece of my brain out so I never had to have feelings again. I started fantasizing about lobotomies a lot. And my play partner and I already do a lot of torture kink stuff. So, I started to be like, "Oh, I just want to get lobotomized so badly, I need part of my brain cut out." And we started to build a scene around that. And we decided that it would be really fun to do it as a way for me to explore my medical trauma. And we started brainstorming, what are the things about my traumatic experience with my medical traumas that we can touch on here? What are the safety things that need to be in place for me to not get re-traumatized through this experience? And we decided that the things I wanted to explore were the feelings of vulnerability, and the removal of autonomy. And I wanted it to be super CNC-based [Consensual Non-consent] where I was having things done to me that I was not aware of or consenting to. So, we planned the scene around that. I wanted to be bound to something in some way, and I don't have a bedframe. So, we just tied my arms to a broom handle because, you know, kinky people are inventive with kink [laughs]. And I actually got to wear one of my medical robes that I had taken from a hospital at one point, it was really fun. Yeah, I was getting to do props like that [laughs]. And my partner had on nitrile gloves and surgeon's mask and was wearing—we didn't have like a proper doctor or nurse outfit. So, it was just wearing a black jumpsuit that it has and that we use for kink sometimes because it's a great way to kind of take away identity during scenes, which can be really fun.

We started with me bound. We actually found a sound clip of a heart monitor on YouTube and just played that, which was a great way to create a little bit of ambience. One of my limits for the scene was I didn't want to be left bound and alone for too long at any point. Because I thought that could be pretty triggering. So, we made sure that as a safety thing, I was never going to be left alone in the room for longer than a few seconds. So, I think my partner gave me poppers to start.

We actually use poppers a lot for scenes to kind of simulate different sensations. And we use poppers as a stand-in for anesthetic. And my partner woke me up by rudely slapping me in the face after getting knocked out via poppers. I wanted to play off of the confusion and disorientation that I felt so I sort of played into how this would maybe be a scenario where I was waking up in a hospital with no awareness of how I got there. So, I was acting very confused and scared and my partner was alternating between doing a condescendingly nice nurse voice and talking to me the way that nurses will kind of sometimes talk to you where they're being nice, but you can tell they're a little bit annoyed with you, and they just sort of want to get through whatever they're doing. And when I wouldn't be compliant, my partner would switch to being really stern and mean with me and punishing me. Because I really wanted to explore that power imbalance, where medical professionals can be nice to you, but at the end of the day, they're just going to get the thing they need to be done.

So, we did a lot of invasive body exploration while I was bound, we like to do this thing in scenes where we'll stick our fingers in the hole underneath your tongue, where there's that piece of connective flesh, but if you kind of push there's these two holes under your tongue, and it feels awful to have touched and we like to touch each other there a lot for scenes. These are creative ways of touching each other. And basically, my partner did a lot of that to me and was pushing on my tear ducts and touching me really hard on pressure points. And they were touching my body in very invasive ways that were not based on my pleasure, and that would be really uncomfortable to me so that no matter how much I complained it was just going to be this thing that was happening to me. And then I have a septum piercing. And we were in the process of stretching the hole size up. So, we decided that we could do that during the scene as this way of doing something that felt a little bit medical and body altering, and also incredibly painful and uncomfortable. So, my partner stretched my septum jewelry up, which sucks to have done during a scene, but I was very into it. Because again, it was like doing a little procedure. And then I think we did some knife play, which was mostly just a lot of poking me and scratching me with the tip of a dull knife. One of my boundaries is I don't get cut when we do knife play. I will do things with knives, but I don't want any cuts on my body. So, a lot of scraping and a lot of weird pressure points with the knife, and things like that. And eventually, my partner decided that I was just not being compliant enough and that I needed to be fixed. And it told me that it was going to perform a lobotomy on me and gave me more poppers to anesthetize me and then use the knife to kind of scrape across my forehead. I wanted the lobotomy procedure to be a little bit medically accurate. And I didn't want to do anything with my eyes, because normally you do a lobotomy through tear ducts, the orbital part of your bone, and I didn't want my eyes getting poked. So, we decided that we would do the procedure where you cut off a little bit of the skull and then remove a piece of the prefrontal cortex. So, we simulated that by having my partner scrape me a bunch with the knife on my forehead and then take its fingers in, which is something we've actually done in different kinds of scenes before, but it's always—once you're in the mindset that this thing is happening to you, it's a very intense experience and something I really like. So, we did that. And then once the lobotomy procedure was done, I role-played acting incredibly docile and confused and complacent. And then we played in that for a little bit and had sex and I got untied, and we did more of like a submissive scene with me, but where I have now had my mind changed, which was fun, and I've never really explored approaching things like mind control through a medical context. And that was a really fun way of doing it. And the scene basically ended the way we always do our scenes where we cuddle a lot. And once it's done, we'd go into like very strict aftercare mode and do a lot of cuddling and affirmations and touching and things like that.

I was extremely turned on through the entire thing. Generally when we do a scene that involves this much prep and discussion, we kind of set a point where we're going to start actually having sex. But often that point could take an hour into the scene. But we're both very, very into what's going on before that point. And it's the most elaborate foreplay ever. We could basically do an entire scene without any sexual touching, and it would be intensely sexual for both of us.

Usually, I like a slow transition out of the scene. So, we might even bring some of our role-playing into the aftercare and do a little bit of aftercare as the characters that we've been role-playing. But usually, by the time that we're making each other laugh and we're talking about what we're going to have for dinner, it's sort of how we know that the scene is officially over [laughs]. That's a good indicator that we're not role-playing anymore if we're talking about, should we order pizza or something.

I think for me, it's really about the way that re-experiencing feelings I had during a traumatic event in a safe environment with somebody I love and trust, is it's my way of exploring what those feelings felt like to me, but where I'm safe and have control over the situation. And I think I'm just sort of wired to get a lot out of re-experiencing horrible things that have happened to me. I'm somebody who will poke my own bruises until they don't hurt anymore. It's almost this way of like, weathering down the bad, scary feelings, to the point where they don't feel bad and scary and overwhelming anymore. Yeah, I'm not sure exactly how it is that I can just function in this way. Where if I feel fear, in a genuinely traumatic moment, it causes trauma. But then if I feel the exact same kind of fear, but in an erotic sense, where I'm safe and have control, it's not scary at all, and it's great and it's healing for me. I guess it's just sort of how I work through things.

Religious Reflections

For centuries, Christian religious scholars and theologians have struggled with the question of theodicy: If God is all-good and all-powerful, why is suffering allowed?[34] Jung wrote extensively about the religious function of the psyche and, for several years, maintained a close friendship and correspondence with the religious scholar Victor White.[35] Ultimately, both their friendship and intellectual collaboration ran afoul of the question of theodicy and the role of suffering and evil in human affairs.

In particular, their disagreement concerned details in Jung's[36] late essay *Answer to Job*, in which he argued that Christianity is psychologically incomplete and one-sided, having split off what was once the left hand of God, that is, the destructive, diabolical aspect of the God image. With the left hand as a separate image, the divine became a dualistic entity. Jung found fault with the Christian doctrine of *privatio boni*, the privation of good, which explains the presence of suffering in the world as an absence of God's will. In other words, suffering is the result of evil, which is the absence of good. Jung regarded the Old Testament figure of Job as the iconic example of "the shattering emotion which the unvarnished spectacle of divine savagery and ruthlessness produces in us."[37] Having lived through the destructive savagery of two world wars and the detonation of two atomic bombs, Jung was particularly concerned with both the literal and archetypal manifestations of suffering and evil in the human psyche. Job is intentionally degraded by God, and ever the obedient servant, he suffers miserably.

Any serious consideration of suffering and degradation inevitably leads to some reflection on how frequently their fantasy-images have a religious context. Suffering has been a topic addressed by every major world religion, particularly regarding why it occurs and what meaning can be derived from it.[38] As archetypal presences, suffering and degradation are part of the Christian world beyond the theological debates over theodicy, perhaps most vividly in the central iconography of the martyred Christ: his naked, bound, flagellated body covered in blood, with hands and feet pierced with nails, hung upon the cross to die. Jesus's mutilated body is the ultimate symbol of his suffering, and its influence on the sexual imagination is undeniably potent.[39] Its reappearance in BDSM scarcely needs overt mention.

As a scholar of mythology, Joseph Campbell recognized the mythic initiatory aspect of the Christ image, which archetypally resembles the initiatory aspect of suffering and degradation in BDSM:

> We crucify our temporal and earthly bodies, let them be torn, and through that dismemberment enter the spiritual sphere which transcends all the pains of earth. There's a form of the crucifix known as "Christ Triumphant," where he is not with head bowed and blood pouring from him, but with head erect and eyes open, as though having come voluntarily to the crucifixion.[40]

Campbell calls attention to the voluntary and conscious element of the crucifixion's dismemberment as an initiation. The consensual (i.e., conscious and voluntary) element of contemporary BDSM is in fact a *spiritual element* of radical sexuality. Figuratively speaking, BDSM aficionados face their ordeals as "good" suffering with eyes open and head erect.

Beyond the mythic theme of initiation with its sadomasochistic undertones, trace elements of Christian culture and thinking reach far into the erotic imagination of alternative sexualities. On a superficial level, there are the blasphemous transgressions, such as dressing up as priests or nuns to enact scenes of confession, penitence, and abuse with the submissive supplicant. Depending on one's personal history and relationship with the church, such scenes can reflect deeper scars of psychological and sexual trauma, in some cases, repeating and in others, healing past wounds. In such enactments, there is permission to play with what was once devastating and scarring, turning the archetypal dynamics of authority, trust, betrayal, and abuse into the subject of the scene.

Given the influence of the Middle Ages on the paraphernalia and the activities of BDSM, the Christian inflections of the medieval imagination are particularly salient. The horrors of the Inquisition, the threat of hellfire and damnation, and the pervasive domination of the medieval Church's demand for absolute obedience and submission from all those tainted by original sin provide much of kink's source material. The sadomasochistic fetishizing of Catholicism is robust in the novels of the Marquis de Sade as, for instance, in Justine's appalling sexual misadventures at a monastery and the religiously themed orgies in *120 Days of Sodom*.[41] More recently, Peter Tupper, writing about Catholic-themed erotica during the Victorian Gothic revival, noted:

Even though the Gothic was supposed to have finished 200 years ago, it keeps recurring, which is fitting because Gothic is all about the return of the repressed. BDSM is about the return of ideas and symbols and relationships that have supposedly been abandoned in liberal history's march towards Utopia.[42]

Like depth psychology itself, the overt transgressive tendencies of kink and BDSM reach back into the neglected shadowy aspects of Western culture to reclaim and make explicit the difficult truths we have forgotten collectively.

The convergence between suffering and degradation, religious or spiritual transcendence, and erotic pleasure is not limited to the Western Christian tradition. Kaldera[43] has recognized the numinous potential of BDSM as a modern iteration of ancient pagan and shamanic practices, in which suffering and degradation participate in the same dizzying sexual-spiritual synthesis. He described three major applications of BDSM for spiritual transformation: to bring individuals closer to spirit by working with the endorphins released during the careful application of pain; to create "psychological theater in a ritual context," guiding individuals through the mythic underworld journey; and to engage the dynamics of the full-time Dominant/submissive relationship as a spiritual path.[44]

The connection to the divine through the ordeal path of BDSM has much in common with the concept of the *numinous* as it was originally described by Rudolf Otto:

The feeling of it may at times come sweeping like a gentle tide, pervading the mind with a tranquil mood of deepest worship. It may pass over into a more set and lasting attitude of soul, continuing, as it were, thrillingly vibrant and resonant, until at last it dies away and the soul resumes its "profane," non-religious mood of everyday experience. It may burst in sudden eruption up from the depths of the soul with spasms and convulsions, or lead to the strangest excitements, to intoxicated frenzy, to transport, and to ecstasy. It has its wild and demonic forms and can sink to an almost grisly horror and shuddering. It has its crude, barbaric antecedents and early manifestations, and again it may be developed into something beautiful and pure and glorious. It may become the hushed, trembling and speechless humility of the creature in the presence of—whom or what? In the presence of that which is a Mystery inexpressible and above all creatures.[45]

Many BDSM practitioners will recognize something of their own personal experience in Otto's description. Jung[46] asserted that numinous experiences emanate from archetypes as an expression of their primordial nature. By pairing the numinous with the archetypal, he expanded the concept beyond the confines of religious thought to encompass psychological experiences of intensity, mystery, and transformation. Thus, the numinosity of religious experience is comparable in its power to the numinosity of sex and aggression.[47]

When suffering becomes a numinous experience, then there is an opportunity for deeper transformation and healing that can be at once spiritual and psychological. Jung famously stated:

> [T]he main interest of my work is not concerned with the treatment of neurosis but rather with the approach to the numinous. But the fact is that the approach to the numinous is the real therapy and inasmuch as you attain to the numinous experiences you are released from the curse of pathology.[48]

How do Jungians imagine potential healing and transformation actually occur through numinous experience? Because archetypes operate at the core of our complexes as well as in the mystery of the *numinosum*, there is the potential to resolve or restructure the personality through the emotional intensity of such experiences.[49] When archetypal energies are allowed to emerge in a secure container, such as exists in a risk-aware, negotiated, mutually consensual BDSM scene, then the numinous aspect of suffering and degradation can reveal itself.

As these religious reflections draw to a close, a word of caution is in order. Because of the archetypal nature of numinous experiences, there is a psychological risk present in engaging with suffering as an agent of transformation and growth. Corbett[50] cautioned that numinous encounters can be overwhelming in their affective power. Sometimes the psychic energy of the archetype transits over into the literal physical reality of the practitioner with too great a valence to integrate into consciousness. If a practitioner's personality is fragile or lacks resiliency, unmanageable anxiety or even psychosis can occur when one is engulfed by the numinous. There is also the risk of identifying with the archetype on the personal level, a state that can lead to destructive feelings of inferiority and self-loathing on the one extreme or grandiose self-importance and power on the other. Approaching the numinous with respect and humility and gradually growing familiar with the depths of transformative suffering in the context of a trusting relationship are essential. Learning about the ordeal path with experienced practitioners, having the support of a kink-affirming community, and seeking the assistance of a knowledgeable therapist can also help.

Discussion

In his discussion of pathologizing, Hillman suggested that the appropriate psychological response to the presence of suffering and degradation in our lives was to identify their psychological necessity, including "purposes which we have misperceived and values which must present themselves necessarily in a distorted form."[51] For people who find themselves unable to relate to the pleasure and intimacy that suffering and degradation provide for many BDSM enthusiasts, Hillman's words offer a reminder that psychological necessities operate autonomously from the ego. These necessities are expressions of soul, whose purposes and values we misperceive because we try to understand them from the perspective of the conscious personality. We are trained to think in more literal, less poetic terms regarding our own welfare and personal advancement, but soul communicates through pathos and disorder. As with any foreign language, we understand little of what soul has to say on its own behalf. For Jung,[52] the psychological necessity of such experiences was the displacement of the ego in the interest of psychic integration and growth.

There is another form of suffering that has yet to be mentioned, and that is the suffering that occurs when one's destiny is thwarted. To some, it may sound grandiose to suggest that to enter upon the ordeal path of BDSM and its application of pain and suffering constitute a kind of yielding to one's destiny. Yet the numinous experiences that many encounter and the self-identity some discover through relationships based on domination and submission often evoke a deeper sense of meaning, purpose, and fulfillment, of being on the path of individuation. When someone blocks or denies the individuation process, ego defenses dam up psychic energy, and a neurosis may develop.[53] Although it may be difficult to understand how people can find pleasure and intimacy by playing with suffering and degradation, most people are familiar with what it is like to suffer the effects of a life unlived, a destiny refused. We feel inauthentic in our relationships and our activities, we suffer from inertia and stagnation, and we feel so very empty inside. Inauthenticity is a form of suffering that no one desires. It is bad suffering because it is vacuous and recursive.[54]

There is a distinction between good suffering and bad suffering. In his discussion of Job's degradation, Corbett[55] maintained that the numinous encounter with the brutal and destructive aspect of the divine is an example of how suffering can be a catalyst for transformation and growth through the creation of new meaning from firsthand experience. Kaldera[56] made a similar point in his overview of neo-pagan BDSM. These are examples of good suffering because the experiences lead toward greater maturity, healing, psychic growth, and progress toward one's destiny. The world is full of examples of bad suffering, most often rendered bad by the contra-psychological effects of literalism, which prevent the flow of psychic energy and the genesis of new meaning.

Hillman[57] said that soul is what makes meaning possible, which is an idea that concurs with Corbett's[58] assertion that meaning is the psychic agent that makes suffering transformative. Jung wrote, "The least of things with a meaning is always worth more in life than the greatest of things without it."[59] Nietzsche had reached a similar conclusion: "Man, the most courageous animal, and the most inured to trouble, does not deny suffering *per se*: he wants it, he seeks it out, provided that it can be given a meaning."[60] When we *psychologize* our suffering and degradation, then some meaning may emerge, and the experience becomes psychologically valuable.

Through suffering and degradation, an archetypal dimension opens, and the intensification of physical pain and emotion can constellate a numinous experience.

When this happens in BDSM, it diminishes our identification with the person we imagine ourselves to be, the burden of personhood is lightened, and the deeper transformative potential of radical sexuality emerges. The argument put forth here is that the archetypal forces of suffering and degradation are emissaries of soul, which produce similar patterns and effects in various contexts. Suffering and degradation can be intensifiers and catalysts of psycho-spiritual transformation that operate within mythic, archetypal structures of initiation.

Conclusion

It is important to offer a concluding word of caution and clinical concern regarding suffering and degradation. The established practices of the BDSM community, which include progressive familiarity and trust with an established partner, negotiation and consent, aftercare, and de-briefing all provide a structure and container for the volatile numinous forces that practitioners encounter. These structures provide a safeguard, creating a modern alchemical vessel for deeper psychological experience. However, in BDSM as in therapy, the structures are not failsafe. Potential transcendence can turn into trauma. Approaching that breaking point is what some practitioners refer to as edgeplay.[61] It is risky by definition and, like most of the practices described here, should be undertaken only with established partners with care and preparation. When trauma occurs, the conscious personality can fragment and splinter, causing dissociation, psychic numbness, or compartmentalization within the psyche's self-care system. Jungian analyst Donald Kalsched has written two superb books on this topic, *The Inner World of Trauma*[62] and *Trauma and the Soul*.[63] Both books are highly recommended to anyone in need of healing from such experiences and to the clinicians providing their care.

In the world of BDSM, suffering and degradation open a unique psychological nexus where paradox and potential are simultaneously destructive and generative. As agents of erotic pleasure, they can intensify and deepen sadomasochistic play by privileging the fantasy shadow elements hidden in daily life. Beneath the surface of BDSM's iconic tropes and ribald imagination, there is archetypal numinous energy at play. Suffering and degradation can serve more profound ends, such as intimate bonding between partners, restructuring of the conscious personality, and catalyzing spiritual revelations. Soul is involved in suffering and degradation as the factor that makes meaning out of adversity. When the struggle to bear the unbearable and endure the morbid brutality of loss becomes meaningful, then the literal details of an event can become a true symbol, capable of re-shaping the stories we tell ourselves about who we are and generating new psychic growth.

Notes

1 Psychoanalyst Avgi Saketopoulou (2014) has written insightfully about the psychological nexus of pain, suffering, disgust, and pleasure as coextensive rather than incommensurate. She has reached a similar conclusion regarding the transformative potential of the pain-pleasure convergence.
2 Dynock as cited in Goerlich, S. (2021, p. 60).
3 Rinder, I. D. (1960).
4 Stein, D. (2016).
5 Jung, C. G. (2009, p. 354).
6 Hillman, J. (1975/1992, p. 56).
7 Hillman, J. (1975/1992).
8 Merriam-Webster (n.d.-b).
9 American Heritage (2011a, p. 1266).
10 Cassell, E. J. (2004, p. 32, emphasis added).
11 Ibid. (p. 35).
12 Hesse, H. (1946/1971, pp. 98–99).
13 Stoller, R. (1991).
14 Kaldera, R. (2006).
15 American Heritage (2011b, p. 1742).
16 Merriam-Webster (n.d.-a).
17 Burton, N. (2014).
18 Hillman, J. (1975/1992, p. 23).
19 Hillman, J. (1972); Hillman, J. (1975/1992); Hillman, J. (1979); Hillman, J. (2004).
20 Hillman, J. (1975/1992, p. xvi).
21 Jung, C. J. (1958/1969c, p. 88 [*CW* 8, para. 184]).
22 Kaldera, R. (2006, p. 27).
23 Glucklich, A. (2001).
24 Mayell, H. (2003).
25 Ibid.
26 Sunda, M. (2015).
27 Lee, A. (2017).
28 Ugobude, F. (2018).
29 Patterson, O. (1982), The word "dehumanization" should not be confused with Hillman's archetypal term *dehumanizing*. Chapter 6 discusses in depth the significant difference between the two terms.
30 Cassell, E. J. (2004).
31 Ibid. (p. 42).
32 Ibid. (p. v).
33 Ibid. (p. xii, emphasis in original).
34 Hall, Langer, & McMartin, 2010;Hall, M. E. L., Shannonhouse, L., Aten, J., McMartin, J., & Silverman, E. (2018); Lammers, A. (2007); Pihlström, S. (2019).
35 Lammers, A. (2007).
36 Jung, C. G. (1952/1969a).
37 Ibid. (p. 366 [*CW* 11, para. 561]).
38 Hall, M. E. L., Shannonhouse, L., Aten, J., McMartin, J., & Silverman, E. (2018).
39 Monick, E. (1993).
40 Campbell, J. (1988, pp. 138–139).
41 Sade, M. D. (1904/2016).
42 Tupper, P. (2009, para. 15).
43 Kaldera, R. (2006).
44 Ibid. (pp. 4–6).
45 Otto, R. (1917/2023, p. 19).

46 Jung, C. G. (1948/1969b, p. 149 [para. 222]).
47 Ellenberger, H. F. (1970, p. 724).
48 Jung, C. G. (1973, p. 377).
49 Corbett, L. (1996, p. 22).
50 Corbett, L. (1996).
51 Hillman, J. (1975/1992, p. 57).
52 Jung, C. G. (1952/1967).
53 Jung, C. G. (1934/1981, p. 183 [*CW* 17, para. 313]).
54 Jungian psychologist Rosemary Gordon published a paper in 1987 that is representative of the clinical concerns of many professionals, namely, that sadomasochism is itself inherently vacuous and recursive because it is the perversion of an archetypal necessity. Gordon argued that the archetypal impulse was a need for veneration and worship that had gone astray. Although the idea that masochism bears an archetypal imprint was original, the presumption that masochistic sexuality is a clinical problem in need of solution is not supported by the preponderance of research over the past 20 years. Any behavior that becomes fixated, repetitive, joyless, and non-generative is a legitimate cause for psychological concern, but the historic tendency of the profession unilaterally to pathologize non-normative sexualities is of equal or greater concern. For kinksters who no longer find intimacy, pleasure, or growth from their activities, psychotherapy should be a safe harbor for supportive introspection. But patients' dysphoria should not suggest that their sexuality is itself a symptom of something disordered and illegitimate in need of a cure.
55 Corbett, L. (2007).
56 Kaldera, R. (2006).
57 Hillman, J. (1983/2004).
58 Corbett, L. (2007).
59 Jung, C. G. (1935/1966, p. 45 [*CW* 16, para. 96]).
60 Nietzsche, F. (1887/1956, p. 298).
61 Goerlich, S. (2021).
62 Kalsched, D. (1996).
63 Kalsched, D. (2013).

References

American Heritage. (2011a). Pain. In J. P. Pickett (Ed.), *The American heritage dictionary of the English language* (5th ed., p. 1266). Houghton Mifflin Harcourt.

American Heritage. (2011b). Suffer. In J. P. Pickett (Ed.), *The American heritage dictionary of the English language* (5th ed., p. 1742). Houghton Mifflin Harcourt.

Burton, N. (2014, August 27). The psychology of humiliation. *Psychology Today*. www.psychologytoday.com/us/blog/hide-and-seek/201408/the-psychology-humiliation

Campbell, J. (1988). *The power of myth with Bill Moyers* (B. S. Flowers, Ed.). Doubleday.

Cassell, E. J. (2004). *The nature of suffering* (2nd ed.). Oxford University Press.

Corbett, L. (1996). *The religious function of the psyche*. Routledge.

Corbett, L. (2007). *Psyche and the sacred*. Spring Journal Books.

Ellenberger, H. F. (1970). *The discovery of the unconscious*. Basic Books.

Glucklich, A. (2001). *Sacred pain*. Oxford University Press.

Goerlich, S. (2021). *The leather couch*. Routledge.

Gordon, R. (1987). Masochism: The shadow side of the archetypal need to venerate and worship. *Journal of Analytical Psychology, 32*, 227–240.

Hall, M. E. L., Langer, R., & McMartin, J. (2010). The role of suffering in human flourishing: Contributions from positive psychology, theology, and philosophy. *Journal of Psychology and Theology, 38*(2), 111–121.

Hall, M. E. L., Shannonhouse, L., Aten, J., McMartin, J., & Silverman, E. (2018). Religion-specific resources for meaning-making from suffering: Defining the territory. *Mental Health, Religion & Culture*, *21*(1), 77–92.

Hesse, H. (1971). *If the war goes on . . .* (R. Manheim, Trans.). Farrar, Straus and Giroux. (Original work published 1946)

Hillman, J. (1972). *The myth of analysis.* Northwestern University Press.

Hillman, J. (1979). *The dream and the underworld.* HarperCollins.

Hillman, J. (1992). *Re-Visioning psychology.* HarperPerennial. (Original work published 1975)

Hillman, J. (2004). Archetypal psychology: A brief account. In *The uniform edition of the writings of James Hillman* (Vol. 1, pp. 13–94). Spring. (Original work published 1983)

Jung, C. G. (1966). General problems of psychotherapy (R. F. C. Hull, Trans.). In H. Read et al. (Eds.), *The collected works of C. G. Jung* (Vol. 16, 2nd ed., pp. 3–128). Princeton University Press. (Original work published 1935)

Jung, C. G. (1967). Symbols of transformation: An analysis of the prelude to a case of schizophrenia (R. F. C. Hull, Trans.). In H. Read et al. (Eds.), *The collected works of C. G. Jung* (Vol. 5, 2nd ed.). Princeton University Press. (Original work published 1952)

Jung, C. G. (1969a). Answer to Job (R. F. C. Hull, Trans.). In H. Read et al. (Eds.), *The collected works of C. G. Jung* (Vol. 11, 2nd ed., pp. 355–474). Princeton University Press. (Original work published 1952)

Jung, C. G. (1969b). A psychological approach to the dogma of the trinity (R. F. C. Hull, Trans.). In H. Read et al. (Eds.), *The collected works of C. G. Jung* (Vol. 11, 2nd ed., pp. 107–200). Princeton University Press. (Original work published 1948)

Jung, C. G. (1969c). The transcendent function (R. F. C. Hull, Trans.). In H. Read et al. (Eds.), *The collected works of C. G. Jung* (Vol. 8, 2nd ed., pp. 67–91). Princeton University Press. (Original work published 1958)

Jung, C. G. (1973). *Letters* (Vol. 1; R. F. C. Hull, Trans.; G. Adler, & A. Jaffe, Eds.). Princeton University Press.

Jung, C. G. (1981). The development of personality (R. F. C. Hull, Trans.). In H. Read et al. (Eds.), *The collected works of C. G. Jung* (Vol. 17, pp. 167–186). Princeton University Press. (Original work published 1934)

Jung, C. G. (2009). *The red book, Liber Novus: A reader's edition* (M. Kyburz, J. Peck, & S. Shamdasani, Trans.; S. Shamdasani, Ed.). W. W. Norton.

Kaldera, R. (2006). *Dark moon rising: Pagan BDSM and the ordeal path.* Asphodel.

Kalsched, D. (1996). *The inner world of trauma.* Routledge.

Kalsched, D. (2013). *Trauma and the soul.* Routledge.

Lammers, A. (2007). Jung and White and the god of terrible double aspect. *Journal of Analytical Psychology*, *52*, 253–274.

Lee, A. (2017, September 11). CE 1100. The Baekjeong: Medieval outcasts. *The History of Korea.* www.thehistoryofkorea.com/ce-1100-the-baekjeong-medieval-outcasts

Mayell, H. (2003, June 2). India's untouchables face violence, discrimination. *National Geographic.* www.nationalgeographic.com/news/2003/6/indias-untouchables-face-violence-discrimination/

Merriam-Webster. (n.d.-a). Degrade. *Merriam-Webster.com dictionary.* Retrieved February 21, 2020, from www.merriam-webster.com/

Merriam-Webster. (n.d.-b). Suffer. *Merriam-Webster.com dictionary.* Retrieved February 21, 2020, from www.merriam-webster.com/

Monick, E. (1993). *Evil, sexuality, and disease in Grünewald's Body of Christ.* Spring.

Nietzsche, F. (1956). *The birth of tragedy & The genealogy of morals* (F. Golffing, Trans.). Anchor Books. (Original work published 1887)

Otto, R. (2023). *The idea of holy* (J. W. Harvey, Trans.). Pantianos Classics. (Original work published 1917)

Patterson, O. (1982). *Slavery and social death.* Harvard University Press.

Pihlström, S. (2019). A Pragmatist approach to the mutual recognition between ethico-political and theological discourses on evil and suffering. *Political Theology, 20*(2), 157–175.

Rinder, I. D. (1960). Degradation, abnegation, debasement of self—a dynamic in role change. *Psychoanalytic Review, 47c*(3), 106–116.

Sade, M. D. (2016). *The 120 days of Sodom* (W. McMorran, & T. Wynn, Trans.). Penguin Random House UK. (Original work published 1904)

Saketopoulou, A. (2014). To suffer pleasure: The shattering of the ego as the psychic labor of perverse sexuality. *Studies in Gender and Sexuality, 15*(4), 254–268.

Stein, D. (2016). From S&M to M/s: How consensual slavery became visible in the gay leather community, 1950 to 1999. In P. Tupper (Ed.), *Our lives, our history* (pp. 75–110). Perfectbound.

Stoller, R. (1991). *Pain and passion*. Plenum.

Sunda, M. (2015, October 23). Japan's hidden caste of untouchables. *BBC News*. www.bbc.com/news/world-asia-34615972

Tupper, P. (2009, February 10). Nuns are the original fetish object: Catholicism, sexual deviance, and Victorian Gothic culture by Patrick R. O'Malley. *The History of BDSM*. https://historyofbdsm.com/2009/02/catholicism-sexual-deviance-victorian-gothic-culture-patrick-omalley/

Ugobude, F. (2018, November 18). Culture: The Osu caste system in Igboland. *The Guardian*. https://guardian.ng/life/culture-the-osu-caste-system-in-igboland/

6

THE SPECTER OF EVIL

Introduction

In her 2017 book, *The Evil of Banality*, moral philosopher Elizabeth Minnich built on the work of her teacher, Hannah Arendt, making the case that evil, from a secular rather than religious perspective, pertains to acts that evoke such a sense of moral horror that we experience them as unimaginable, unthinkable, and unspeakable. Yet paradoxically, the banality of everyday life facilitates large-scale atrocities, such as the Nazi Holocaust and the Rwandan genocide, by providing an unquestioning citizenry to support and collude with the operations of evil. Minnich argued that the lessons of such human catastrophes warn of a greater danger than the romanticized notion of moral monsters or sociopathic madmen, and that is the danger of the ordinary, rooted in the average person's lack of moral imagination and their failure to self-reflect and evaluate the destructive impact of their own actions and ideas. Minnich's book is insightful, persuasive, and challenging. Her work provides a helpful point of reference in the present discussion about the specter of evil as a soul-image and its relationship to BDSM.

Minnich made an oblique reference to BDSM and kink among the examples she provided of popular culture's penchant for adopting the specter of evil in video games, slasher movies, comic books, biographies of serial killers, and Nazi-themed parties and social events. She suggested that such examples are evidence "that a tamed evil still sizzling with a bit of hell-fire, romanticized and intense, flourishes" in modern society.[1] She continued

 DOI: 10.4324/9781003223597-8

with a strong word of caution that is relevant to the present argument and the dangers of literalism:

> *Evil*, reduced to cultural specter with which to scare ourselves silly as well as theme for playacting transgressive acts, can provide a kind of vacation from the frustrating bonds of convention and consideration of others. Sometimes, then, people seek release and relief in safely crossing those boundaries into a super-dramatic fantasy, a break from reality from which they easily return to acceptable social lives. Pressed into service by a system going wrong, however, what was known to be transgressive can be transmuted into, rather than used as defiant escape from, the conventional.[2]

Although there is appreciation here for the value of fantasy as a given of psychological life, there is also a concern that what begins as elaborate play with malicious and destructive psychic elements can devolve into complicit acceptance of evil as ordinary. The risk depends on a fundamental question: What is the difference between a recreational enactment of evil and the perpetration of evil acts? That is the psychological concern of this chapter.

As discussed in the previous chapter, human consciousness negotiates an edge between psychic reality and literal reality. Although literal thinking aspires to make the dividing line simple and distinct, the transformative power of play discussed in Chapter 4 demonstrates that the edge in question is the blurred liminal zone of potential space. Fantasy-images shape our perceptions and reactions to the reality of everyday life. The difference between a recreational enactment of evil and the commission of evil acts rests on a pivot point: on the one hand, playing with the fantasy-images of psychic reality and on the other, concretizing them through literalism. Minnich was right to sound a note of caution about the dangers of collapsing fantasy elements into the banality of literal thinking, although she may have underestimated both the value and the autonomous character of what we are calling the imaginal element in psychological life. The edge between psychic reality and literal reality is the zone where BDSM practitioners and kinksters play. When the specter of evil appears in the play space, some psychological care is indeed warranted.

The world of kink and BDSM is fascinated with evil. The visceral thrill of exploring the unthinkable and the unspeakable is almost emblematic of kink. The sinister aspect of the medieval fantasy so central to many BDSM scenes has a peculiar appeal because it implies that something horrible and merciless might happen in the dungeon, something worse than anything we can imagine. Like devotees of slasher movies or neighbors who turn their suburban home into a blood-soaked haunted house for Halloween, we all recognize that there is something in us that wants to scare and be scared. A gasp of simultaneous terror and delight is a cherished moment in the modern BDSM dungeon. Psychoanalyst Avgi Saketopoulou[3] believed we are born with an innate impulse to venture into the realm of the unthinkable and unsayable to experience a psychological state she called *overwhelm*. Such encounters with the darkness of the unconscious can break down the ego and allow a freshly integrated self-image to emerge. *Overwhelm* is related to that bit of sizzling hellfire that Minnich[4] described. In such experiences, the specter of evil is often close at hand.

The present discussion proposes a depth psychological orientation toward the subject: *evil is a particularly potent archetypal pattern characterized by malice, ruthlessness, intentional cruelty, and moral horror, giving expression to the unthinkable and unspeakable in their most destructive aspects.* The archetypal perspective affords some psychological space for reflection between evil as soul-image and the literal atrocities perpetrated throughout history that bear its sinister imprint. History will be a particular concern here because a psychological understanding of evil always occurs within a historical context. It is not the history of human evil per se that will be the focus but rather the operation of the archetypal pattern through history, sometimes as fantasy-image, sometimes as literal atrocity.

There are four major sections to Chapter 6. First, Jungian and archetypal perspectives on evil establish a depth-psychological understanding of the topic, augmented by the psychological and philosophical work of Julia Kristeva. Second, we consider the historical context of the present moment by examining the painful legacy of a specific world event: the transatlantic slave trade. BDSM and kink incorporate psychological elements of slavery, sometimes overtly, sometimes less consciously, which raise ethical and moral questions the BDSM community is itself now debating. Third, the discussion turns to Black voices from the BDSM community who share in their own words how modern consensual Master/slave relationships affect them. The concluding discussion considers the pain and difficulty the topic elicits and how coming to terms with evil as it manifests in the progression of history traverses the edge between psychic reality and literal facts.

A Psychological Understanding of Evil

Ideas about evil occupy an unusual place in the human imagination. Throughout history, the subject appears to oscillate between being seen in exclusively human terms and being recognized as having a cosmic dimension. In some cases, evil is viewed in relation to morally abhorrent acts enacted by individuals or collective humans. In others, it refers to the presence of a supernatural force to which humans are subject. As is the case with any major archetype, evil travels far and deep into the psyche on both personal and collective levels. It has understandably aroused the interest of theologians and philosophers as well as psychologists. Over the past several years, there have been numerous books devoted to the topic, a trend that suggests interest in evil remains vivid for the psychologically minded as well as the wider public.[5] Lionel Corbett's[6] recent survey of the existing psychological literature cannot be improved upon for anyone interested in a thorough review of diverse perspectives on evil. These works share a central question: *How can we understand the abhorrent moral atrocities our species perpetrates, and how can we reduce or eliminate such behavior?* It is an important question and the consensus at present is that the answer is complicated. In considering how the specter of evil as a soul-image operates in the world of BDSM, it becomes clear that the usual framing of the question overlooks a fundamental element: the imaginal basis of psychic reality (first, fantasy, then reality). The contemporary discussion tends to address evil as a human behavioral problem, whereas a Jungian and archetypal approach would ask: *What is it that fascinates us about fantasy-images of evil? And is there a way to balance risk and caution in engaging such potent psychic energy?*

A Jungian Perspective

For Jung, the topic of evil was "a constant preoccupation that would not leave him alone."[7] Jung saw enough devastation in his lifetime to recognize evil as a real and potent force in human affairs. Having witnessed the blood-soaked devastation of two world wars, the atrocities of the Holocaust, and the detonation of two atomic bombs, Jung regarded evil as an urgent psychological concern. However, the metaconcept of wholeness was the greater overarching principle guiding his psychology.[8] Jung encountered an unusual problem reconciling the psychological question of good and evil with his concept of the Self. If one embraces good and rejects evil, following the established moral injunctions of Western thought, how can one achieve psychological wholeness? His efforts to sort out the paradox led to several fundamental conclusions about the nature of evil, which together form the basis of a Jungian perspective.

They include the following features. First, evil is a category of human thought—a subjective judgment reached through the operations of the conscious moral mind.[9] Through the work of differentiation, we recognize that our inner world is comprised of disparate psychic elements. As we mature and attain higher levels of consciousness, we develop the discernment to judge some of these elements as evil. They are evil by virtue of our subjective moral perception.

Second, evil is best understood in a historical context.[10] Our subjective moral judgment is contextualized by the historical traditions that shaped our values and beliefs. Psychologically speaking, we are the products of our history. The conclusion that an idea or an impulse is evil always bears the traces of a historical perspective.

Third, the human shadow is the great danger—it is our disavowal of our own capacity for evil that leads to projections and the justification to perpetrate evil acts.[11] As we learn what others around us view as good or evil, we learn to suppress what they might recognize as evil within ourselves. By not allowing these unacceptable elements to come into consciousness, they easily become shadow projections that we cast on to others whom we then perceive as evil. Such projections form the justification for fighting and annihilating the evil other. Because psychic material that is repressed into the shadow always has a strong archetypal character, evil has a strong capacity to attract and to fascinate.

Fourth, the psychological task is to work out the problem of evil on the personal level because individual change begets social change.[12] Jung was not optimistic about the prospects of a collective solution to the problem of evil. He believed that the work of confronting one's own personal shadow and reclaiming the projected parts of our own soul would lead to a collective comprised of more psychologically conscious individuals. If we understand individually the risks of projecting our shadow on to others, the risk of collective stigma against ostracized groups will decrease.

Fifth, when we encounter evil as a part of our own nature, we encounter our fate and our guilt, which are essential for integrating the shadow.[13] The great task of individuation is to come to terms with the ways in which we differ from the society around us. We are each peculiar, a unique expression of soul. The experience of our peculiarity can involve feelings of guilt for not conforming to collective norms, but that same nonconformity designates the fate that is uniquely ours to carry in life. Often, our uniqueness includes aspects that the ego views as evil. The challenge of individuation is to accept those aspects hidden in the shadow and integrate them as part of our identity.

And sixth, wholeness comes through introspection, reflection, inner struggle (soul work), and a personal system of morality and ethics, which must be constantly tested and revised.[14] Accepting and integrating the evil that is uniquely ours is no easy task. It requires a serious and often painful struggle between contradictory elements within our own soul. This struggle is the essence of the individuation process. A more mature consciousness recognizes the necessity of introspection and reflection to identify the disparate contradictory elements of our own nature and to take personal responsibility for those aspects we deem to be evil. The insights we gain through inner work form the foundation of a more sophisticated personal system of morality and ethics. Because the individuation process is never complete, it is incumbent upon us to continually interrogate and refine the values and beliefs that help us determine what is evil.

What do these conclusions have to do with kink and BDSM? It is probably best to address BDSM enthusiasts directly in answering the question. Here is a proposed set of kinky axioms inspired by Jung's approach to evil:

Evil is real—you need to take it seriously. But it is up to you to reach your own conclusions about how and where it is present in your BDSM play and in your life. You must use your subjective judgment and develop your own system of morals and ethics to guide your choices. You can develop an archetypal morality that recognizes the unique character of each figure that animates your erotic imagination. It will help you recognize the presence of evil and help you develop an ethical attitude toward it.

History is kinky, and evil runs through it. The specter of evil is with you in your creative play when you draw upon the images of history to build your fantasy scenarios and BDSM style. The Gothic is a tradition that brings with it monsters, horror, the abject, and the medieval imagination. The dungeon, the torture chamber, the instruments of pain and suffering, all carry with them their own histories, which include the literal degradation and torment of people who were harmed and destroyed without their consent or negotiation. The presence of the past is part of what makes BDSM exciting and sometimes overwhelming. Your play will deepen when you contemplate the presence of evil that lives in the historical artifacts of the scene. The historical will draw you into the archetypal.

Know your shadow. For many kinksters, the play space is shadow space, a zone where the unknown images of the deep psyche are invited to emerge and present their truth. That truth often occurs as self-discovery and sometimes as troubling revelation. Your personal shadow may confront you with the pleasure you feel in your sadism or your masochism as something within you that is real and vital. BDSM play supports shadow integration. But the shadow is exciting and fascinating because part of its potent allure comes from the evil that also resides there. Sometimes a scene comes close to the edge of what either you or your partner can control, and when one of you loses control, when consent evaporates and safe words are ignored, then evil has jumped from the imaginal to the literal. The negotiation of hurt becomes the perpetration of harm, and the consequences can be disastrous.

Your kink will make you whole. If you can recognize the presence of evil as a soul-image without falling into an archetypal possession, you can integrate aspects of your inner world into consciousness and achieve a greater level of psychological wholeness that will serve you in life. Your upbringing may have taught you to reject and discard certain aspects of who you are on a deeper level. Your kink restores those lost parts and can lead to a richer imagination and fuller range of emotions.

Your kink will reveal your guilt and your fate. Others often cannot understand why BDSM brings you so much pleasure. Your desires express your subjective truth, and when you can recognize a flicker of evil in them (i.e., the impulse to harm and destroy or to be destroyed with horrific malicious intent), you will discover that you are living your fate. Owning the evil that is uniquely yours also involves feeling the guilt that makes you unique. Guilt becomes a catalyst for developing your personal morality and ethics. At such a moment, play becomes craft, and BDSM becomes a path of personal development.

If you want the most out of your kink, treat it as psychological work. Your scenes require introspection, reflection, and ethical appraisals. These practices help you identify and evaluate when evil has appeared in your play, sometimes invited and sometimes unbidden. Reflecting on what has happened develops self-knowledge. You increase sensitivity and attunement toward your inner life and that of your partner. If you build these practices into your play, you will find that your kinky life yields psychological growth that carries over into other areas.

What about Hitler and the Nazis? Any exploration of evil sooner or later will lead you back to Germany and World War II. Hitler and the Nazis are perhaps the unrivaled image of evil in the contemporary Western imagination. Jung[15] referred to them throughout his writing as does almost every author featured in the present discussion. "Nazis came to have a symbolic function as a floating signifier for the abject in simplistic narratives of good and evil."[16] The connection between the BDSM aesthetic and the Nazis is close indeed: the iconic look of gay leather motorcycle culture immortalized by Tom of Finland was appropriated from the Nazi uniforms designed by Hugo Boss.[17] Many of the founding members of the gay leather motorcycle clubs were returning World War II veterans, and some had been prisoners of war.[18] It is reasonable to speculate that the specter of Nazi evil was a looming shadow, ripe for eroticization, in the psyches of early BDSM practitioners.

Jung's approach to evil primarily concerned the individuation process and the challenge each of us faces to achieve psychological wholeness. A healthy society is obliged to reject evil, and yet each of us individually must reckon with it as an interior reality. Jung's emphasis on personal responsibility is likely to fit well with the values of BDSM practitioners who are accustomed to community standards that highlight personal agency and accountability in negotiating and consenting to the pursuit of transgressive pleasures.

Hillman's Next Step: Pleasure Beyond Humanism

Hillman's[19] fundamental concern was the restoration of soul to the logos of psyche. He advocated for a full-scale re-visioning of psychology oriented toward the primacy of fantasy-images, which constitute autonomous imaginal reality. Although he never devoted an entire paper or book to evil, his concept of *dehumanizing* suggests how one might use an archetypal approach to understand it.

Let us recall that Hillman[20] regarded the soul's imaginal world to be populated by a seemingly endless panoply of fantasy figures. As personifications, they possess considerable power to structure and inflect our perception, our emotion, our cognition, and our action. Because of their archetypal nature, these images precede us and outlast us. Hillman asserted that their time-less durability makes them more real than we are, so the primary task of psychology is to study the nature of their reality. Making such a re-vision asks a lot of the Western mind, which has been captivated by the principles of humanism as it developed during the Protestant Reformation and the Age of Enlightenment. By contrast, Hillman was a passionate admirer of humanism as it existed in the era of classical Greece and the Renaissance, when it celebrated the mythic imagination and a poetic sensibility. Hillman offered a compelling inventory of the modern maladies large and small that have proceeded from the dominance of rational humanism, including con-crete thinking and literalism. Worse still is the conflation of human real-ity with psychic reality so that they are misperceived as one and the same. *Dehumanizing* repopulates the human imagination with the primal vivid reality of fantasy soul-images. Thus, *dehumanizing* is based on a compensa-tory move away from rational humanism. It is a term that privileges the soul rather than the human. It does not intend to degrade or negate the human except to "upgrade" fantasy-images as the subject of psychology.

How can *dehumanizing* contribute to a psychological understanding of evil? Hillman[21] was concerned with the effects of rational humanism on dichotomous thinking. Initially, it is simple enough to distinguish the human from the nonhuman, but that quickly leads to evaluations of good versus bad, right versus wrong, and superior versus inferior as manifestations of the human/nonhuman binary. The development of Christian morality also intensified the dichotomy between good versus evil. "Before Christian-ity, evil was not quite as evil," Marie-Louise von Franz once said. "The rise of Christianity added a kind of spirit of evil which it did not have before."[22] What was polytheistic in ancient Greece and Rome became monotheistic in Europe, and what was pagan in the classical imagination became evil in the Christian age.[23] That monotheistic symbol of ultimate cosmic evil, the Devil, was a condensation of several pantheistic figures: the wild nature god Pan; that divine trickster Hermes; and the Underworld's hidden ruler, Hades.[24] In ancient times, no one regarded these deities as evil, and nobody considered their counterparts on Mount Olympus as supremely good. *Dehumanizing* invites us to step back from the binary of good and evil and seek out the plurality of fantasy-images that are present but occluded by dualistic thinking.

What Hillman proposed is not simple. When we contemplate evil's appearance throughout history in horrific human atrocities, it is indeed difficult to look beyond the human perpetrators to the primordial images of the soul that are urging on the destruction. Who among us can look at the tattooed forearm of a Holocaust survivor and tell her that fantasy preceded the real horrors of gassing and incineration at Auschwitz? Yet Jung himself noted that the Nazi endeavor had its origin not in fantasies of genocide and global chaos but in the idealism of uplifting the German *volk* and achieving a new world order.[25] Behind the obscene inhumanity of the death camps was a fantasy of purification and decontamination, a fantasy that grew unchecked into fanaticism so extreme that its shadow side could not remain hidden from the world. Before the final solution (and prior to Hillman's concept), Jung had already demonstrated how *dehumanizing* can reveal the archetypal dimension behind human events. He responded to the rise of Nazism in an extraordinary 1936 essay entitled "Wotan."[26] Consistent with Hillman's concept, Jung stepped back from the literal human details of Hitler's rise and suggested that there was no better explanation for the bellicose idealism sweeping through the German people than the mythic Norse-German god of war, who had seized the national imagination in his archetypal grasp. *Dehumanizing* evil involves stepping back from the literal material facts of human atrocities to seek out the deeper necessities of the soul, whose destructive fantasies are giving rise to unspeakable ideas and horrific acts.

Several points of clarification are necessary to avoid confusion. First, *dehumanizing* in no way provides moral cover for people (or nations) who perpetrate intentionally destructive malicious crimes. "The devil made me do it" may be a sly hint at the realities of archetypal possession, but it is never a legitimate excuse for sociopathy. Judgment, punishment, and expiation are also fantasy-images of soul, and they must play their part in the drama of life along with evil. "Morality is rooted in psychic images and psychic images are moral powers," Hillman wrote. "These images remind us that we are not alone, choosing and deciding, but that in our choices and decisions we are always reflecting mythic stances."[27] Hillman's argument for a life lived in soul imagines a psychic reality in which fantasies of moral horror find their place alongside images of moral justice, thereby reducing the risk of evil physical enactments.

Second, *dehumanizing* is conceptually very different from *dehumanization* (a similar-sounding term), which refers to the psychological act of ascribing a subhuman essence to a group of people as moral justification for unequal treatment and lethal violence against them.[28] Nazi propaganda portrayed the Jews as vermin, and the Rwandan Hutus described their Tutsi victims as cockroaches to cite two examples of *dehumanization*. Examples like these appear throughout human history in racism, colonialism, slavery, warfare, mass violence, and genocide, which expose our less-than-human attributes. *Dehumanization* has been a catalyzing force of evil in the world. It begins as a way of thinking and then becomes a way of behaving (first, fantasy, then reality). When we condemn perpetrators as monsters, the fantasy-image behind our outrage appears as the projection of our own shadow. We dehumanize the dehumanizers, as philosopher David Livingstone Smith put it.[29] In a similar vein, Jung wrote, "The flame of evil glowers in our moral indignation."[30] Evil as an archetypal force is contagious. It is present in both acts of perpetration and condemnation.

Finally, there is the question of pleasure, which is central to the intimate transgressions of BDSM and kink. What does the archetypal understanding of evil offer those who are pursuing pleasure as practitioners? First, there is pleasure in psychological liberation. Hillman's psychology offers a release from the bondage of humanism and its constraining patterns of judgment based on human virtue. Kink and BDSM delight in blurring the lines between right and wrong, good and bad, kindness and cruelty, tenderness and violence, purity and filth. The traditional axioms of humanism are not up to the task of enjoying these ambiguities. Hillman described the archetypal mode as "subtle, complex, and ambiguous, a composite of thinking, erotic feelings, and imagination."[31] The release from dualistic thinking liberates the soul's imaginal possibilities. Where monolithic evil once stood in opposition to virtue, there is now a diverse pantheon of numinous figures, some terrifying, some disgusting, some beautiful, some deceptive, some seductive, some destructive, each worthy of admiration, discernment, and caution. They are among the most incandescent figures of the soul, the keepers of the hellfire that Minnich[32] wrote of. In their presence, BDSM practitioners must balance attuned, hot-blooded action with cool, vigilant reflection—pleasure is the ultimate reward of both. In mythology, pleasure—*Voluptas*—was the child of flighty Eros and contemplative Psyche.

Pleasure beyond humanism also includes pleasure in the paradox of the unknown and the abject. In BDSM, the mind is allowed to swing and pivot between contradictory modes of imagining. When the specter of evil appears during a scene, it can elicit a burst of joy with a simultaneous grimace of horror. Such paradoxical spontaneous reactions can fascinate, delight, and perturb. "Why did I do that? I can't believe that turned me on. I turned into somebody else under your control." Such self-revelations exemplify the paradoxical pivots of character and personality that occur as the psyche oscillates between established identities of the personal and the unplumbed depths of archetypal possibilities. *Dehumanizing* necessitates releasing the possessive grip of the ego. The scene is more than a means of personal gratification—it becomes an act of service to imaginal possibilities.

Evil as an archetypal mode of experience is always adjacent to the unknown and the unimaginable. Feminist philosopher and psychoanalyst Julia Kristeva[33] developed this insight when she wrote *Powers of Horror* as a treatise on that realm of the psyche she named the *abject*. It is a domain beyond the more conventional fantasies of the unacceptable and the repressed—a psychic dumpsite of our earliest unspeakable and unknowable personal refuse. We cannot bear to go there, yet we cannot stay away. The experience induces a state of horrifying otherness and uncanny paradox. For Kristeva's theoretical leanings toward the Oedipal complex, the *abject* is the mother lode. Working from the psychologies of Sigmund Freud and Jacques Lacan, it signifies a primal psychic zone of chaos and annihilation before the differentiation between self and other and the development of language to represent that distinction. She sees the abject as a wellspring of the Gothic imagination (that evocative synthesis of fear and desire[34]). The vampire, a paragon of Gothic horror, finds a psychic home here, where the *abject* elements of predatory danger, erotic seduction, and death converge in a single figure (Kristeva designated the corpse as "the utmost of abjection,"[35] and the vampire represents the return of the undead corpse as a living predator). It is no accident that *Fifty Shades of Grey* began as a work of fan fiction based on the characters from the *Twilight* vampire series.[36] The *abject* horror of the Gothic monster forms the archetypal relation between Edward Cullen and Christian Grey.[37] The vampiric pedigree of *Fifty Shades* illustrates how the *abject* draws the erotic imagination toward its most frightening and morbid fantasies.

When Hillman's concept of *dehumanizing* is applied to BDSM's eroticization of evil, the fantasy figures of the *abject* start to reveal themselves with overwhelming effect. Here, the sensory deprivation of hoods, gags, and sleepsacks induces a different kind of deep surrender into the unknown. Someone or something is in control, it is coming for us, it is ruthless, it is vicious, it is a beast, it has us, and we are defenseless and powerless. If fear and desire are the objectives of the scene, then the Gothic unknown becomes the way in. The fantasy world begins to animate with *abject* forms: here is the filth, the rotted, the necrotic, the expulsions and excretions, the worms, the maggots, the primal fundament, the corrupted, the misshapen, the inside-outs, and the unformed ("a 'something' I do not recognize as a thing," wrote Kristeva).[38] Here is the rusty laboratory door so easily unhinged with the mad scientist's failed experiments clawing on the other side. Here is the churning graveyard where death is the ultimate image of the unspeakable and the unknowable. Be careful here. The thrills are intense, but things are always quickly turning in a bad way because the *abject* lives in a climate of revolting violent disorientation and inversion. Such inherent unpredictability is why a BDSM scene can be terrifying fun in one moment and suddenly become deadly serious and trauma-inducing in the next. Saketopoulou's[39] concept of *overwhelm* is a valuable aide here because it helps explain the irresistible draw we feel, like children who want the scary monster to take us beyond what we can stand. Touching into the horror of the *abject* is risky, but it is also transformative and restorative. Through *dehumanizing*, we reemerge from these experiences with a self-image newly re-formed and in-formed.

Let us return to the two questions that guided the discussion of evil as soul-image in the direction of depth psychology: *What is it that fascinates us about fantasy-images of evil? And is there a way to balance risk and caution in engaging such potent psychic energy?* From an archetypal perspective, the fascination comes from the numinous *overwhelm* of experiencing the reality of the *abject*. The psyche draws us into its *dehumanizing* expressions beyond our human measure as a means of bringing soul into the world. When we know we are dealing with greater-than-human powers, ritual provides the structure that can balance risk with caution. The BDSM tradition knows all about the importance of ritual. Most serious practitioners have developed a craft that includes inflection points to support a shift in consciousness to mark the entry into a scene (preparing the play space, setting out the gear, donning the finery, creating a personal induction with the partner); to establish points of reference during the scene (check-ins, rest periods, transitions); and to reemerge from the experience (ending time, closing the space, and aftercare). There is another dimension to balancing risk and caution when one knows beforehand that there will be some hellfire present in the play. That dimension concerns the psychological bridge (or downward ladder) that is gradually constructed between the conscious personality and the greater reality of the archetypal unconscious. Admiration and respect toward the personified soul-images are always advisable, along with periods of deep self-reflection.

The field of psychology has attempted to address the question of evil from standpoints that oscillate between human acts and fantasy-images. BDSM partakes of both dimensions: human bodies become the theater of imaginal possibilities. Although seldom acknowledged, the development of BDSM and kink as an ethically engaged erotic practice has contributed to a cultural broadening of the moral imagination. However, Jung believed that the specter of evil in the world requires each of us to formulate a personal moral and ethical response to its ruthless, intentional, malicious, destructive character. When evil is present, even if it is imagined as a drop of transformative venom, serious reflection is warranted.

Slavery: Historical Legacy Versus Soul-Image

The discussion now turns to a moral and ethical question that the BSDM community is currently posing to itself regarding a particular form of societal evil: the issue of systemic racism and the enduring harm of the transatlantic slave trade on the human community, especially the harm inflicted on Black people in the United States. In 2016, a BDSM blogger published a post entitled "Is BDSM inescapably racist?"[40] Five years later, she posted a follow-up piece that reported on the increasing attention the original question had been receiving, particularly regarding the use of the terms *Master* and *slave* in a world that is increasingly aware of the harm these words have caused in the American psyche over the past 400 years.[41] The conversation is contentious and painful, and it has everything to do with how we address the specter of evil embedded in our midst.

The fantasy-image of master and slave runs deep through the Western (white-dominated) imagination. G. W. F. Hegel[42] employed the image as a metaphor to describe the dialectic of self and other that drives the development of self-consciousness. Hegel originally described the roles as Lord and Bondsman (subsequently mistranslated from German), and he believed it was the consciousness of the Bondsman that led to a clearer, more sophisticated understanding of reality. Friedrich Nietzsche[43] invoked master and slave as signifiers of two contrasting moralities that shape the structure of individual personality, society, and civilization. Frantz Fanon,[44] one of the great firebrands of post-colonial thought, took up Hegel's dialectic of master and slave and argued against applying it to the social and political struggles of Black people in the modern era. Fanon showed how Hegel's valuation of work as a pathway to consciousness breaks down because slavery perverts the dignity of work through objectification and violence. More recent scholars have addressed the progression of thought from Hegel to Fanon as a chronicle of the West's troubling history with race, slavery, and violence.[45] The use of the historical master/slave relationship as an image by influential Western philosophers and scholars suggests that there is something emblematic and archetypal about the extreme power imbalance of the relationship.

Philosophical ideas are one thing, and historical facts are another. The use of the master/slave fantasy-image as a philosophical signifier risks neglecting the appalling atrocities that the historical institution of slavery has inflicted upon human communities. Historical and cultural sociologist Orlando Patterson commented on the pervasive presence of slavery in human communities spanning both time and geographical region:

> It [slavery] has existed from before the dawn of human history right down to the twentieth century, in the most primitive of human societies and in the most civilized. There is no region on earth that has not at some time harbored the institution. Probably there is no group of people whose ancestors were not at one time slaves or slaveholders.[46]

The institution of slavery is a troubling, ubiquitous, and enduring aspect of human existence. However, there is growing consensus that the transatlantic slave trade as it developed in the United States was unique and extreme as an elaborate state-sanctioned system that turned human beings into units of commerce and enforced the practice intergenerationally.[47] The work of Black writers like Fanon,[48] Angela Davis,[49] and James Baldwin[50] paved the way for a new generation of Black scholars like Sheldon George,[51] Ibram X. Kendi,[52] and Isabel Wilkerson.[53] They have traced the roots of America's present inequities and injustices visited upon Black people back to the colonial fantasy of race. Their analysis exposes race as a social construct, a fantasy of difference that white people constructed out of economic necessity to justify the slave trade. The consensus is clear: the route traveled by generations of Black lives in the U.S. from antebellum slavery to systemic racism today is as direct as the passage traveled by the slave ships for over 200 years from Western Africa to the Americas.

There is no question that the institution of American slavery was evil. In every aspect, it fit the definition that appears at the start of Chapter 6: *evil is a particularly potent archetypal pattern characterized by malice, ruthlessness, intentional cruelty, and moral horror, giving expression to the unthinkable and unspeakable in their most destructive aspects.* Historian Edward Baptist[54] emphasized the overt and creative sadism of slave masters exerting power over their chattel as well as the willful denial of white people that the U.S. economy was based fundamentally on torture at its inception. Incidentally, the word *chattel* has a telling etymology: it evolved as a derivative of *cattle*,[55] which came from the Latin word for head, *caput*. The same Latin root led to the word "capitalism."[56] The legacy of chattel slavery in the U.S. lingers in the American psyche through systemic racism and the assumptions of a free-market capitalist economy.

To what extent are the historical atrocities of the transatlantic slave trade relevant to the modern consensual structure of Master/slave (M/s) BDSM relationships? Whereas many in the lifestyle will insist that one has nothing to do with the other, some argue that to make such an assertion requires willful ignorance. At the time of this writing, journalists and commentators are describing the present historical moment as a time of moral reckoning on race in the United States,[57] which means that any ethical discussion of modern M/s relationships cannot ignore it. BDSM blogger Rebecca Blanton wrote a post in early 2021:

I have been trying to figure out how to deal with the [Master/slave] language for years, and pretty unsuccessfully. At the core, I discovered that we cannot continue to use the language because it will never be decoupled from American slavery. The debasement of enslaved people, the harm done to them, their descendants and Black folks today has never been dealt with by America. This means that the link between M/s language and American slavery cannot be broken. Continuing to use the language is continuing the harm.[58]

Like Blanton, many white members of the BDSM community are recognizing that the larger national reckoning on race poses difficult questions for the leather movement, which values inclusivity as well as tradition. A webpage constructed in 2020 by a prominent member of the M/s community featured statements from Black people, who shared a range of opinions about the use of the words *Master* and *slave* in the world of leather.[59] Some expressed the deep pain of intergenerational trauma upon hearing white people use the words, but others considered the terms irreplaceable in the context of leather culture. Slavery has been a recurring practice among human populations around the world prior to recorded history, but the present historical moment, which provides the context for Black pain and racial trauma, concerns the specific practice of chattel slavery in the U.S.

The discussion that follows will employ two techniques to address the question of the relation between the institution of American slavery and modern M/s relationships: a comparative analysis between the historical institution and the elements of the modern relationship and interviews with Black people who either are familiar with or participate in M/s relationships.

Differences and Similarities

There are essential differences between the historical institution of American chattel slavery and the structure of modern M/s relationships. Patterson's[60] definitive study summarized slavery's essential characteristics:

1   The slaveholder employs physical coercion and violence to assert and maintain domination and authority over the slave.
2   The status of *slave* negates and destroys the social personhood of the enslaved individual; the slave becomes a "social nonperson."[61]
3   In most cultures, slavery has been a substitute for death. Patterson wrote, "Archetypically, slavery was a substitute for death in war.

But almost as frequently, the death commuted was punishment for some capital offense, or death from exposure or starvation."[62]

4 Slavery constitutes *natal alienation*, which Patterson described as the denial of ancestral history and heritage:

[Slaves] were not allowed to integrate the experience of their ancestors into their lives, to inform their understanding of social reality with the inherited meanings of their natural forebears, or to anchor the living present in any conscious community of memory.[63]

5 Slavery is unique as a form of relation because it is "perpetual and inheritable."[64]

6 Slavery constitutes implicit dishonor for the slave.

7 Slavery is a special form of "human parasitism."[65]

The modern M/s relationship is very different:

1 The relationship is noncoercive. Individuals negotiate and consent to participate in an extreme dynamic of authority transfer. Violence is not an essential characteristic of the relationship, but if it is present, its use is circumscribed and agreed to in advance.

2 The modern BDSM slave retains a social identity, although social activities are usually subject to some degree of control by the Master. A slave may voluntarily surrender symbols of social identity (e.g., a driver's license or control of finances) as gestures of obedience and sacrifice, but the status of *slave* is not an inherent negation of social personhood.

3 The modern M/s relationship is not a substitute for death.

4 *Natal alienation* is not an essential characteristic of M/s relationships.

5 M/s relationships are neither perpetual nor inheritable. The relationship can be dissolved by the couple. The offspring of the slave are not considered slaves.

6 Participation in a consensual M/s dynamic is not inherently dishonorable for the slave. In fact, many BDSM slaves speak with intense emotion about the honor they feel being of service to their Masters.

7   M/s relationships are not a form of human parasitism. They are essentially concerned with the pleasure of voluntary participation in a dynamic of extreme authority transfer for the mutual personal fulfillment of both parties.

Patterson concluded that the essence of slavery is not the ownership of a human being as another's property—rather, it is the social death of the individual who is enslaved. The substantial differences between Patterson's summary of essential characteristics and modern M/s dynamics indicate that the BDSM relationship does not correspond to literal enslavement as it has historically existed. If these modern relationships are not to be taken literally, then the psychological task is to consider them *imaginally* in a poetic and metaphorical sense. From the psychological perspective, what are the similarities between M/s relationships and historical slavery?[66] Patterson's[67] study helps identify common elements. First, the slave is in service to the Master and operates as an extension of the Master's will. Second, the Master's authority relies upon the manipulation of "private and public symbols and ritual processes that induce (and seduce) people to obey because they feel satisfied and dutiful when they do so."[68] Third, common symbols that support the Master's control include naming, clothing, hairstyle, use of language, and body marks.[69] Fourth, both the historical institution of slavery and M/s relationships are dependent upon the dyadic relational unit of Master and slave. Each role is categorically dependent upon the other.[70] And fifth, honor and power are central themes in the relationship. The list of similarities emphasizes the role played by symbols in establishing and maintaining the relationship and the unique relational bond that defines the dyad. Absent from these elements are malice, ruthlessness, intentional cruelty, or moral horror, in other words, the characteristics of archetypal evil. The diminishment or negation of one's personhood may provoke a feeling of horror for some readers, but as we saw in the previous chapter, BDSM practitioners frequently play with the fantasy of the person without a malicious intent to harm or destroy.

A preliminary comparison between the institution of slavery and the practice of modern M/s relationships suggests that evil as an archetypal soul-image is not inherently a part of the M/s dynamic. However, the M/s leather tradition employs symbols derived from the historical institution of slavery, and those symbols can reignite ancestral traumas for Black people.

Those same symbols also can trouble white people, who are coming to a more complete understanding of the atrocities that were perpetrated by their slave-owning ancestors. Symbols are important and so is language. Hillman wrote that "words bring with them the aura of their origins."[71] In a similar vein, George,[72] working from the depth psychology of Lacan, recognized that because history is buried in language, the modern discourse regarding race and racial identity inevitably evokes the language and trauma of chattel slavery with its attributions of otherness, inferiority, and lack imposed upon Black people. The M/s community's debate over the terms *Master* and *slave* reflects the growing consciousness of many white people that the present injuries and injustices suffered by Black people in the U.S. are linked with a history of dehumanization and oppression spanning over 400 years. It is an evil history. Are the words themselves inseparable from that evil?

The Black Experience in M/s

If the concern is that the words *Master* and *slave* perpetuate harm to Black people, we will, of course, want to understand the experience of members of the M/s community who are Black. The M/s community finds itself at a psychological crossroads between two ethical callings. On the one hand, there is the call to engage in the social justice work of reckoning with the harm that chattel slavery has inflicted upon generations of Black people in the U.S. On the other hand, there is the call to engage with the figures of Master and slave as soul-images, emerging from trauma and chaos as symbols with new meaning and transformative potential. Quite possibly, there is no group within M/s culture more acutely aware of the tension between these two paths than M/s practitioners who are Black. It is important and necessary to listen to their experiences in their own words as they share how they negotiate the space between these two ethical paths.

What follows is a summary of interviews that were conducted with six individuals who are active in the M/s community. Five are Black, and one is white in a M/s relationship with a Black partner.[73]

Miss Dion

Miss Dion described herself as a 51-year-"young" heterosexual woman, who is Black with mixed heritage. She holds a bachelor's degree in psychology, a masters in criminal justice, and a PhD in psychology with a specialization in addiction. In the leather community, she identifies as a Master. Although as a young person, she enjoyed activities and relationship dynamics that she would later learn are part of BDSM and polyamory, she said that she has been active in the community since about 2016.

Authenticity was the prevailing theme in Miss Dion's interview. She shared that part of the appeal of leather and M/s culture for practitioners is that the relationship is not a role-play. It is based on who people really are, and they are acting according to deeply felt values and beliefs:

> I learned it was okay to just be who I am, and to not feel like I had to pretend to fit into what family, religion, and society said I should be or how I should look or how I should act. . . .

> When I spoke to different people, not even knowing what leather was, I realized that I lived by those internal moral codes, which, ironically, are the same, or very similar to military code, which is, you know, honor, integrity, selfless service, authenticity, education, commitment, dedication, structure, respect.

The sense of belonging Miss Dion found through participating in a community that shares her core values has been both affirming and refreshing for her.

Miss Dion emphasized that she was speaking only for herself when she shared that the terms *Master* and *slave* are not problematic for her personally. Although she acknowledged that the terms can be triggering, especially for Black people in the U.S., she regards the words as an established feature of M/s culture. Community members understand that the words mean something distinct and different from historical chattel slavery:

> I don't have an issue with the term[s] *Master* and *slave* in the M/s community, because it's consensual. This is not forced slavery or coercion. Nobody is at risk of death, or having their limbs cut off, or, you know, being beaten or raped if they don't comply with what the master says. . . .

> So, in a way, it's them saying, "I want you to have total control, or whatever you negotiate to have control over." And on the flip side is me accepting that. And so, it's consent on both sides. And so, I don't

have a problem with the terms *Master* and *slave*. This is actually a way of life. . . . The way my moral codes are, it's not something I'd just be like, "Oh, today, I'm going to be a person of integrity. Today, I'm going to be respectful," it is who I am. It's not role-play. . . .

I know it can be triggering for Black people, especially those of us who definitely know that we're direct descendants of slaves to say, how can you call yourself a slave?

Regarding the question of how chattel slavery was the source for systemic racism and intergenerational trauma for Black people in the U. S., Miss Dion took a pragmatic view:

I do believe history can play a factor into your daily life, but it doesn't have to have a negative impact on your life. And for someone who struggles with that, my take on that is, just learn who you are today as a person. Because what happened is what happened, you can't change what happened.

In her opinion, the M/s community should not discontinue the use of the terms:

To change the wording of an entire subset of a community, just for the ones who may be offended, I don't think that's a good idea. . . .

And I just think people need to do some self-reflection. And if they have a problem with the terms, to just search within themselves as to *why* they have a problem with those terms. Like is this something that happened to *you*? Or are you just hanging on to the history of legalized slavery and not looking at what the term means consensually, in today's M/s dynamics?

Mister Blue and BlueFrost

Mister Blue and BlueFrost have been in an M/s relationship for four years and in a Dominant/submissive power exchange for eight years. Mr. Blue described himself as "a [49-year-old] Black heterosexual male-identified

Master within the M/s life choice," and BlueFrost described herself as a 45-year-old Black woman with a fluid sexual orientation in an M/s dynamic with Mr. Blue. They hold titles as 2017 Northeast Master and slave and as 2018 and 2021 International Master and slave. They currently both serve on the board of MTTA (Master Taíno's Training Academy), which produces the M/s Conference.

Mr. Blue said that their Dominant/submissive dynamic "blossomed with our personal relationship" over a period of years. Eventually, they arrived at a consensual M/s dynamic. One of the major themes of the interview was the explicit distinction people in the M/s community make between their modern consensual relationships and the historical trauma of chattel slavery. BlueFrost described her personal journey:

> The relationship had evolved organically to TPE [Total Power Exchange] but I had an issue with the word *slave*. . . . My initial reaction was negative for obvious reasons, given America's history of chattel slavery. . . . The trauma in our DNA from chattel slavery in America has us react to images of slavery in two opposite ways. Either we don't want to address it at all, or it is so painful that it is overwhelming.

The initial difficulty with the words *Master* and *slave* led them to do their own historical research. BlueFrost said:

> Being Black people, we know a lot about slavery. We've learned it from our youth. . . . We wanted to address the triggers and the trauma, so that the words didn't have power over us as we walked through the M/s community or as we walk through life in general. We did extensive research into chattel slavery in America, why it existed, how it existed. We took away from that a lot of knowledge.

Mr. Blue shared the first of two important conclusions the couple reached:

> One of the reasons why our relationship works is because it's consensual. It's something that we both *want*—is something that we both *discussed*. It's something that we both architected, and it's something that we both constantly work on to maintain, grow and

rebuild *daily*. . . . But it remains work that we believe in at our core. We live as consensual Master and slave. That reality has absolutely nothing, *zero*, to do with and has no parallel with chattel slavery. Those folks were enslaved.

BlueFrost shared the second conclusion the couple reached:

> There's just so much hidden power in the strength of our ancestry. . . . We can and should revere what our enslaved ancestors went through. . . . That same power, that same strength, that built everything that is on these shores, is in you. . . . I stand on that power of my ancestors. Those enslaved people did so much to build this country that stands as the most powerful country in the world. So, I don't have a problem connecting or identifying with their struggle or their ability to survive.

BlueFrost shared a further insight:

> Words have meaning, and words are powerful. And for me, *slave* is an identity, just like any that I get to choose for myself. Enslaved people didn't get to choose. I'm not sure why the word *slave* hasn't been reclaimed. . . . Slaves have never had the power and didn't set up the powers that be, for things to be this way. So, I'm trying to figure out why we have yet to stand and be proud of the word.

For the Blues, the words *Master* and *slave* describe a highly organized and codified structure for a relationship and a household. The word *Master* signifies a creator, visionary, leader, and guide. *Slave* signifies the implementer and the foundation of vision. Surrender and alignment to the Master's will are key. BlueFrost also finds a spiritual component in the experience of surrender. The Blues said that it is a valid choice for other M/s couples to adopt different terms, such as *Owner* and *property*.

The couple believed that rejecting the words *Master* and *slave* for the M/s community would not be realistic or constructive. BlueFrost said:

> The funny thing about it is . . . the harder someone fights against the fact they don't want something, the more people will fight back

with it. . . . You can call it anything you want. It's up to you . . . which is why we call ourselves Masters and slaves because it's up to us.

The couple acknowledged emphatically that the words can be painful for some Black people because, as BlueFrost said, "It's painful to have to think about those things and the residual effects of slavery that still hit us to this day as Black people." For those who find the terms objectionable, the Blues suggest that people have personal work to do.

BlueFrost identified what she regards as a social problem larger than the question of the specific words, and that is the conflation of slavery with blackness as something bad, wrong, or evil. She concluded:

> Those are the things that I really want people to think about when they think about race, more so than slavery. Let's talk about what's really keeping the stereotypes going because slavery was abolished. But we're still living in a world where blackness is negative and/ or dangerous and it's Black folks that bear the burden of that fact.

Doc Coral

Doc Coral uses the pronouns she/her and identifies as African American. She described herself as "heteroflexible, but mostly heterosexual," and in Dom/sub dynamics, she identifies "on the upper side of the slash," meaning the Dominant role. She works professionally as a physician. Doc Coral knew she was kinky from an early age, years before she got involved with the BDSM community. Initially, she learned about the world of BDSM through reading comic books and literature and later through online activity.

Doc Coral regarded the essence of power-exchange relationships as a couple's co-creative pursuit of personal excellence. This aspiration is primary, more important than kinky sex, the external symbols of control and ownership, or the words people use to designate their roles.

> I am not looking to belittle anyone, or I am not looking to own anyone to be honest. I'm looking to exceed at the highest level of my ability to making a relationship, a partnership, the best it can be. And that doesn't require a collar, that doesn't require branding.

That doesn't require anybody to acknowledge that relationship but
me and the person I'm in a relationship with.

Coral's opinion that M/s relationships are idiosyncratic and deeply personal
was a point she made repeatedly.

She also spoke at length regarding the complex range of opinions regarding the terms *Master* and *slave* in the M/s community: "There are multi-
generational party members who will say, 'Do we still need to call it M/s?
Can we move away from M/s? . . . Can we just call it a power exchange
relationship?'" Coral concurred, "Is that not the whole purpose? . . . We're
not just BDSM. You know, why does *M/s*, that title, have to incorporate the
values exclusively? No."

Doc Coral said the hurt these words cause to Black people is "blatant,"
but she also recognized that there are Black people in the community who
accept the terms and use them. She finds the terms problematic in the
leather world because they are "almost like a glamorization of slavery, a
glamorization of ownership." Sometimes individuals who carry the title of
Master receive preferential treatment that is neither merited nor warranted.
She expressed concern that privilege based on the titles themselves leads to
injustice and non-consensual harm, especially of women. She pointed out
that a number of people choose other words to designate their D/s role and
identity, including her own choice to use the title *Doc* because "I earned that
position."

For Doc Coral, the words *Master* and *slave* remain problematic and hurt-
ful because of the history of chattel slavery in the U.S. and the fact that slavery persists internationally in the present day: "In the 21st century . . . do
these titles make sense? Can you really divorce something that still exists?"
In her view, people who argue that the words have nothing to do with a historical context are being "willfully ignorant." She argued that Black people
have a personal ancestral understanding of slavery that other races do not.
The stigma, oppression, and discrimination they face today are tied to this
history. White people are able to adopt the monikers of *Master* and *slave*
from a place of privilege and adjust the outward expression of their M/s
identity accordingly.

No white person who's walking around saying, "I have a heart of
a slave," is going into the general population, screaming that out

to the world, they're screaming it within the enclosed space where they're accepted. And they can turn it off when they go out into the main world.

By contrast, she spoke of how chattel slavery and its modern legacy have shaped every Black person's experience of race and racial identity. The context of racial discrimination and oppression makes the widespread unexamined use of the terms in a white-dominated space problematic.

> Every Black child remembers the first time they realized that the majority of society around them thought they were less than. Every Black person can tell you that first time it became clear to them that their life was at risk because they were less than. So no, you're never going to hear a Black person say, "I was born to be a slave."

Master Jess and boi Kaseem[74]

Master Jess and boi Kaseem began their relationship as play partners in a "paradigm-shifting" scene, which initiated an egalitarian romantic partnership between them. Over time and with intentionality, their relationship has become a formal Master/slave dynamic. boi Kaseem described himself as a 26-year-old "Black, queer, trans-masculine, butch dyke, Leatherboi, switch . . . slave and property." And Master Jess, a therapist with over 20 years in the leather world, described himself as a 42-year-old white "trans-masculine butch Leatherdyke." As activists, students of life, and "folx" outside of the binary, they interrogate complex social inequities regarding race, history, and justice in the context of their consensual, negotiated Master/slave relationship.

The couple emphasized that their decision to form an M/s relationship involved a very serious and careful relational process. Prior to their meeting, boi Kaseem "ran left side," meaning that he identified as a Top or Dominant in BDSM spaces. However, with Master Jess, boi Kaseem "felt safe to be a boi with him," in part because he felt fully seen in all his complexity. "I'm very service-oriented," Kaseem said. "I wanted Him to be the Master that I serve." Initially, Master Jess recalled:

> I demurred. I was like, no, no. For a host of reasons, no. And I made very clear to him that it was not for a lack of desire for his service, because I had been feeling that call as well. But it was a case of his

heart being ready in some ways, his head being ready in some ways, but some other parts of him that were not . . . I told him that there was work that he had to do before I could feel ethical about step-ping into any sort of authority imbalance.

With a deep knowledge of boi Kaseem's personal history as well as the personal and systemic harm done to Black folx in the United States, Master Jess supported and encouraged boi Kaseem's engagement in healing work around that history:

> I told him, "Some of the work that you have to do is work that I can't do for you. It has to start first with acceptance of your Blackness and move into pride and ownership of that. You're going to have to move into recognition and ownership of who you are . . . and you're not doing this for me. You're doing this for yourself."

As part of their discernment process, Master Jess tasked boi Kaseem with a rigorous program of journal assignments and in-depth conversations. Master Jess also delineated circumscribed periods of time in which they trialed an authority-imbalanced dynamic together. Eventually, the couple entered a Master/boi relationship, and in time, boi Kaseem began to feel called to *slave* as an identity:

> *slave*, for me, in my opinion, is not something that is taken on lightly. If you choose to step into an identity like *slave*—especially if you are not Black—and you haven't done the introspective work that comes with stepping into that space, then I don't feel that you can truly have an awareness of the reckoning that (I feel) is required to bear a moniker with such an intensely traumatic cultural layer that *cannot* be removed from its story. There were months of conversations, not just with Him, but with other slave-identified folx who supported me and had some hard con-versations with me about what slave felt like for them. And, yeah, I got to have conversations with Black slave-identified folx, and also white slave-identified folx. And at the end of those conversations was when I realized that this felt like the natural path that my life

was supposed to take, as far as my ability to sit in my skin and feel clean and feel closer to whole.

boi Kaseem also described how the identity of *slave* helps him through periods of challenge:

> Being His slave feeds every aspect of who I am . . . that wasn't something that I expected to come out of our relationship. That wasn't something that I expected when I stepped into the space of *slave* full time. But it is something that I am finding out has been a joyous benefit. And that is the thing that allows me to exist comfortably, even in the challenge, even in the struggle.

Master Jess noted the relationship's intentional nonegalitarian structure, which consistently provides a powerful framework that supports communication and conflict resolution when the couple encounters challenges:

> We do not step into egalitarian space. This is the way we have chosen to move through the world and we lean into that when there are struggles or challenges. We don't step out of it. It is the framework on which our relationship is built.

They both expressed that personal growth has been a major theme throughout their relationship and agreed that working through conflict by leaning into the structure of their relationship has been supportive of that growth.

The couple also emphasized that they have tailored their long-term M/s dynamic to their individual circumstances and what they both need; their solutions are not generic. For example, boi Kaseem explained how some of the rituals and practices Master Jess has implemented address challenges boi Kaseem faces as someone who is neurodivergent:

> I do really well with ritual. I appreciate consistency. I appreciate knowing this is what is expected of me. This is the time in which I have to do it . . . and I can rise to meet that expectation pretty much every time.

The couple described a flexible structure to their communication that encourages boi Kaseem to express when he is struggling with changes to scheduled plans. Master Jess noted how their M/s relationship differs from some others regarding the emphasis he places on ritual and protocol as solutions:

> Every protocol and every ritual we have in place is process-and-solution driven. . . . If it doesn't answer a problem, or a challenge, or a struggle . . . for me as a leader, it doesn't sustain. I don't need the showy, the pretty, the "you're going to kneel this particular way and do this." And I know and I understand for some people, that's the meat and potatoes, and that's perfectly valid. But I want the things that create solutions to stumbling blocks, I want things that work to [facilitate] us leaning into our relationship.

There are two further themes that characterize boi Kaseem's experience of being in the M/s relationship: feeling fully seen and surrender as the essence of being a slave. Master Jess touched on their view of "slavehood," emphasizing the personal nature of their definition:

> This is somewhere we allow everyone to explain what these words mean to them . . . slavehood to us is about shaping. He has made a conscious and active choice to surrender to my will, to align himself to me. It's about surrender. Yes, there is definitely a guidance component to it, but in boihood, guidance was the primary component. . . . It is now surrender.

boi Kaseem described the difference he experiences between acts of surrender and those of submission:

> Surrender is an active choice and it is an act of choice. Folx who are the submissive in their dynamic [may] have the option to say no. They can choose whether or not to abide the order that they were given. In my surrender to Master, even and especially when I struggle with a directive He has given, my internal "no" is acknowledged and overridden by the "Yes!" that I have chosen to give to Him in every instant and situation. To me, surrender is not the absence of a *No*. My surrender is most evident to me when I acknowledge my *No* and still choose to give Master my *Yes*.

In other words, boi Kaseem regards submission as actions that express a temporary consensual yielding to the authority of another, whereas he views surrender as a consciously sustained consignment of his will and agency to his Master. Surrender is primarily an act of alignment with his Master's will:

> I know there are a lot of folx who feel that in order to be a slave, you are required to be submissive, you are required to submit. I don't submit to Him. As slave, one of my main jobs is to align with His Will and manifest it. He sets his goals for us, and it is my responsibility to help Him get us there.

Master Jess clarified that it was important to him to receive Kaseem's surrender as a voluntary act:

> For me to feel clean in my leadership, especially in something that is a total authority transfer, the surrender has to be proactive. For example, he gave up his *No*, I didn't ask for it. He put it on the table and said, "I don't want this anymore."

boi Kaseem also emphasized how he feels fully seen in this relationship, which fosters his surrender:

> I can honestly say that I don't know I am seen truly and fully by any other individual on the planet. I am seen in parts and pieces by people that I love . . . I don't feel with others that I can just exist in the space and just be me in my wholeness and my fullness, to the extent that I can with Him. . . . no one else has seen my soul the way that He does. And that has taken a lot of very intentional and very energetic work that we have both put into our relationship together.

The couple spoke in depth regarding the controversy in the leather community over the words *Master* and *slave*. boi Kaseem shared some of his own experience regarding conversations with other members of the M/s community:

> I have zero issue with folx who want to sit down and have conversations about how *Master* and *slave* make them uncomfortable. I've had conversations with many slave-identified folx—most of whom

were white—who came to me wanting to engage in hard conversations around the acknowledgement of the history of slavery. Their discomfort with the conversations that were being had in majority-white M/s circles—the notion that *Master* and *slave* were words that white folx needed to stop using—was conflicting with the fact that they felt Called to slavehood as their Path. They wanted to hear my perspective on what *slave* felt like for me, and in the vast majority of those conversations, there was a significant amount of alignment that helped them feel better about standing firm in their identity. And I am generally willing to have those conversations.

However, boi Kaseem went on to assert clear limits regarding his participation in such conversations:

I'm *really* not here for white folx telling me that the history of my people is something that I need to completely disengage with because it makes them uncomfortable. Like, yes, I acknowledge the fact that the history of slavery in this country is incredibly uncomfortable for you to reckon with. And I acknowledge the fact that there are white folx who are just now starting to look at history for what it is. . . . No one expects that to be easy for you. It's hard to sit with the knowledge that your ancestors chose to enslave an entire race of people for centuries. But that is not mine to handle for you, and you should not expect me to be willing to hold space for you to process through that while you simultaneously point fingers and tell me that my choice of identity is wrong. Don't tell me that identifying as *slave* means that I am stepping back into that space. What I do is consensual, what you did to us was not.

boi Kaseem emphasized several times that the words themselves are not inherently problematic—it is the context and the tone with which they are employed that convey a different meaning and intention when he hears them as a Black person:

The words *Master* and *slave* are very heavy words, regardless of whether or not someone is in a kink space. If I were to see a non-kink person refer to themselves as Master, that would hit very, very different. Would it be painful? Depending on who the person was. Depending on what they look like, depending on the space they're taking up at the time. But it's not guaranteed to be painful. I think anything that has the weight that *Master* and *slave* have, that has the weight that *Owner* and *property* have, that has the weight that *boy* and *girl* have, can be painful. But I don't think that they are inherently painful.

Master Jess described the process that he went through to clarify what accepting the title of Master meant for him:

It [*Master*] is not something that I felt was acceptable to pick up without wrestling with the history of chattel slavery in the United States. It was something that I had to do work around and see if I was willing to carry all of it, if I was willing to hold the conversations. If I was willing to take up space when space needed to be taken up and step back and defer when that was warranted. Because I feel that along with picking up that title—in the United States in particular because of our history—that there is a social justice component that *must* go along with it. And it *must* be more than "Oh, I'm doing this just so I can use this naughty word." It [social justice work] has to become, if it isn't already, integral to who you are and how you move through the world.

Master Jess shared what it has meant for him to be a white Master during a period of controversy in the M/s community regarding the use of the words:

It's [Mastery] calling people out when it's uncomfortable. It's standing up and telling other white Masters, "No. Black Masters [and] Black slaves have been coming and saying that this is the language they are choosing to express who they are at their core. Please stop telling them how to use it." Even if those white Masters are esteemed. It's being willing to listen during these conversations that were happening a couple of years ago. It's being willing to sit and listen to Black folx before jumping into the fray and defending my language. . . . Black folx . . . were saying, "No, these are my words, this is what we mean. We have no problem with folx that have done the work using these words." My slave said, in fact, "If you say these words can only be used by Black people, you're fetishizing us."

Master Jess and boi Kaseem said several times that white people "have to do the work" if they intend to use the words. They explained in more detail what it means to "do the work":

MASTER JESS: Self-reflection and showing the fuck up. Understanding that even if, for example, I say something that I just grew up saying or grew up hearing and he looks at me and is like, "That's racist as shit." I don't get to be defensive about that.

BOI KASEEM: He doesn't get to tell me that it's not racist.

MASTER JESS: Exactly. And he doesn't have to tell me nicely. . . . I don't get to tone police that sort of thing. And understanding if that is to happen: One, he is not telling me that I'm a terrible person. Two, he is spending the energy on me sharing that information with me because he believes I am capable of doing better. . . . And three . . . that while I'm not responsible for the way in which I learned that [i.e., racist ideas and language], I am responsible for my behavior moving forward. We have no control over the way in which we learn things. . . . I grew up in a very conservative, very Christian, very white, very Southern household. . . . But it is my responsibility as a grown-ass adult who is responsible for their own behaviors and their impact, for their own growth, to do better. And that's part of the work.

Master Jess went on to say that "doing the work" also means being anti-racist, which requires active engagement (versus the passive nature of simply being "not racist") and stepping up to call out other white people when they engage in racist behavior and language. "Doing the work" also refers to the ongoing process of recognizing the effects of having been raised to view the world through a white Eurocentric lens. Finally, it requires considering the unintended negative impact on Black people and people of color when white people pursue well-intentioned social policies.

boi Kaseem offered concluding thoughts about what it means to "do the work":

Many white folx are taught from birth that they are better, superior, the norm, the standard that everyone else must live up to. And while you are not to blame for the things you were taught as you were growing up, once it's called to your attention, it is wholly your responsibility to change your actions, to change your words, to change your behaviors. If you refuse to do that Work, you are telling the person who gave their labor to you that you are no longer worth their time. . . . Even if the thing is ingrained in you . . . when someone has called this to your attention, it deserves enough effort from you to pause and honestly commit to never doing it again. If you cannot commit . . . understand that your lack of commitment may very well cause some folx to grow apart from you . . . and [you need to] be okay with that.

Major Themes and General Structure

There were two questions that prompted a phenomenological exploration of the Black experience in M/s relationships: What is it like to be a Black member of the M/s community? And as people well-acquainted with the modern consensual M/s dynamic as well as the historical weight the words carry, how are Black M/s practitioners navigating the complexity of language and culture in the present moment?

An analysis of the interview material found six major themes. These themes describe the general structure of the phenomenon:

1   Collaborative discernment process. The decision to form a M/s relationship often occurs as a natural, organic progression in the relationship dynamic based on who the two people are. The process is often slow, deliberate, and deeply collaborative. Ideally, the process considers the individual circumstances and desires of both people and how the relationship can be tailored to support each person's development.

2   Domestic and relational structure based on surrender and responsibility. For some practitioners, the modern M/s relationship is different from sexual activities and more oriented toward adhering to a highly codified domestic and relational structure that strives for a co-creative experience of excellence. The fundamental elements of the M/s relationship involve surrender and alignment with the Master's will for the slave and responsibility, guidance, and vision

for the Master. Trust, obedience, vulnerability, and respect are other essential characteristics.

3   Wholeness and authenticity. Being in an M/s relationship can foster personal growth and a sense of wholeness, completion, and authenticity. Sometimes the trust and intimacy of M/s relationships carry people through periods of extreme crisis and personal hardship.

4   Use of controversial language, personal work, and personal choice. The monikers *Master* and *slave* are not for casual use. The words are linked to the intergenerational trauma of Black people in the U.S. from chattel slavery. The use of the words is controversial, but many Black people in the community believe that it is a legitimate personal decision whether to use the words to identify a modern consensual authority-imbalanced relationship. There is disagreement over whether the words can be separated ethically from the history of chattel slavery. Some say the modern relationship has nothing to do with the historical institution.

5   Consent and empowerment as distinguishing factors. Identifying as a slave in M/s culture today is substantively different from being an enslaved person, primarily due to the element of consent. For Black people in the M/s dynamic, participation in the relationship itself can become an empowering act of reclamation and healing of lost choices and freedoms that were denied to ancestors during generations of enslavement.

6   White privilege and racial justice. Taking on the identity of Master or slave in the M/s leather community requires psychological work to face the impact of historical facts on modern race relations between Black people and white people. However, many white people avoid addressing this issue. Black people cannot. Ideally, participation in an M/s relationship involves doing the work of racial justice and empowerment in support of Black people. White people need to be vigilant to recognize the negative effects of their own fragility, their defensiveness, and a belief in their own exceptionalism. White people should consider Black people as individuals. It can be exhausting for Black people to keep engaging in dialogue around race with white people.

Synthesis of the General Structure

When Black members of the M/s community decide to create a formal Master/slave or authority-imbalanced relationship, it typically involves a slow, deliberate, and deeply collaborative process. Couples tailor the details of the relationship to their unique personalities and circumstances, but there are essential characteristics that do not change: the slave surrenders independence and autonomy and lives in alignment with the Master's will; the Master not only assumes responsibility for the well-being of both the slave and the relationship but also creates a vision for the couple's pursuit of excellence in multiple life domains. Often, M/s couples report their relationships foster personal transformation and growth toward a more complete and authentic expression of who they really are. Black people and their allies in the M/s community are very aware of the historical connections between the words *Master* and *slave* and the evils of chattel slavery in the United States. There is a legacy of violence, inequality, and injustice that continues to the present day. Part of the psychological work confronting Black people in modern M/s relationships is to address the shadow of intergenerational trauma due to chattel slavery. In some instances, confronting the past can become an act of ancestral reclamation and a source of pride and empowerment. Although controversy exists, the use of the words *Master* and *slave* is an established practice in M/s culture, and many Black practitioners support and respect the use of the words as a personal choice within the community. Regardless of one's race, the decision to take on the identity of Master or slave requires one to face the impact of historical facts on modern race relations between Black people and white people. The broader social context within which M/s culture exists places a demand on practitioners to embrace a social justice component as part of their identities.

Discussion

The interview process revealed the deeply personal nature of the debate in the M/s community regarding the words *Master* and *slave*. For many, the words have placed them at an ethical crossroads between a reckoning with ancestral trauma and a healing affirmation of an authentic identity. For Doc Coral, it was self-evident that the "words bring with them the aura of their origins."[75] The evil that brought the first slave ships to the U.S. is still a presence in the language and the national culture of today. Other participants regarded the convergence of the historical and the personal as a calling to do their own psychological work. For BlueFrost, the experience of the M/s dynamic has been a deeply spiritual act of surrender, an empowering affirmation of her identity, and an expression of ancestral reverence. The aim of the Jungian individuation process is to achieve a state of greater psychological wholeness. The inner journey described by many of the participants is consistent with Jung's model of psychological growth. However, *the interviewees offered no indication that evil is a spectral presence in their relationships or their aspirations.* On the contrary, each participant spoke of the vision of co-creating a highly structured life of personal excellence, fulfillment, and authenticity with their partner.

The interview process also drew attention to the challenges of being Black in the white-dominated leather world. The question of whether one can use the words *Master* and *slave* in an ethically inclusive and affirming way has not been the only issue. White people in the M/s world have their own psychological work to do, which Master Jess and boi Kaseem referred to as "doing the work." Back in 1991, leatherman Scott Tucker acknowledged the troubling presence of racism in his community when he wrote, "Leatherfolk cannot erase history or refuse responsibility; we must use our heads when we play with power, or by default we allow ourselves to be playthings of powers we should resist."[76] In a community that is fascinated with expressions of power and authority, white BDSM enthusiasts have a particular responsibility to reflect deeply on how power and race have intersected in the United States (and beyond) to support systems of white privilege. The psychological work of becoming conscious of the forces that animate one's inner world constitutes the work of the soul, especially when those forces are historical, oppressive, destructive, and malicious. Master Jess cautioned that even when one does the work, the work is never done. His words apply equally to the work of social justice and to the inner work of individuation as a continual process.

Beyond the M/s community, collective sensitivity to the impact of the word *slave* is on the rise.[77] In a recent interview, the originator of the *New York Times*'s 1619 Project, Nikole Hannah-Jones, spoke of her editorial decision not to use the word:

> Language is important—particularly in the past, but, of course, in all contexts—because it can either clarify or obscure. It can either justify or explicate, right? And one of the things I did early on was

I created a guide on language, so the language would be uniform. And that said, we won't call human beings slaves. We're not going to use the euphemism of a plantation. We don't use blacks as a noun. And that language was important because when you call someone a slave, you're saying that's who that person was. But slavery was a condition. And of course, the entire reason people were defined as slaves was to strip them of their humanity, to treat them as something that could be owned, not as someone—a human being. So it was really important to me to not continue to dehumanize people who had been dehumanized, but also to force an understanding that these were people who had a condition forced upon them. But this was not their identity.[78]

Hannah-Jones called attention to the operations of dehumanization that continue to operate behind the connotations of the word in its cultural-historical context. In contrast, BlueFrost expressed an opinion shared by many of the interview participants: the condition of enslavement is substantively different from the identity of slave adopted by people in modern consensual relationships, in which their humanity and their inherent dignity remain intact. For the Black people interviewed, dehumanization was not something they played with in their relationships. Participants shared that the focus of their relationships was instead on developing themselves into people of character, strength, and integrity. The interviews suggest that Black people in the M/s community are interrogating and deconstructing the specter of evil as it lives through language and history in their midst.

Conclusion

The lexicon of BDSM activities includes extreme acts that some outside the community may regard as malicious and destructive: inflicting pain, inciting terror, manipulating suffering, degrading and humiliating partners, and playing at the edge of the body's physical integrity. It is a mistake, however, to judge these activities as evil per se. The present discussion has made the case for differentiating between evil as a potent fantasy-image and evil as the commission of unspeakable human atrocities. The objective here has been to create a psychological mode of ethical attention rather than urging the reader to draw moral conclusions.

As Minnich[79] acknowledged in the passage quoted at the opening of the chapter, the imaginal presence of evil can lend a little hellfire to recreational activities that indulge our fascination with terror and desire. The play element discussed in Chapter 4, along with the elements of consent and negotiation referenced by several M/s participants in this chapter, function as a boundary between a scene that serves the imaginal possibilities of the soul and a hazardous zone of unchecked violence and destruction. Incorporating ritual into the creation of a container for the scene can strengthen the boundary that holds evil's presence as a spectral soul-image.

However, Minnich rightly emphasized a word of caution. The pleasures of evil and the *abject*[80] can take a sudden sinister turn. As Lacan once said of his own concept of *jouissance*, "It begins with a tickle and ends in a blaze of petrol."[81] There is also a concern that play becomes routine to the point that one regards the presence of evil and the psyche's protean nature as banal. If it becomes a night just like any other in the dungeon, there is a risk that one will neglect the skills of ethical discernment, and evil then can have its way. Minnich's advice regarding these hazards is consistent with Jung's own counsel: if the psyche is split between good and evil, reconciliation comes through introspection, self-reflection, and developing and exercising one's own system of moral judgment.[82]

Having confronted and reflected deeply on the intergenerational atrocities of the past, the M/s practitioners interviewed here appear to be uncovering new imaginal possibilities alive in the words *Master* and *slave*. How is it possible to work psychologically beyond (or is it within) the specter of evil? Hillman's concept of *dehumanizing* offers a means for developing an ethical attunement toward fantasy-images of evil. "Images are to be left free of judgments, good or bad, positive or negative," he said.[83] The distinct differences between modern M/s relationships and chattel slavery are more apparent when *dehumanizing* reveals the contrast in the fantasy-images operating behind the two situations. The interviews with modern M/s practitioners revealed images of authority and control paired with surrender, intimacy, belonging, devotion, wholeness, excellence, and honor. Let us add integrity, trust, commitment, and harmony. In contrast, the imaginal world that animates the historical record includes images of human livestock, monetization, natal alienation, broken families, social death, relentless violence, destruction, and cultural genocide. The images themselves lead to different psychic realities with different ethical and moral conclusions.

The archetypal character of the modern M/s relationship demonstrates a fundamental difference from the evils of the historical record.

Regrettably, space has not allowed consideration of another significant controversy between BDSM practitioners and their critics, which concerns the violence, exploitation, and oppression perpetrated against women. Acts against women are an all-too-frequent occurrence of evil roaming through human communities regardless of race, socioeconomic status, sexual orientation, or nationality. The plight of women has been particularly relevant to the world of BDSM and its history. Concerns that kink celebrates a culture of violence against women has been a hotly contested topic for decades, particularly among feminists. The debate was probably the most intense during the so-called Lesbian Sex Wars of the 1980s.[84] In her essay, "S/M: Some questions and a few answers," Carol Truscott addressed the most frequent concerns raised by second-wave feminists regarding the treatment of women in BDSM. She wrote, "Consensual sadomasochism has nothing to do with violence. Consensual sadomasochism is about safely enacting sexual fantasies with a consenting partner. Violence is the epitome of non-consensuality, an act perpetrated by a predator on a victim."[85] Truscott expressed one of the main themes of the present discussion: consent is an essential feature in BDSM activities. However, as Saketopoulou[86] has noted, consent as a psychological construct is not fail-safe, especially when the deeply charged regions of the *abject* are involved. Fantasy-images of inexpressible horror always bring with them the risk of boundary violations as part of their volatile hellfire. As previously stated, mindfulness and ethical care are always warranted.

Encounters with evil and the *abject* offer a glimpse of the unspeakable and the unknowable that draws us beyond the fantasies of our human measure. We find ourselves *dehumanized* by the numinous power of the images. They can induce the terror of annihilation, but the displacement of ego domination during such experiences can also catalyze indecipherable pleasure and psychological growth.[87] BDSM practitioners are familiar with the language of ecstasy to describe such intoxicating mysterious moments of altered consciousness.

Notes

1 Minnich, E. (2017, p. 79).
2 Ibid. (pp. 79–80, emphasis in original).

3 Saketopoulou, A. (2019).
4 Minnich, E. K. (2017).
5 Baumeister, R. (1997); Buss, D. (2006); Corbett, L. (2018); Jung, C. G. (1995); Minnich, E. K. (2017); Naso, R. C., & Mills, J. (2016); Smith, D. L. (2011); Shaw, J. (2019); Von Franz, M.-L. (1995); Zimbardo, P. (2008).
6 Corbett, L. (2018).
7 Stein, M. (1995, p. 1).
8 Ibid. (p. 15).
9 Jung, C. G. (1943/1967, p. 199 [*CW* 13, para. 247]); Jung, C. G. (1959/1970c, p. 467 [*CW* 10, para. 883]); Jung, C. G. (1961/1989, p. 329); Stein, M. (1995, p. 7).
10 Jung, C. G. (1944/1968, p. 27 [*CW* 12, para. 32]).
11 Jung, C. G. (1946/1970b, p. 223 [*CW* 10, para. 455]; Stein, M. (1995, p. 13).
12 Jung, C. G. (1945/1970a, p. 215 [*CW* 10, para. 440]); Jung, C. G. (1946/1970b, p. 223 [*CW* 10, para. 455]); Jung, C. G. (1961/1989, pp. 330–331); Stein, M. (1995, p. 17).
13 Jung, C. G. (1944/1968, p. 30 [*CW* 12, n. 17]); Jung, C. G. (1945/1970a, p. 203 [*CW* 10, para. 416]).
14 Jung, C. G. (1946/1970b, p. 221 [*CW* 10, para. 451]); Stein, M. (1995, pp. 9–10).
15 Jung, C. G. (1936/1970d); Jung, C. G. (1945/1970a); Jung, C. G. (1946/1970b).
16 Tupper, P. (2018, p. 154).
17 d'Avignon, A. (2017).
18 Stein, D. (2016, p. 76).
19 Hillman, J. (1975/1992).
20 Ibid.
21 Ibid.
22 Von Franz, M.-L. (1995, p. 211).
23 Hillman, J. (1975/1992, p. 171).
24 Hillman, J. (1975/1992).
25 Jung, C. G. (1945/1970a, p. 223 [*CW* 10, para. 454]).
26 Jung, C. G. (1936/1970d).
27 Hillman, J. (1975/1992, p. 179).
28 Smith, D. L. (2011).
29 Ibid. (p. 135).
30 Jung, C. G. (1945/1970a, p. 200 [*CW* 10, para. 410]).
31 Hillman, J. (1975/1992, p. 198).
32 Minnich, E. K. (2017).
33 Kristeva, J. (1982).
34 Halberstam, J. (1995).
35 Ibid. (p. 4).
36 Business Insider (2015).
37 The nexus of the *abject*, the Gothic, and BDSM also intersects with Jungian psychology. Susan Rowland (2002) has described Jung as a Gothic author (e.g., his fascination with the medieval discussed in Chapter 2, his privileging of the irrational, and the shadow's concealment of the monstrous other are all equally Jungian, Gothic, and kinky). For an in-depth discussion of BDSM and the Gothic idiom, see Chapter 8.
38 Kristeva, J. (1982, p. 2).
39 Saketopoulou, A. (2019).
40 Blanton, R. E. (2016).
41 Blanton, R. E. (2021).
42 Hegel, G. W. F. (1807/1977).
43 Nietzsche, F. (1887/1956).
44 Fanon, F. (1952/2008).
45 Kistner, U., & Van Haute, P. (2020).
46 Patterson, O. (1982, p. vii).

47 George, S. (2016); Kendi, I. X. (2016); Wilkerson, I. (2020).
48 Fanon, F. (1952/2008).
49 Davis, A. (1983).
50 Baldwin, J. (1998).
51 George, S. (2016).
52 Kendi, I. X. (2016).
53 Wilkerson, I. (2020).
54 Baptist, E. E. (2016).
55 Maimonides, the medieval Torah scholar, compared foreign slaves to cattle (Patterson, 1982, p. 40).
56 American Heritage (2011, p. 2046).
57 Batrawy, A. (2020); Elving, R. (2020); Glaude, E. S. (2020); Seaquist, C. (2020).
58 Blanton, R. (2021, para. 5).
59 Sexsmith, S. (2020).
60 Patterson, O. (1982).
61 Ibid. (p. 5).
62 Ibid. (p. 5).
63 Ibid. (p. 5).
64 Ibid. (p. 9).
65 Ibid. (p. 14).
66 The use of the term *historical* should not suggest that slavery no longer exists in the modern world. On the contrary, human trafficking remains an urgent human crisis on a global scale, and the enslavement of prison inmates remains a constitutionally legal practice in 20 U.S. states (Jackson, 2022).
67 Patterson, O. (1982).
68 Ibid. (p. 2).
69 Ibid. (pp. 8–9).
70 In the interviews that follow, Master Jess offers a counterargument: one can earn the designation of Master through the rigorous practice of introspection, discipline, and self-mastery without owning a slave.
71 Hillman, J. (1975/1992, p. 195).
72 George, S. (2016).
73 Interview participants were contacted through established organizations in the M/s community, and they gave their written consent to have interviews recorded, transcribed, and summarized. Consent forms reviewed the purpose of the interviews as well as the potential benefits, risks, and limitations. Participants reviewed and approved transcripts for accuracy, and they gave final approval of the interview summaries that appear here. All participants were financially compensated for their time and contributions. One participant requested a donation be made in her name to an M/s organization of her choice in lieu of compensation. The approved transcripts of each interview underwent a phenomenological analysis using the Giorgi and Giorgi (2004) Descriptive Phenomenological Psychological Method, which distilled the major themes that emerged from each person's experience.
74 In the interview excerpts that follow, the participants have designated their preferred spelling and punctuation for writing out their spoken language. Their editorial preference to use the word *folx* indicates a direct acknowledgment of non-binary and gender expansive individuals. While *folks* is not inherently binary, the dominant culture is; to be inclusive beyond the binary requires an active shift in lexicon.
75 Hillman, J. (1975/1992, p. 195).
76 Tucker, S. (1991/2004, p. 12).
77 Another important contribution to the present debate has been Jeremy O. Harris's (2019) *Slave Play*, which confronts audiences with the intergenerational traumas of chattel slavery as volatile fantasy material in modern interracial relationships. Saketopoulou

(2020) has written about the play's implicit discourse regarding the eroticization of racial trauma and the questionable validity of consent when indecipherable overwhelming psychic material is at play.

78 Arablouei, R., & Abdelfatah, R. (2021, para. 42).
79 Minnich, E. K. (2017).
80 Kristeva, J. (1982).
81 Lacan, J. (2007, p. 72).
82 Jung, C. G. (1946/1970b, pp. 215–217 [*CW* 10, para. 440–443]).
83 Hillman, J. (1975/1992, p. 179).
84 Tupper, P. (2018).
85 Truscott, C. (1991/2004, p. 30).
86 Saketopoulou, A. (2020).
87 Saketopoulou, A. (2014).

References

American Heritage. (2011). Kaput. In J. P. Pickett (Ed.), *The American heritage dictionary of the English language* (5th ed., p. 2046). Houghton Mifflin Harcourt.

Arablouei R., & Abdelfatah, R. (Hosts). (2021, November 18). Nikole Hannah-Jones and the country we have [Audio podcast episode]. In *Throughline*. NPR. www.npr.org/2021/11/17/1056618320/nikole-hannah-jones-and-the-country-we-have

Baldwin, J. (1998). *Collected essays*. Library of America.

Baptist, E. E. (2016). *The half has never been told: Slavery and the making of American capitalism*. Basic Books.

Batrawy, A. (2020, September 26). The U.S. reckoning on race, seen through another nation's eyes. *Apnews.com*. https://apnews.com/article/voting-fraud-and-irregularities-race-and-ethnicity-police-united-arab-emirates-violence-6c3a73366d92e30260d5201e6434c43f

Baumeister, R. F. (1997). *Evil: Inside human violence and cruelty*. Henry Holt & Company.

Blanton, R. E. (2016, October 11). Is BDSM inescapably racist? *Love Letters to a Unicorn*. https://loveletterstoaunicorn.com/2016/10/11/is-bdsm-inescapably-racist/

Blanton, R. E. (2021, January 11). Is BDSM inescapably racist: 4 years later. *Love Letters to a Unicorn*. https://loveletterstoaunicorn.com/2021/01/11/is-bdsm-inescapably-racist4-years-later/

Business Insider (2015, February 17). *'Fifty Shades of Grey' started out as 'Twilight' fan fiction before becoming an international phenomenon*. www.businessinsider.com/fifty-shades-of-grey-started-out-as-twilight-fan-fiction-2015-2

Buss, D. (2006). *The murderer next door*. Penguin.

Corbett, L. (2018). *Understanding evil*. Routledge.

D'Avignon, A. (2017, May 3). Nazi chic. The style that just won't go away. *Medium*. https://medium.com/s/aesthetics-of-evil/nazi-chic-the-style-that-just-wont-go-away-f886cd58e38a

Davis, A. (1983). *Women, race & class*. Vintage Books.

Elving, R. (2020, June 13). Will this be the moment of reckoning on race that lasts? *NPR*. www.npr.org/2020/06/13/876442698/will-this-be-the-moment-of-reckoning-on-race-that-lasts

Fanon, F. (2008). *Black skin, white masks* (R. Philcox, Trans.). Grove Press. (Original work published 1952)

George, S. (2016). *Trauma and race: A Lacanian study of African American racial identity*. Baylor University Press.

Giorgi, A. P., & Giorgi, B. M. (2004). The descriptive phenomenological psychological method. In P. M. Camic, J. E. Rhodes, & L. Yardley (Eds.), *Qualitative research in psychology: Expanding perspectives in methodology and design* (pp. 243–274). American Psychological Association.

Glaude, E. S. (2020). *Begin again: James Baldwin's America and its urgent lessons for our own.* Crown.

Halberstam, J. (1995). *Skin shows: Gothic horror and the technology of monsters.* Duke University Press.

Harris, J. O. (2019). *Slave play.* Theater Communications Group.

Hegel, G. W. F. (1977). *Phenomenology of spirit* (A. V. Miller, Trans.). Oxford University Press. (Original work published 1807)

Hillman, J. (1992). *Re-Visioning psychology.* HarperPerennial. (Original work published 1975)

Jackson, M. S. (2022, February 28). When I did time, I was—technically, legally, constitutionally—a slave. *Esquire.* www.esquire.com/news-politics/a39252495/prison-slavery-13th-ammendment-essay/

Jung, C. G. (1967). The spirit Mercurius (R. F. C. Hull, Trans.). In H. Read et al. (Eds.), *The collected works of C. G. Jung* (Vol. 13, pp. 191–250). Princeton University Press. (Original work published 1943)

Jung, C. G. (1968). Introduction to the religious and psychological problems of alchemy (R. F. C. Hull, Trans.). In H. Read et al. (Eds.), *The collected works of C. G. Jung* (Vol. 12, 2nd ed., pp. 1–38). Princeton University Press. (Original work published 1944)

Jung, C. G. (1970a). After the catastrophe (R. F. C. Hull, Trans.). In H. Read et al. (Eds.), *The collected works of C. G. Jung* (Vol. 10, 2nd ed., pp. 194–217). Princeton University Press. (Original work published 1945)

Jung, C. G. (1970b). The Fight with the Shadow (R. F. C. Hull, Trans.). In H. Read et al. (Eds.), *The collected works of C. G. Jung* (Vol. 10, 2nd ed., pp. 218–226). Princeton University Press. (Original work published 1946)

Jung, C. G. (1970c). Good and evil in analytical psychology (R. F. C. Hull, Trans.). In H. Read et al. (Eds.), *The collected works of C. G. Jung* (Vol. 10, 2nd ed., pp. 456–468). Princeton University Press. (Original work published 1959)

Jung, C. G. (1970d). Wotan (R. F. C. Hull, Trans.). In H. Read et al. (Eds.), *The collected works of C. G. Jung* (Vol. 10, 2nd ed., pp. 179–193). Princeton University Press. (Original work published 1936)

Jung, C. G. (1989). *Memories, dreams, reflections* (R. Winston & C. Winston, Trans.; A. Jaffe, Ed.). Vintage Books. (Original work published 1961)

Jung, C. G. (1995). *Jung on evil* (M. Stein, Ed.). Princeton University Press.

Kendi, I. X. (2016). *Stamped from the beginning: The definitive history of racist ideas in America.* Bold Type Books.

Kistner, U., & Van Haute, P. (Eds.). (2020). *Violence, slavery and freedom between Hegel and Fanon.* Wits University Press.

Kristeva, J. (1982). *Powers of horror* (L. S. Roudiez, Trans.). Columbia University Press.

Lacan, J. (2007). The other side of psychoanalysis (R. Grigg, Trans.). In J. A. Miller (Ed.), *The seminar of Jacques Lacan* (Book XVII). W. W. Norton & Company.

Minnich, E. K. (2017). *The evil of banality: The science behind humanity's dark side.* Rowman and Littlefield.

Naso, R. C., & Mills, J. (Eds.). (2016). *Humanizing evil: Psychoanalytic, philosophical and clinical perspectives.* Routledge.

Nietzsche, F. (1956). The genealogy of morals. In *The birth of tragedy and the genealogy of morals* (F. Golffing, Trans.; pp. 147–299). Anchor Books. (Original work published 1887)

Patterson, O. (1982). *Slavery and social death.* Harvard University Press.

Rowland, S. (2002). *Jung: A feminist revision.* Polity.

Saketopoulou, A. (2014). To suffer pleasure: The shattering of the ego as the psychic labor of perverse sexuality. *Studies in Gender and Sexuality, 15*(4), 254–268.

Saketopoulou, A. (2019). Draw to overwhelm: Consent, risk, and the re-translation of enigma. *Journal of the American Psychoanalytic Association*, *67*(1), 133–167. http://doi.org/10.1177/0003065119830088

Saketopoulou, A. (2020, January 10). #consentsowhite: On the erotics of slave play in "slave play." *Los Angeles Review of Books*. https://lareviewofbooks.org/article/consentsowhite-on-the-erotics-of-slave-play-in-slave-play/

Seaquist, C. (2020, June 23). With racial and sexual reckoning, a moral awakening in America? *Medium*. https://carlaseaquist.medium.com/with-racial-and-sexual-reckoning-a-moral-awakening-in-america-259560597cd7

Sexsmith, S. (2020). The impact of M/s language: Voices from the community. *Sugarbutch Chronicles*. https://sugarbutch.net/2020/07/ms-language-impact/

Shaw, J. (2019). *Evil: The science behind humanity's dark side*. Abrams.

Smith, D. L. (2011). *Less than human*. St. Martin's Griffin.

Stein, D. (2016). From S&M to M/s: How consensual slavery became visible in the gay leather community, 1950 to 1999. In P. Tupper (Ed.), *Our lives, our history* (pp. 75–110). Perfectbound.

Stein, M. (1995). Introduction. In M. Stein (Ed.), *Jung on evil* (pp. 1–24). Princeton University Press.

Truscott, C. (2004). S/M: Some questions and a few answers. In M. Thompson (Ed.), *Leatherfolk: Radical sex, people, politics, and practice* (3rd ed., pp. 15–36). Daedalus. (Original work published 1991)

Tucker, S. (2004). The Hanged Man. In M. Thompson (Ed.), *Leatherfolk: Radical sex, people, politics, and practice* (3rd ed., pp. 1–14). Daedalus. (Original work published 1991)

Tupper, P. (2018). *A lover's pinch: A cultural history of sadomasochism*. Rowman & Littlefield.

Von Franz, M.-L. (1995). *Shadow and evil in fairy tales*. Shambhala.

Wilkerson, I. (2020). *Caste: The origins of our discontents*. Random House.

Zimbardo, P. (2008). *The Lucifer effect: Understanding how good people turn evil*. Random House.

7

THE DEPTHS OF ECSTASY

Introduction

Sometimes during a BDSM scene, something magical happens. Moments of synesthetic wonder take practitioners by surprise: sensations turn into colors or pain becomes an inner landscape that surrounds the individual. Feelings of bliss, euphoria, or serene calm emerge from the experience of surrender. Consciousness floats away from the ego, boundaries blur between self and other, and sometimes a transcendent out-of-body experience occurs. Firsthand accounts by practitioners are vivid and impressive.

A few examples of BDSM practitioners' descriptions of altered states convey the emotional intensity and the psychic impact of such transcendent moments when they occur during scenes. Moth Meadows, an experienced BDSM player from Montreal, Canada, who was an interview participant, shared the following:

> I find [BDSM] sex to be a very synesthetic experience for me. I often will see a lot of colors internally. And I can have closed-eye hallucinations during intense moments of pleasure. I find that having intense moments of ecstasy during kink, and play, and sex, is usually a complete letting go of my body and my faculties and fully surrendering to the experience I'm having. Sometimes I've experienced full beautiful, almost like angelic visions. And sometimes I

DOI: 10.4324/9781003223597-9

just get feelings and colors and things like that. So yeah, it's a really, really sensory, intense and synesthetic experience for me.

Almost 20 years earlier, gay leatherman Joseph Bean described one of his first S/M experiences while being whipped:

> At some point, like a cool rain falling directly from my brain and heart, there began to be spots of painlessness, points of lightness. It was as though the pained, suspended boy of eighteen or so was being left behind, an object barely remembered, not identified with my self at all. Something else, something that I recognized as myself was being liberated. Like a stamp peeling loose, as the raindrops of coolness touched me, I floated free.[1]

BDSM practitioner Carol Truscott described how her experience of a scene became an immersive mental landscape:

> In an S/M scene I remember with much fondness, I was able to see what my limits for receiving intense pain looked like, although I was nowhere near reaching them or wanting my partner to stop. What I think of as "I" was in the middle of a vast gray plain. My "limits" were a border of darker gray mountains, far in the distance. Behind them were other mountains composed of many bright, flashing, crystalline colors and music. This vivid mental picture meant that if I were to reach my limits, if I were able to let go and let myself expand to the edges of what I could see (the colored mountains), I would become part of something quite wonderful.[2]

These three afficionados describe similar experiences of slipping into an altered dream-like state with blurred boundaries and vivid transcendent imagery. Although all three were in the role of submissive or "bottom" when their shifts in consciousness occurred, Bean has reported that Dominants or Tops can also slip into altered states when they are empathically attuned to the inner world of their partner.

Ecstasy is the word that typically encapsulates the experiences described in these BDSM scenes. In 1961, British author Marghanita Laski published a rigorous study of the experience of ecstasy, based on a series of interviews and analyses of published texts, both religious and secular. Her list of descriptive feeling words compiled from her findings provides a nuanced distillation of the elements that make up ecstatic experience:

> Feelings of new life, satisfaction, joy, salvation, purification, glory; new and/or mystical knowledge; loss of words, images, sense; knowledge by identification; unity, eternity, heaven; loss of world-liness, desire, sorrow, sin; up-feelings; contact; enlargement and/or improvement; loss of self; inside-feelings; loss of difference, time, place; light and/or heat feelings; dark-feelings; loss of limitation.[3]

Although many of the words on her list match the accounts of the BDSM practitioners, Laski made no mention of sadomasochism in her research—the correlations she found between pain, pleasure, and ecstasy mostly had to do with the experience of childbirth. Considering that she included histor-ical literary sources as part of her exploration, one imagines it was modesty that prevented her from including the graphic ecstatic encounters chroni-cled by the Marquis de Sade and Leopold von Sacher-Masoch.

Philosopher Jules Evans[4] was more inclusive in his recent survey of ecstatic experience. He recognized in Sade's writings a pursuit of the ecstatic as part of a larger cultural reaction against the hyper-rationalism of the Age of Enlightenment. Evans also credited French philosopher Georges Bataille and English occultist Aleister Crowley as forerunners of contemporary BDSM because of their endorsement of ecstatic states achieved through transgressive sexual violence. He defined ecstasy as an experience of going beyond one's ordinary sense of self and feeling con-nected to something larger than one's individual identity.[5] Evans noted that the word ecstasy originates from the Greek *ekstasis*, meaning to stand outside. When we are in ecstasy, we find ourselves standing outside the conventional boundaries of ego consciousness and outside our familiar assumptions about what is real.

Recent authors have turned to the language of neuroscience to explain how the pain associated with S/M induces pleasurable ecstatic states through the production of endogenous opioids.[6] Social psychologist Brad Sagarin and his associates have investigated changes in hormonal activity during BDSM activities.[7] Thus, scientific studies of ecstatic states provide objective measurable evidence that specific systems within the body produce pleasurable endorphins and natural analgesics. Yet although it is beneficial to identify the hormones that interact during ecstatic experiences, the brain is not the psyche. Understanding the psychological necessity of such experiences and what they mean to the soul calls for a different kind of research.

Although Jung repeatedly criticized the Western world's habitual neglect of the irrational, his views on ecstatic experience were also ambivalent—he recognized that ecstasy can manifest in destructive behavior and madness.[8] Laski's[9] study made a similar observation, and many others have recognized that the pursuit of ecstasy can represent an addictive escapist longing to be free of ego restraints.[10]

Due to their numinous archetypal nature, ecstatic experiences can simultaneously fascinate, exhilarate, and terrify. Examples throughout history demonstrate the impact and the value people have found in such pursuits. Two historical examples of ecstatic practices have often been discussed by depth psychologists: the indigenous shamanic healing traditions and the ancient Greek cult of Dionysus. Henri Corbin's[11] formulation of the *mundus imaginalis* and Jung's[12] concept of the psychoid both provide a context for examining the relationship between ecstasy and soul in BDSM.

Shamanism and the Practice of Ecstasy

Historically, "shamanism" has referred to the mystical religious practices of ancient nomadic tribes in Siberia and Central Asia that date back to the Paleolithic era.[13] However, the term has also been applied more broadly to the similar magico-religious practices of tribal cultures around the world, in the Americas, Oceania, Indonesia, and Africa.[14] Magic and mysticism are part of religious life worldwide, but what distinguishes shamanism is its emphasis on mastering techniques of ecstatic trance. Indeed, such techniques are so central to shamanic healing that religious historian Mircea Eliade defined shamanism as the "technique of ecstasy."[15]

The shaman's ecstatic practice has specific identifying characteristics. Traditionally, an aspiring shaman underwent "an initiatory sickness" that included an out-of-body soul journey.[16] The initiate suffered a symbolic death, descended to the land of the dead, endured physical dismemberment, communicated with the spirits and souls of dead shamans, was initiated into the secrets of the shamanic tradition, often experienced an alteration in gender identity, reintegrated the body, and ascended to the sky for further dialogue with gods or spirits followed by a return to the terrestrial dimension.[17] Animal spirits played an important role in shamanic practices, either guiding or accompanying the shaman through the ecstatic journey. In some cases, the shamans even became the spirit animal as they transited between realms. The supportive presence of such guardian spirits authenticated the shaman's mastery of ecstatic techniques. In each subsequent healing ritual, the shaman underwent the mythic trajectory of death and resurrection on behalf of a suffering supplicant in order to recover the primordial human connection with the divine that existed before the break between heaven and earth.[18]

John Merchant[19] has cautioned that a consensus on a precise definition of what a shaman is has remained elusive. Scholars debate about the element of control in the shaman's technique, with some emphasizing that the shamans had learned to control entry into trance states and visualizations for ceremonial purposes. Others argue that shamanism involves spirit possession or involuntary psychosis (a distinctly Eurocentric view imposed on an ancient indigenous practice). Merchant believed that the ability to control the transit into and out of trance states while remaining lucid—able both to participate in and to recall the revelations experienced—suggests that the practitioner retained elements of ordinary consciousness while having visionary out-of-body experiences. The shamanic experience of a direct lived encounter with imaginal beings, and with an "inner" reality experienced as an out-of-body revelation, have something in common with the ecstatic practices of BDSM. However, contemplating the similarities between shamanism, Jungian psychology, and BDSM merits some care.

It is seldom useful to regard the culturally embedded practices of one community as directly analogous to those of another. Kinksters are not modern shamans (although some may adopt the title in an aspirational evocative manner), and ancient shamans were not Paleolithic kinksters. The startling similarities between shamanic practices all over the world throughout history indicate a common engagement with the deep primordial structures of the mind, structures that Jung regarded as archetypal and invaluable to the individuation process.[20]

Jung and Shamanism

Jung repeatedly expressed his interest in shamanism[21] and described the modern neuroses as comparable to a shamanic loss of soul, a state of self-division, in which the conscious personality is cut off from the regenerative archetypal depths.[22] He looked upon the shaman's initiatory ordeal as a metaphor for the ego's need to undergo a symbolic death as part of the individuation process.[23] The shaman's ecstatic dismemberment illustrates the Jungian concept that psychological healing involves meaningful suffering.

Post-Jungian authors such as Broderson,[24] Groesbeck,[25] Merchant,[26] and Ryan[27] have written in detail about the similarities between shamanism and Jungian psychology. Their work emphasizes the significance of the shamanic experience as an archaic forerunner to Jung's concept of the individuation process. "For Jung, shamanism represents something from an earlier stage in the cultural development of the individuation archetype and which may be closer to its unalterable core, hence 'archaic' and 'primordial.'"[28] Both Merchant and Ryan view shamanism as itself archetypal due to its ubiquitous and transhistorical presence. Their perspective fits in with the Jungian approach to world cultures that tends to associate the archaic and aboriginal with what is psychologically pristine, archetypal, and illustrative of the deepest structural elements of the psyche. Although they recognized ecstasy as an essential element in the shamanic tradition, they did not discuss ecstasy's relevance to the individuation process.

Some Jungians have referenced the shamanic tradition when delineating the relationship between the personal and archetypal levels of the psyche. They focus on the shaman's particular role in the tribal community as an individual capable of leaving the physical dimension and traveling to other realms for a direct encounter with spiritual forces that were creating disturbances in communal life.[29] They suggest that, from the Jungian perspective, the shaman developed facility traveling between personal and transpersonal dimensions of the psyche.

Jungians have also noted the correspondence between the shaman's multidimensional facility and the archetype of the wounded healer.[30] They have drawn a direct comparison between shamanic suffering, the wounded healer archetype, and the episode in Jung's personal life involving his prolonged immersion in the chaotic forces of the unconscious, which produced *The Red Book*.[31] But again, these authors have not addressed the role played by ecstasy as a common denominator. For shamans, ecstasy was the catalyzing agent that facilitated spiritual transits beyond the terrestrial and the cosmic; ecstasy was both the technique and the conveyance that led to wounding, transformation, revelation, and healing.

Yet the wound essential to the archetype of the wounded healer does display an ecstatic aspect. James Hillman[32] saw woundedness as an archetypal condition that transports us beyond our fantasies of self-sufficiency and self-control. The wound forces us to confront the reality of other imaginal possibilities more powerful than our conscious selves (a state of being that many masochists and submissives appreciate). None of us can escape our wounds—they serve as a portal (or a ladder) for the soul to enter our world. We imagine that our wounds befall us—that they come upon us. But if we follow the shamanic model, it is we who leave the confines of ego consciousness and are drawn into the wound's encompassing reality. We find ourselves displaced (transported) by the wound into fantasies of infirmity outside our healthy and intact ideas of who we are. *Wounded consciousness signifies an ecstatic displacement of ego consciousness.* There are many mythic tales that further illustrate the role of ecstasy as an essential feature of archetypal woundedness: Adonis, Attis, Wotan, Tristan, the Fisher King, and yes, Jesus, all bear the imprint of the ecstatic wound.

As the archetypal wound grew active during Jung's period of personal psychic distress, ecstasy was present as a source of both torment and education. He learned about the reality of the objective psyche through his own imaginal journeys into mystical regions beyond his ordinary life. Scholars have debated whether the experiences of ego fragmentation suffered by both Jung and the shamans who preceded him were instances of ecstatic suffering or of psychopathology.[33]

Ecstasy functions as an archetypal agent of the psyche, bridging together the realms of the personal and collective. The Jungian perspective has found correspondences between ancient shamanism, the individuation process, and the wounded healer archetype. The ecstatic wound is the soul-image that draws these disparate exemplars of archetypal experience together. Ecstasy and wounding also converge in the world of BDSM.

BDSM and Shamanism

The accounts of BDSM practitioners featured at the start of this chapter clearly have some important elements in common with shamanism: synesthetic visions, intentional states of extreme physical and psychological stress, lapses into trance states, and out-of-body transits between levels of reality. But missing are the details of a culturally sanctioned spiritual narrative that describes direct encounters with demons and spirit guides in the Underworld and the heavens. Also different is that the shaman's mastery of the techniques of ecstasy was for the specific purpose of supporting and healing members of a small tribal community.

However, shamanism has been a conscious reference point for some BDSM practitioners who find a vital spiritual dimension to their activities. Mark Thompson's[34] anthology *Leatherfolk* contains four interviews with S/M practitioners who identified as shamans.[35] Each used the word "shamanism" as a moniker for a nonsectarian, pagan-oriented personal spirituality, which fused the practice of radical sexuality with direct unmediated experiences of divine ecstasy.

BDSM neo-paganism is another subgroup that has much in common with shamanism as a structured psychospiritual practice. Raven Kaldera has documented the points of correspondence between the modern movement and ancient ritual practices, and he describes himself as a modern shaman. He explained how he came to adopt the title:

> I have died and come back (literally, had a near-death experience, a series of divine visitations, and a sex change, and that's about as severe as a shamanic rebirth gets in our modern culture) and everything I do must be channeled toward the sacred.[36]

In his book *Dark Moon Rising*, Kaldera envisioned BDSM scenes as underworld journeys. He provided detailed practical advice on how to create a ritual container for inflicting and receiving pain as a sacred act. The intentional use of BDSM to facilitate transformation and healing is a common theme in his work. Much like ancient shamans, neo-pagan BDSM practitioners believe that ecstasy serves a curative purpose. An archetypal structure related to sacred ecstatic wounding as a method for psychological healing and transformation appears to be subliminally present in these carefully designed activities.

Many BDSM practitioners who do not identify as shamans have developed their craft according to principles that resemble shamanism. For example, Master Jess, who participated in the interviews discussed in the previous chapter, described how he works with intuition in his scenes. He believes that his role as a sadistic Top is to serve as an ethical conduit for a greater intelligence that guides his actions when participating in a scene. His aim goes farther than his own pleasure—he seeks to facilitate catharsis and growth in the partners who place themselves under his control:

> In the process of Ordeal Work, your ego gets set way over there. It's not just sat down [close at hand], it's in another room somewhere; it's not invited to the party. Your skills are invited to the party and that's it. That starts literally with the scene creation—if something keeps jumping out, even though I think something else might work better, if the Universe keeps putting this thing in front of me, that's the thing I'm going to go with, because experience has taught me that's The Thing. Whether I know why or not. I don't have to know why, I just have to bring the tools and the hands and the presence and show up and do my work and make myself available to those that need it that don't have the physical presence to be able to actually insert a needle or throw a liquid cane or something like that. And that is again, going through the scene, paying attention to [the bottom], listening to [the Universe], listening to that instinct, listening and just being open. When I say in Ordeal Work you're a conduit, I mean that quite literally. . . . The Universe is telling me what this person needs in this moment.

Master Jess described an intentional displacement of ego consciousness in his work as an ordeal Top. The idea that the Top can function as a conduit for information from another source (i.e., the Universe) to discern what the bottom needs is consistent with shamanic practice. In the ancient tradition, the shaman accessed instruction from ancestral figures and spirit guides, many of whom appeared as animal presences, on how to heal a particular affliction.

Animal presences in the form of fantasy-images or spirit guides often are also part of BDSM scenes. Modern petplay and the broader classification of animal play are vibrant subcategories of BDSM in which participants explore varying degrees of immersion in role-plays as animals, most typically dogs (pups), kittens, ponies, or mythical creatures.[37] Petplay puts a lighthearted and creative spin on the traditional Dominant/submissive dynamic. Iconic leather or neoprene pup masks, plug-in tails, kitten ears, and dressage equipment, such as bridles and reins, are familiar items to

BDSM practitioners. In some cases, petplay does not involve sex or erotic undertones. Immersion into the inner world of the animal can go quite deep. For some enthusiasts, the animal-being becomes a spirit guide or an expression of their essence (their totem). boi Kaseem, another BDSM interview participant in the preceding chapter, said that he identifies so deeply as a pup that he had a pup paw branded on his arm after a lengthy process of reflection and discernment. Perhaps the archetypal pattern that supported the shaman's ecstatic relationship with animal guides also contributes to the essential identity that a modern practitioner finds through animal embodiment.

Hillman was intrigued by the archetypal nature of our fascination with animals. He recalled that the *Zohar* regarded an animal as "the highest grade of angel."[38] He shared an insight that affirms the vital meaning many find in petplay:

> In terms of human lives, each kind of animal backs a style of human behavior, showing us in their display our traits and our sustaining natures, which we have named "instincts." We meet animals out there, in the bush, in the streets, but they also live in the psyche transmitting behavior patterns.[39]

Hillman dug deeply into the archetypal psychology of the dog (quoted here with apologies to kitten and pony enthusiasts): "All our behaviors, even our faces, as caricaturists have shown, betray some animal trace. The *canidae* (dog, wolf, jackal, fox, dingo) are present in our very structure. Those incisors in our mouths are 'canines.'"[40] Part of the fascination and love we feel for the dog lies in its distillation of loyalty and devotion, which may lie behind this particular animal's compatibility with BDSM dynamics.

Can animal play constitute a form of ecstasy? Serious practitioners can spend hours immersed in the world of their spirit animal, playing fetch with their handler, chasing a ball of yarn, or practicing the finer points of equestrian dressage technique. Petplay afficionados who spoke with Ana Valens[41] commented on the pleasure of transitioning into animal headspace, which frequently included relinquishing speech as a mode of communication. When fully immersed in the role, ego consciousness appears to be altered if not abandoned. Such altered states can include feelings of spontaneous joy, disinhibited energy, timelessness, intimate bonding with one's partner, and as already noted, loss of speech and loss of self—all feelings associated with ecstasy.

A final point of correspondence between shamanism and the modern practices of BDSM concerns the element of theatricality. The ancient rituals of shamanic healing ceremonies made overt use of theatrical elements. These included the ambience of the darkened tent, the use of costumes and masks, ventriloquism and sound effects to convey the presence of spirit beings, slight-of-hand illusions that mimicked pulling spiritual impurities from the body of the patient, and acrobatic dramatizations of the shaman's descent to the Underworld and ascent to heaven for direct communication with ancestors and divinities.[42] Ernest Kirby[43] believed that these archaic productions expressed a primordial urge to mystify and transport the audience through an enactment of spiritual experience. He theorized that the theatrical elements of the shamanic séance are the origins of drama and theater. Rogan Taylor[44] believed that the shaman's miraculous feats were commodified gradually as street magic and slowly evolved into modern entertainment and show business.

Contemporary BDSM displays a similar taste for theatrical effect and dramatization. Chapter 1 surveyed elements of the BDSM world that suggest a theatrical pedigree: the reference to a BDSM session as "a scene", the alternate meaning of "play" as dramatization, the darkened ambience of the dungeon as a setting, the elaborate construction of the role-play, the evocative fantasy-inspired costumes and masks, the transition into alternate identities and personalities, the intention to create an enlivening experience through enactment, and the psychologically cleansing effect of catharsis. Kaldera wrote, "There's a lot about BDSM play that is similar in tone to a pagan ritual, in that it is theatrical and uses lots of props."[45] The scene creates a performance space for the embodiment of fantasy-images and the ecstatic liberation of imaginal possibilities. The shaman's employment of archaic theatrical elements suggests that the impulse to dramatize emanates from the deepest regions of the psyche. Perhaps theatricality itself, like play, is a pristine archetypal pattern, which helps explain the numinous power that often emerges during the carnal enactments of BDSM play.

Dionysus, God of Ecstasy

The mythic figure of Dionysus occupies an unusual place in the Greek pantheon. The list of his epithets and attributions demonstrates the profound ambiguities and contradictions essential to his nature: "the Roarer, the Loud-Shouter, the Loosener, the Beast, the Mountain Bull;"[46] "the womanly god," "the phallic one," and "the twiceborn god;"[47] "the one who is born of fire;"[48] "The Hybrid" and "The God of many forms;"[49] "the exultant god, the god who brings man joy" and "the suffering and dying god, the god of tragic contrast;"[50] "the raging one" and "the mad one;"[51] and perhaps most important to depth psychology, "the Lord of Souls."[52] He was revered as the god of the vine and of wine, a god associated with intoxication, mysticism, and the dissolution of boundaries.[53] The whirling of ecstatic dance was his, as well as the frenzy of dismemberment, cannibalism, and horrific, violent death.[54] The mask was a symbol of his paradoxical nature, and he was the creator of theater, giving life to both comedy and tragedy.[55] "Wherever ambivalence appears," wrote Hillman, "there is a possibility for Dionysian consciousness."[56]

Other characteristics attributed to Dionysus include transgression, intensity, and overflowing life force.[57] "The womanly god" is inherently androgynous, transgressing established gender lines.[58] For the women who were his most ardent followers, worshipping him provided a temporary release from the social limits that confined them to their roles as wives and mothers: "On the mountaintops in the company of one another and the god, they allowed themselves to experience their own pent-up instinctual energies."[59] Liberation and freedom, those great heralds of transgression, were among his greatest gifts.[60]

Dionysus is also a god of intensification.[61] The ecstasy promulgated by Dionysian worship occurs through a surplus and overflow of bodily sensations to the point of intoxication and madness: "body and soul are mutually stirred."[62] The Maenads were his crazed, ecstatic female followers (their name, which signifies raging madness, comes from the Greek word *mainas*, which is also connected to mania, money, and monster);[63] legend has it that they dismembered wild game and unfortunate humans with their bare hands and devoured the raw flesh.[64] It is believed that Dionysian rituals included a whirling ecstatic trance-dance of intensification, which quickened worshippers' altered state of arousal through rhythmic drumming and movement.[65] Although the god is primarily associated with transgression and intensification, he also stands apart. At the end of Euripides's[66] *Bacchae*, we see him dispassionately observing the havoc his interventions have provoked. Notwithstanding the orgiastic rituals in his honor, he was faithful to his wife, Ariadne, and unlike other male divinities, his exploits never included seduction or rape.[67]

The classical scholar Walter F. Otto appears to have himself been touched by the god's gift of intensification when he described Dionysian ecstasy:

> The elemental depths gape open and out of them a monstrous creature raises its head before which all the limits that the normal day has set must disappear. There man stands on the threshold of madness—in fact, he is already part of it even if his wildness which wishes to pass on into destructiveness still remains mercifully hidden. He has already been thrust out of everything secure, everything settled, out of every haven of thought and feeling, and has been flung into the primeval cosmic turmoil in which life, surrounded and intoxicated with death, undergoes eternal change and renewal.[68]

Otto emphasized several of the god's main characteristics: his ability to blur and transgress limits, the monstrous wildness and madness that he brings, his capacity to induce intoxication and dissolution, his appetite for intensification, and his intimate relationship with death. Dionysus is an intoxicating expression of nature's overwhelming power to create and to destroy simultaneously: "The rapture and terror of life are so profound because they are intoxicated with death."[69] In one version of his creation myth, Dionysus is the son of Zeus (king of the gods) and Persephone (Queen of the Underworld).[70] He was born from the union between the ecstatic peaks of Olympus and the unknowable depths of Hades. The potent fusion of the ecstatic and the abject, which Dionysus embodies, prompted archetypal psychologist Rafael Lopez-Pedraza to describe him as the god who provokes the most repression in the classical tradition.[71] Many will go to great lengths to avoid an encounter with a force so threatening to the control and coherence of the ego.

There are noticeable similarities between the characteristics of Dionysus and those of ancient shamanism. The initiatory illness of the shaman—which involved trance, visions, ecstatic journeys to the land of the dead, dismemberment, being eaten by demon spirits, reconstitution, shape-shifting, androgyny, and encounters with spirit guides—can be seen as a form of divine madness.[72] Myths about Dionysus as a child include a terrible encounter with the Titans in which the child is dismembered and eaten (Athena was able to recover only the heart or phallus, which she gave to Zeus for a subsequent second birth).[73] The origin myth served as a template for Dionysian rituals, which reenacted the themes of dismemberment, ingestion of the god, and regeneration, much as did the earlier shamanic rituals. Both traditions viewed the intimate relationship with death and the Underworld as a prerequisite of spiritual transformation. For both, the tree was an important symbol. For the shaman, the tree was the bridge or the ladder that led to encounters with spirit beings in non-physical dimensions. For Dionysus, the tree was a symbol of the god's vegetal identity. He was known as "the god of the tree" and "the Power in the tree."[74] Similarities also include theatrical elements such as the significant use of trance-dance, masks, costumes, and dramatic enactment. The early Dionysian satyr plays (the satyr's hybrid form being another similarity with shamanism) led to the classical traditions of theatrical comedy and tragedy.[75] Although Eliade dismissed the similarities between shamanism and Dionysian observances as simply an indication that both participate in a pattern characteristic of all ancient religions, Kirby believed that the shamanic tradition was a source for the mystic rituals of Dionysus. He pointed out further similarities, which included symbolic gender switching; mystical initiations that involved a direct, unmediated experience of the divine; and shapeshifting into animals (particularly the eagle, bull, and horse). Classical scholar E. R. Dodds[76] agreed that shamanism influenced Greek culture in the seventh century, but he did not believe that the Dionysian cult was its direct descendant. From an archetypal perspective, the particulars of an anthropological pedigree between shamanism and the cult of Dionysus are less significant than the evidence that there is a recurring pattern of deep psychic structures at work in both.

Ecstasy is a fundamental feature of both shamanism and the Dionysian experience. However, Dionysian ecstasy has some distinct qualities. First, unlike shamanism, the Dionysian mode emphasizes a frenzied dissolution of the self as a sacred tribute to divinity. In contrast, Eliade[77] emphasized that the ecstatic techniques of the shaman had the objective of mastering communication with spirits without becoming possessed by them. The possessive ecstasy associated with Dionysian ritual is not madness per se. The frenzy of the Maenads was a temporary condition, a liberation from a life of civilized domesticity and a compensation for its restrictive effects. However, true madness was indeed a hazard of crossing the god, especially as punishment to those who defied him, such as Lycurgus and Pentheus.

Second, there is an extreme physicality and earthiness to Dionysian experience. "Dionysian ecstasy is reached through an *intensification of bodily feelings.*"[78] It is not the case that the soul leaves the body to travel to other realms so much as that the body and soul together escape the inhibitions of intellect and reason to deepen into the wildness of the life force in nature (what the Greeks called *zoe*).[79]

Finally, ecstatic dismemberment occupies a different place in Dionysian consciousness. The shaman undergoes dismemberment in the Underworld as an initiation to a vocational path, whereas Dionysian dismemberment is a reenactment of the god's origin story and a tribute to his divinity. To dismember as a tribute to Dionysus is to participate in the god's power to rob another of their individuality and very life. To tear apart a living creature, as Agave does in *The Bacchae*,[80] is to feel the Dionysian paradox of life and death, the wild forces of primeval nature surging through and around one's own blood-soaked hands. On the other hand, to be dismembered in the Dionysian sense is to experience the disintegration of one's carefully crafted ego through the terrifying primordial energy of *zoe*.

Dionysus and the Jungian World

Jung's references to Dionysus over the course of his career reveal an evolution in his view of the god.[81] Early in his career, the tragic figure of Nietzsche colored his interpretation. Nietzsche[82] had strongly identified with Dionysus, both in his writing and in his life. The fact that the great German philosopher descended into madness and signed several of his final letters as Dionysus provided ample fodder for nineteenth-century minds to speculate on the dangers of the pagan unconscious.[83] In his autobiography, Jung recalled his student days at the University of Basel, where he associated with people who had personally known Nietzsche—Jung secretly feared that he might "be like him."[84] In 1917, as he was dealing with his own confrontation with the spirit of the depths, Jung attributed Nietzsche's illness to the perils of Dionysian pagan ecstasy. He wrote, "The ecstatic by-passes the law of his own life and behaves, from the point of view of nature, improperly."[85] It seems likely that Jung's school-age fears and his own brush with madness had helped consolidate an attitude of mistrust and caution toward the ecstatic power of Dionysus. Perhaps Jung's apprehension conflated divine ecstasy with the pathology of mental illness.

By 1940, however, Jung had come to appreciate the spiritual aspect of Dionysian ecstasy as representing a necessary loosening of the conscious personality in service to the irrational numinous mysteries of the individuation process. He compared the mythic dismemberment and reconstitution of Dionysus to the psychological process of gathering (recollecting) the split-off and discarded "shadow" aspects of the personal psyche as part of the move toward individual wholeness.[86] He grew to recognize the spiritual value of ecstasy separate from his earlier fears of psychic fragmentation and madness.

Hillman[87] brought attention to Dionysus as a god intimately associated with women and the feminine. He suggested that a Dionysian mode of psychology would restore value to psychic elements such as intuition, emotion, receptivity, and interconnection. The dismembered Dionysian body also interested Hillman.[88] He suggested that a body broken into pieces could remain in a state of paradox, holding the consciousness of differentiated parts, each with symbolic value, while also retaining its coherence. The ecstatic move that situates consciousness outside the body can also be a Dionysian move outside the mind and *into* the body, facilitating an awakened consciousness of our physical form. Practitioners of BDSM are familiar with such awakenings, for example, when the body becomes a landscape of altered consciousness.

Lopez-Pedraza[89] focused on the Dionysian body as the symbolic locus of Western cultural repression. Because Dionysus presents the contradictory, problematic, and mad aspects of our own natures, Lopez-Pedraza asserted that the god was both "the most psychiatric"[90] and "the most repressed"[91] of the Greek pantheon. He thought that Dionysiac ecstasy constitutes an embodied mysticism, which is difficult for a Christian monotheistic culture to grasp or appreciate. The Christian repression of the body and of emotion leads to a regular distortion in how Dionysus is represented and (mis-) understood. Lopez-Pedraza cautioned that to repress Dionysus is to defy his divine necessity and that the consequences for his detractors have always been tragic.

Jungian analyst Lyn Cowan found archetypal aspects of masochism present in the mythic themes associated with Dionysus: "Humiliation and submission, pleasure and ecstasy, suffering and madness, death and mortification, sexuality and religiosity, necessity and fate—come together to tie a knot of paradox."[92] The Dionysian spirit is present both in masochism's paradoxical synthesis of pleasure and pain and in its longing to escape the burdens of selfhood through dissolution. Like Hillman and Lopez-Pedraza, Cowan found that Dionysus restores value to the experiences of the body and of the feminine in a culture that represses both.[93] The ecstasy of masochism honors the Dionysian mode:

> In masochistic experience, every bit of flesh comes alive in an agony of trembling ecstasy. All is sensitized almost beyond endurance. How can it not be sexual? How can it not be religious? One is taken out of oneself and beyond all law and duty and custom, and yet utterly reduced, pressed down, made small. It is a defeat and a glory.[94]

The Dionysian mode of ecstasy involves simultaneously standing outside of law and duty on the one hand and deeply inside the exquisite details of sensory overload on the other. Cowan recognized and dignified the spiritual aspect of masochism by bringing it under the aegis of Dionysus.

Dionysus and BDSM

Among his many names, Dionysus was known as "the Lord of Souls."[95] His mythic pedigree makes him an ideal guide to explore the soul's presence in BDSM and kink: his connection to the Underworld, pagan spirituality, transformative manipulations of extreme body sensations, and theatricality all suggest that the god is in our midst. We will consider three elements associated with the Dionysian realm that are relevant to BDSM: the mask, bondage, and flogging.

The Mask

One of the representations of Dionysus in ritual and ceremony was a mask, sometimes mounted on a column.[96] However, it was not simply a representation. It was believed that Dionysus actually *was* the mask. The god was in attendance as the mask—Otto said that the mask was Dionysus "at his epiphany,"[97] meaning his appearance in the physical world. Masks and hoods are an iconic element in BDSM and kink. What does it mean to call a mask an epiphany of the Lord of Souls?

The mask holds the paradox of simultaneous concealment and revelation. From the conventional standpoint of the ego, the mask serves as a disguise, as a concealment of personal identity—a masquerade. Some kinksters may regard masks as accessories that support the ambience of the scene or as a means of "getting into the role." In more extreme cases, such as hoods without openings for eyes, mouth, or ears, the garment is a form of sensory deprivation and a negation of the personal dimension—in the absence of the face, the hood reduces a person to a *sense-less* object. At the same time, however, the mask reveals secrets and truths that are deeper than ego consciousness. The sadist dons the mask of the executioner and feels more fully embodied as the master of pain and suffering, carried by the ecstatic flow of the craft. In pup play, the mask evokes the deeper canine nature of the individual who wears it. When the mask goes on, the dog comes out. These examples illustrate the ecstatic nature of the mask—placing the mask over the ordinary face transports one outside the conventions of ego identity.

However, the ancient Greeks had an insight that was deeper than the mask's *effects* upon the ego. The mask was an epiphany of the god. Some of the Dionysian masks were made of marble on a scale that a human could never wear.[98] What is a mask that is not made to be worn? It stands outside the human context, autonomous and ecstatic, as a numinous presence that has come into the material world from the world of subtle material, the dimension Corbin[99] called the *mundus imaginalis*. Even without wearing it, one experiences the mask as soul made tangible. From this perspective, the mask is not an accessory we use to "get in the role;" *the mask-as-god uses us to come more fully into this world from the imaginal world*. Dionysus establishes the paradox of fantasy material made into material fantasy.

Dionysus-as-mask reveals that ecstasy is not in service to the desires and pleasures of the ego when it wishes to step outside its own conventions. *Ecstasy is the enactment of imaginal possibilities*. In ecstasy, we do not stand outside ourselves as torturer, gimp, or pup—the images made manifest now stand outside us.

Bondage

There is a tale that a very young Dionysus was once kidnapped by a group of pirates who planned to sell him into slavery. The god punished their attempt to hold him captive by turning their oars into giant snakes, sending vines of ivy over the sails and masts, flooding the decks with wine, striking the crew with madness, and turning them into dolphins as they jumped overboard.[100] Johnson offered an interpretation: "The flow of life cannot be bound by ropes or rules. In the same way, we cannot ultimately control or deny within ourselves the inherent freedom of this ecstatic archetype."[101] Dionysus is *zoe*, the wild libidinal life force surging through nature, which cannot be contained or restrained. Many BDSM enthusiasts think of rope play and restraints in connection with the pleasure of restriction and surrender, but the Lord of Souls offers a different insight into the magical ecstasy that can occur during bondage activities.

The BDSM experience of restraint and immobilization places an individual in an erotic vise between power and vulnerability. Arousal and fear constellate with growing intensity when the dynamic works properly. The submissive bottom savors concurrent feelings of vulnerability and erotic excitement, trusting yet not knowing how far the Dominant Top will push the limits of pain and pleasure. The Top seizes control over the bottom, and when the Top is unafraid to meet the bottom's vulnerability with a fierce but controlled predatory joy, the Dionysian spirit of destruction, ecstasy, and merger is liberated. Guy Baldwin[102] has written about such encounters in the context of the potential of BDSM's scenes to become a transformative rite of passage; Baldwin's metaphorical image of the black hole represents the unknowable, indecipherable power of numinous experience:

> Real vulnerability is scary stuff. It must be so before it can do the job in a scene. The fear and intensity tells [*sic*] you that the vulnerability is authentic. It is upon this platform of vulnerability that Tops master their internal beasts. It is at this moment, this place which lies within the Black Hole, that Tops and bottoms fuse and become one. We go together, or else, we don't go at all.[103]

Baldwin's account illustrates how elements of the Dionysian mode come together in bondage. The appreciation of intensification, authentic fear as a catalyzing agent, the image of the instinctual beast, the paradox of destruction merged with creation, and perhaps most significantly, the experience of mystical ecstatic fusion are all examples. Dionysus consecrates the mad, joyous struggle between vulnerability and power that can make a scene a rite of passage.

According to the legend, the god cannot be bound or restrained. We can interpret the myth as a soul-image of what occurs internally for a bondage bottom. When we subject ourselves to the forces of restriction and immobilization, Dionysus is the wild force of nature that appears in our embodied fear and vulnerability. With the recognition that one is no longer in charge, the ego is no longer "captain of the ship." Bondage arouses the god as a primordial life force of resistance (we struggle internally with psychic ambivalence and externally with embodied pushing and pulling against the restraints). In the ensuing struggle, there is a psychic regression to a more primal state. The energy that was propelling us forward in life regresses to a reptilian slither (oars become snakes); the wind in our sails is overtaken by a vegetal regression into primal emotions (vines grow over the rigging); and wine, the classical agent of intoxication and drunken ecstasy, covers the decks. The crew of the conscious personality abandons ship; they dive into the waters of the unconscious and are transformed into aquatic soul-animals. And then Dionysian ecstasy brings psychic renewal.

Baldwin[104] made it clear that the ecstasy he had in mind does not come from a simple equation: immobilization plus consensual surrender plus menacing stimulus does not equal ecstasy. The story that connects Dionysus with bondage teaches that the restriction of the life force in bondage can summon the wild, destructive aspect of the god's ecstasy as potent fantasy-images for both the bondage bottom and the Top. The Dionysian spirit can materialize in overwhelming pleasurable fear for the bottom and in the liberation of the primordial beast for the Top. True vulnerability leads to ambivalence and struggle, and Baldwin advised that it must be authentic and intense for ecstatic madness to transform the players.

Flagellation

In the ancient Roman city of Pompeii, there is a site known as the Villa of Mysteries. Beautifully preserved frescoes in the interior depict what many scholars believe is a Dionysian initiation rite.[105] One image in the series depicts a young woman on her knees being scourged by an angelic figure holding a staff crowned with pinecones (the *thyrsus* of Dionysus). "We can read this initiation scene as an initiation of soul, through submission, to *enthusiasmos*—possession by the god."[106] The whip is the medium of the divine message, which teaches reverence and modesty in the face of the ecstatic divinity.[107] The flagellation can also be viewed "as an initiation into Dionysus as an inner experience of the emotional body."[108] Some have speculated that the flagellation was intended to induce ecstatic madness as a direct encounter with the god.[109]

Whipping and flogging are popular modern BDSM activities, which can sometimes induce ecstatic states in practitioners (see Bean's[110] account at the opening of the chapter). The ancient rites remind us that the whip and flogger have a long history as sacred initiatory instruments with numinous power. The Mysteries of Dionysus were among the best-kept secrets of the ancient world. Although scholars are not certain exactly what happened in the rituals,[111] it is clear from the few existing accounts that initiates "were there to learn to experience new states of consciousness, to acquire an intimate knowledge of the immortality of the soul."[112] Jungian analyst Robert Hopcke[113] has noted the archetypal theme of initiation in BDSM activities among gay men. His assessment is consistent with the ancient god's emphasis on embodied experience: "I believe S/M provides gay men with an initiation into the body."[114] Likewise, "Dionysus is always the body," wrote Lopez-Pedraza.[115] In the ancient world, an initiation into Dionysus was always considered a blessing.[116]

What blessings might modern enthusiasts discover through the initiatory power of the whip and flogger? "I think we should all just start admitting that there are at least two reasons why anyone does S/M," wrote Kaldera, "sex and catharsis."[117] The word catharsis comes to us originally from the Maenads of Dionysus,[118] which suggests that the god remains a numinous presence presiding over much of modern BDSM. For example, an impact bottom shared the following account of a whipping scene:

> A pause, then a harder whip. The pain increases, the rhythm quickens and he can no longer keep breathing with it. In and out are now each laced with the sharp redness of blows. It's hard now, not the easy waltz, but a violent dance with a partner who drags him stumbling around a dance floor of spikes. I can't bear it, he thinks, I can't take this, but somehow he does, and then it happens. His arms stretch against the ropes like wings opening to fly, and then he is lifted out of his flesh. Ecstasy pours through him; the blows are still there, still strong, but now they are like the hoofbeats of a running horse that he rides, its muscles bunching as it thunders beneath him. The pain is [no] longer his enemy, but his mount to

bear him. Stars spiral around his head, the web of the universe spin-ning, woven into the ropes that hold him, and there is nothing in the world more important than this.[119]

This account illustrates how modern scenes can induce ecstatic transforma-tion in practitioners. The embodied spirituality of Dionysus appears revived in such numinous experiences. The element of dance, so integral to many Dionysian rituals, helps the bottom keep a rhythmic pace, which acceler-ates into increasingly vivid physical sensations until a simultaneous ecstatic transcendence occurs. The pain has shapeshifted into the fantasy-image of the thundering flying horse.

Perhaps there is something uniquely Dionysian about the archetypal nexus of the whip, the horse, and ecstatic flight. The retinue of the intox-icating god always included satyrs and centaurs, creatures of wild nature composed of parts human and equine.[120] The earliest representations of the centaurs "often have small wings growing from their backs, a symbolism identifying them with the flight of the shaman's horse as trance vehicle."[121] It is interesting to note that *The Satyrs* was the name of one of the earliest motorcycle leather clubs in the gay community, which many consider the inauguration of the modern BDSM movement[122]—yet another instance of the Dionysian presence in BDSM culture. On their motorcycles, the early leathermen took flight from the ordinary world, and through their extreme sexuality, they discovered the ecstasy of liberation from the restrictions of the conventional.

Discussion

For the ancient shamans, ecstasy was a unifying principle around which their mystico-religious practices converged. For the followers of Dionysus in the classical world, ecstasy was the overwhelming experience of the god's wild nature, which could produce emotions ranging from joy to abject ter-ror. An ecstatic encounter with Dionysus could be both regenerative and transformative, but it could also result in madness and violent death. In the present day, BDSM enthusiasts sometimes discover ecstasy by surprise during intense scenes, but more accomplished practitioners are familiar with the potential for intentionally mind-altering transcendent experiences. Neo-pagan cathartic BDSM rituals provide perhaps the clearest example of what knowledgeable practitioners can achieve.[123]

Among the ecstatic practices and experiences explored here, there are some common themes worth noting. First, the experience of ecstasy and trance states is temporary. Shamans, Maenads, and kinksters depart for a time, but they always return to the so-called ordinary world. However, they are changed when they return, which is the second common characteristic: ecstasy promotes transformation. For shamans, the journey to other dimensions initiated them into their spiritual and vocational role and provided them with healing secrets that would enable them to aide afflicted members of their tribe. The followers of Dionysus found themselves rejuvenated by their ecstatic breaks with domesticity and social codes. BDSM enthusiasts describe psychological and spiritual growth issuing from their "initiation into the body."[124] The transformative aspect of ecstasy makes it a potent element in initiatory experiences by making available a nonverbal, often inexpressible level of knowledge that can be life changing. BDSM afficionados also know that ecstasy can be a catalyst for catharsis and healing. Third, ecstasy has a hazardous aspect. It is not limited to pleasure and feelings of transcendent joy. The shamanic tradition, the Dionysian cults, and contemporary kinksters all recognize that valuable ecstatic experiences can also involve pain, suffering, vulnerability, terror, destruction, and the immediacy of death. Finally, ecstasy is inherently paradoxical. Ecstasy has the power to confuse and confound by mobilizing liminal indeterminate states between presence and absence, creation and destruction, inner and outer, living and dead. Paradox frequently appears in ecstatic practices: the shaman is both a mystical holy person and an accomplished illusionist, Dionysus brings intoxicating joy as well as dismemberment and terror, and the ecstasy of modern BDSM pivots between desire and dread.

Jung mistrusted ecstasy in his youth, fearing that he might fall into the same psychic abyss as Nietzsche. As he reached adulthood, those fears intensified due to the psychic and emotional upheaval he experienced. Peter Kingsley[125] has made a strong case that the years following the 1912 break with Freud were more terrifying and dire for Jung than some scholars care to admit. When Jung wrote that he feared he was losing his mind, he was not being euphemistic. His associate R. F. C. Hull once said, "Jung was a walking asylum in himself, as well as its head physician," and that he "went through everything an insane person goes through."[126] Jung was experiencing episodic psychic excursions into the primordial depths of the unconscious. The years he spent creating *The Red Book* taught him that the excursions were temporary, and unlike Nietzsche, he could experience the fearsome spirit of the depths and still return to his mundane life. However, the ecstatic excursions changed him, and he gained insights into the primordial structures of the psyche, which formed the basis of his mature psychology. Ecstasy became a conduit for psychological insight. Jung realized that archetypal reality could function simultaneously as a force behind embodied physical events as well as a formal agent behind psychic images. He referred to the dual nature of the archetype as *psychoid*, meaning it was partly psychic and partly physical in nature yet neither wholly one nor the other.[127] The psychoid is a concept that helps explain the paradoxical nature of ecstatic experience, including the Dionysian mode of embodied spirituality and Hopcke's[128] assertion that BDSM constitutes an embodied initiation that is psychically transformative. When Jung discovered the work of Corbin, which was based on research into ecstatic Islam, it validated the conclusion that primordial archetypal images are psychoid in nature. Corbin[129] asserted that psychic images are ontologically real—they are emanations from the ecstatic land of the *mundus imaginalis*.

What can ecstasy tell us about the presence of the soul in the activities and relationships of BDSM? From the perspective of archetypal psychology, ecstasy displaces the conventional personal fantasy of the ego and reveals the reality of imaginal figures, the unknowns of the soul, who live autonomously according to their own obscure necessities. Our exploration of ecstatic realms has discovered a rich pageant of emissaries from the depths: underworld demons, ancestral beings, animal spirits, and images of death and dismemberment. We have encountered black holes, pirate ships, flying horses, gods as masks, twining vines, and images of the emotional body broken into a field of living symbols. These are soul-images liberated by ecstasy. They release us into a liminal enactment of imaginal possibilities, and we can ponder the meaning of such mysteries for a lifetime.

People have pursued ecstatic experiences for centuries, often for some greater aim than personal pleasure or escapism. The psychological value of ecstasy lies in its capacity to break down established structures of the personality, which can become too rigid and one-sided. Ecstasy draws us outside our established mental habits and compensates for the one-sidedness of everyday consciousness. As such, it can be an agent of psychological healing, growth, and transformation, thereby promoting the individuation process. Yet ecstasy does more than compensate for an unbalanced psyche.

Ecstasy is a potent and mysterious force of nature. Like any archetype, it functions as a psychoid factor, seizing our physical being with overwhelming sensations and transporting the mind into the autonomous psyche. Ecstasy is also a process that facilitates movement between liminal indeterminate states; it confounds the ego, dissolves boundaries, and helps new psychic paradigms to emerge. In BDSM and kink, ecstasy arises and takes flight through combinations of authenticity, intensity, vulnerability, fear, trust, ambivalence, pain, suffering, wounding, destruction, creation, and belonging. In its most extreme form, the ecstatic journey leads to what Hillman referred to as "the incurable possibility"[130] and what Baldwin described as "the Black Hole,"[131] which is the soul-image of death.

Notes

1 Bean, J. (2003, p. 137).
2 Truscott, C. (2004, pp. 24–25).
3 Laski, M. (1961, p. 41).
4 Evans, J. (2018).
5 Ibid. (p. xii).
6 Mains, J. (2002).
7 Sagarin, B., Cutler, B., Cutler, N., Lawler-Sagarin, K. A., & Matuszewich, L. (2009).
8 Jung, C. G. (1917/1966, p. 33 [*CW* 7, para. 41]).
9 Laski, M. (1961).
10 Evans, J. (2018); Johnson, R. (1987).
11 Corbin, H. (1972).
12 Jung, C. G. (1947/1969a).
13 Eliade, M. (1951/1964); Merchant, J. (2012).
14 Broderson, E. (2019).
15 Eliade, M. (1951/1964, p. 4).
16 Ibid. (p. 34).
17 Eliade, M. (1951/1964, p. 34); Dodds, E. R. (1957/2020, p. 140).
18 Eliade, M. (1951/1964, p. 493).
19 Merchant, J. (2012).
20 Merchant, J. (2012); Ryan, R. E. (2002).
21 Jung, C. G. (1918/1970c, pp. 15–16 [*CW* 10, para. 21–22]); Jung, C. G. (1930/1970b, p. 514 [*CW* 10, para. 977]); Jung, C. G. (1931/1970a, p. 48 [*CW* 10, para. 101]).
22 Jung, C. G. (1934/1970d, p. 172 [*CW* 10, para. 367]).
23 Jung, C. G. (1954/1968, p. 256 [*CW* 9i, para. 457]).
24 Broderson, E. (2019).
25 Groesbeck, C. J. (1989).
26 Merchant, J. (2012).
27 Ryan, R. E. (2002).
28 Merchant, J. (2012, p. 21). Jung's interest in developmental stages of cultural history should not suggest that his perspective on shamanism belongs to his more unpalatable ideas on primitivism. Scholars such as Fanny Brewster (2017) have correctly characterized Jung's writing about "the primitive" as indefensibly racist (p. 5).
29 Eliade, M. (1951/1964).
30 Jung, C. G. (1954/1968); Groesbeck, C. J. (1989); Merchant, J. (2012).

31 Jung, C. G. (2009).
32 Hillman, J. (1979).
33 For more on the shamanic debate, see Ryan, R. E. (2002); and Merchant, J. (2012). For the debate over Jung, see Winnicott, D. W. (1964/1989); Kalsched, D. (2013); and Shamdasani, S. (2009).
34 Thompson, M. (1991/2004).
35 See the selections by Bean, Ganymede, Norman, and Thompson in *Leatherfolk* (Thompson, 1991/2004).
36 Kaldera, R. (2006, p. 4).
37 Valens, A. (2021).
38 Hillman, J. (2008, p. 151).
39 Ibid. (p. 151).
40 Ibid. (p. 151).
41 Valens, A. (2021).
42 Eliade, M. (1951/1964); Kirby, E. T. (1975); Taylor, R. (1985).
43 Kirby, E. T. (1975).
44 Taylor, R. (1985).
45 Kaldera, R. (2006, p. 336).
46 Paris, G. (1990, p. 5).
47 Downing, C. (1993, pp. 71–72).
48 Otto, W. F. (1965, p. 146).
49 Cowan, L. (1982, p. 97).
50 Otto, W. F. (1965, p. 78).
51 Ibid. (p. 135).
52 Ibid. (p. 49).
53 Downing, C. (1993).
54 Kirby, E. T. (1975).
55 Otto, W. F. (1965).
56 Hillman, J. (1972, p. 275).
57 Rowland, S. (2017).
58 Downing, C. (1993, p. 72).
59 Ibid. (p. 73).
60 Downing, C. (1993); Otto, W. F. (1965).
61 Paris, G. (1990).
62 Ibid. (p. 6).
63 American Heritage (2011, p. 2051).
64 Otto, W. F. (1965, p. 135).
65 Kirby, E. T. (1975, p. 91).
66 Euripides (2005).
67 Downing, C. (1993, p. 74).
68 Otto, W. F. (1965, p. 140).
69 Ibid. (p. 137).
70 Downing, C. (1993, p. 71).
71 Lopez-Pedraza, R. (2000, p. 26).
72 Eliade, M. (1964).
73 Downing, C. (1993, p. 78).
74 Kirby, E. T. (1975, p. 107).
75 Ibid. (p. 92).
76 Dodds, E. R. (1957/2020).
77 Eliade, M. (1964).
78 Paris, G. (1990, p. 6, emphasis in original).
79 Downing, C. (1993, p. 77).
80 Euripides (2005).

81 Hillman, J. (2007).
82 Nietzsche, F. (1871/1956).
83 Chalakoski, M. (2017).
84 Jung, C. G. (1961/1989, p. 102).
85 Jung, C. G. (1917/1966, p. 33 [*CW* 7, para. 41]).
86 Jung, C. G. (1940/1969b, p. 264 [*CW* 11, para. 400]).
87 Hillman, J. (1972).
88 Hillman, J. (2007).
89 Lopez-Pedraza, R. (2000).
90 Ibid. (p. 22).
91 Ibid. (p. 26).
92 Cowan, L. (1982, p. 97).
93 Writing in 1982, Cowan went to some lengths to clarify that the term feminine designates a set of psychological characteristics that must be considered apart from the gendered reality of people who identify as women. Working with the term as a construct based on patriarchal assumptions, Cowan found in masochism a restoration of value in attitudes regarded culturally as feminine.
94 Cowan, L. (1982, p. 113).
95 Otto, W. F. (1965, p. 49).
96 Ibid. (p. 87).
97 Ibid. (p. 88).
98 Ibid. (p. 88).
99 Corbin, H. (1972).
100 March, J. (1998, p. 266); Paris, G. (1990, p. 19).
101 Johnson, R. (1987, p. 53).
102 Baldwin, G. (2003).
103 Ibid. (p. 233).
104 Ibid.
105 Lopez-Pedraza, R. (2000, p. 32).
106 Cowan, L. (1982, p. 99).
107 Ibid. (p. 100).
108 Lopez-Pedraza, R. (2000, p. 32).
109 Ibid.
110 Bean, J. (2003).
111 Burkert, W. (1987).
112 Paris, G. (1990, p. 16).
113 Hopcke, R. (1991/2004).
114 Ibid. (p. 72).
115 Lopez-Pedraza, R. (2000, p. 31).
116 Ibid.
117 Kaldera, R. (2006, p. 163).
118 Downing, C. (1993, p. 76).
119 Kaldera, R. (2006, p. 26).
120 Kirby, E. T. (1975).
121 Ibid. (p. 134).
122 Thompson, M. (1991/2004).
123 Kaldera, R. (2006).
124 Hopcke, R. (1991/2004, p. 72).
125 Kingsley, P. (2018).
126 As cited in van der Berk (2012, p. 74).
127 Jung, C. G. (1947/1969a, p. 213 [*CW* 8, para. 417]).
128 Hopcke, R. (1991/2004).
129 Corbin, H. (1972).

130 Hillman, J. (1975/1992, p. 110).
131 Baldwin, G. (2003, p. 233).

References

American Heritage. (2011). Men. In J. P. Pickett (Ed.), *The American heritage dictionary of the English language* (5th ed., p. 2051). Houghton Mifflin Harcourt.

Baldwin, G. (2003). *Ties that bind* (2nd ed.). Daedalus.

Bean, J. W. (2003). *Leathersex* (2nd ed.). Daedalus.

Brewster, F. (2017). *African Americans and Jungian psychology: Leaving the shadows.* Routledge.

Broderson, E. (2019). *Taboo, personal and collective representations.* Routledge.

Burkert, W. (1987). *Ancient mystery cults.* Harvard University Press.

Chalakoski, M. (2017, September 1). The "Letters of insanity" and "The Turin Horse": The baffling breakdown of Friedrich Nietzsche. *The Vintage News.* www.thevintagenews.com/2017/09/01/the-letters-of-insanity-and-the-turin-horse-the-baffling-breakdown-of-friedrich-nietzsche/?safari=1

Corbin, H. (1972). *Mundus Imaginalis* or the imaginary and the imaginal. *Spring Journal,* 1–19.

Cowan, L. (1982). *Masochism: A Jungian view.* Spring.

Dodds, E. R. (2020). *The Greeks and the irrational.* Beacon. (Original work published 1957)

Downing, C. (1993). *Gods in our midst.* Crossroad.

Eliade, M. (1964). *Shamanism, archaic techniques of ecstasy* (W. R. Trask, Trans.). Princeton University Press. (Original work published 1951)

Euripides. (2005). *The Bacchae and other plays* (J. Davie, Trans.). Penguin.

Evans, J. (2018). *The art of losing control: A philosopher's search for ecstatic experience.* Canongate.

Groesbeck, C. J. (1989). C. G. Jung and the shaman's vision. *Journal of Analytical Psychology, 34,* 255–275.

Hillman, J. (1972). *The myth of analysis.* Northwestern University Press.

Hillman, J. (1979). Puer wounds and Ulysses' scar. In J. Hillman (Ed.), *Puer papers* (pp. 100–128). Spring.

Hillman, J. (1992). *Re-Visioning psychology.* HarperPerennial. (Original work published 1975)

Hillman, J. (2007). Dionysus in Jung's writing. In *Uniform edition of the writings of James Hillman* (Vol. 6.1, pp. 15–30). Spring.

Hillman, J. (2008). You dirty dog! In *Uniform edition of the writings of James Hillman* (Vol. 9, pp. 150–160). Spring.

Hopcke, R. H. (2004). S/M and the psychology of gay male initiation: An archetypal perspective. In M. Thompson (Ed.), *Leatherfolk: Radical sex, people, politics, and practice* (3rd ed., pp. 65–76). Daedalus. (Original work published in 1991)

Johnson, R. (1987). *Ecstasy: Understanding the psychology of joy.* Harper Perennial.

Jung, C. G. (1966). On the psychology of the unconscious (R. F. C. Hull, Trans.). In H. Read et al. (Eds.), *The collected works of C. G. Jung* (Vol. 7, 2nd ed., pp. 3–122). Princeton University Press. (Original work published 1917)

Jung, C. G. (1968). On the psychology of the trickster figure (R. F. C. Hull, Trans.). In H. Read et al. (Eds.), *The collected works of C. G. Jung* (Vol. 9i, 2nd ed., pp. 255–274). Princeton University Press. (Original work published 1954)

Jung, C. G. (1969a). On the nature of the psyche (R. F. C. Hull, Trans.). In H. Read et al. (Eds.), *The collected works of C. G. Jung* (Vol. 8, 2nd ed., pp. 159–236). Princeton University Press. (Original work published 1947)

Jung, C. G. (1969b). Transformation symbolism in the mass (R. F. C. Hull, Trans.). In H. Read et al. (Eds.), *The collected works of C. G. Jung* (Vol. 11, 2nd ed., pp. 201–298). Princeton University Press. (Original work published 1940)

Jung, C. G. (1970a). Mind and earth (R. F. C. Hull, Trans.). In H. Read et al. (Eds.), *The collected works of C. G. Jung* (Vol. 10, 2nd ed., pp. 29–49). Princeton University Press. (Original work published 1931)

Jung, C. G. (1970b). The complications of American psychology (R. F. C. Hull, Trans.). In H. Read et al. (Eds.), *The collected works of C. G. Jung* (Vol. 10, 2nd ed., pp. 502–514). Princeton University Press. (Original work published 1930)

Jung, C. G. (1970c). The role of the unconscious (R. F. C. Hull, Trans.). In H. Read et al. (Eds.), *The collected works of C. G. Jung* (Vol. 10, 2nd ed., pp. 3–28). Princeton University Press. (Original work published 1918)

Jung, C. G. (1970d). The state of psychotherapy today (R. F. C. Hull, Trans.). In H. Read et al. (Eds.), *The collected works of C. G. Jung* (Vol. 10, 2nd ed., pp. 157–178). Princeton University Press. (Original work published 1934)

Jung, C. G. (1989). *Memories, dreams, reflections* (R. Winston & C. Winston, Trans.; A. Jaffé, Ed.). Vintage Books. (Original work published 1961)

Jung, C. G. (2009). *The red book, Liber Novus: A reader's edition* (M. Kyburz, J. Peck, & S. Shamdasani, Trans.; S. Shamdasani, Ed.). W. W. Norton.

Kaldera, R. (2006). *Dark moon rising: Pagan BDSM and the ordeal path*. Asphodel.

Kalsched, D. (2013). *Trauma and the soul*. Routledge.

Kingsley, P. (2018). *Catafalque*. Catafalque Press.

Kirby, E. T. (1975). *Ur-drama: The origins of theater*. New York University Press.

Laski, M. (1961). *Ecstasy in secular and religious experiences*. Jeremy P. Tarcher, Inc.

Lopez-Pedraza, R. (2000). *Dionysus in exile*. Chiron.

Mains, G. (2002). *Urban aboriginals* (3rd ed.). Daedalus.

March, J. (1998). *Cassell's dictionary of classical mythology*. Cassell.

Merchant, J. (2012). *Shamans and analysts*. Routledge.

Nietzsche, F. (1956). The birth of tragedy. In *The birth of tragedy and the genealogy of morals* (F. Golffing, Trans., pp. 1–146). Anchor Books. (Original work published 1871)

Otto, W. F. (1965). *Dionysus: Myth and cult* (R. Palmer, Trans.). Indiana University Press.

Paris, G. (1990). *Pagan grace*. Spring.

Rowland, S. (2017). *Remembering Dionysus: Revisioning psychology and literature in C. G. Jung and James Hillman*. Routledge.

Ryan, R. E. (2002). *Shamanism and the psychology of C. G. Jung*. Vega.

Sagarin, B., Cutler, B., Cutler, N., Lawler-Sagarin, K. A., & Matuszewich, L. (2009). Hormonal changes and couple bonding in consensual sadomasochistic activity. *Archives of Sexual Behavior, 38*, 186–200. http://doi.org/10.1007/s10508-008-9374-5

Shamdasani, S. (2009). Introduction. In S. Shamdasani (Ed.), *The red book, Liber Novus: A reader's edition* (M. Kyburz, J. Peck, & S. Shamdasani, Trans., pp. 1–96). W.W. Norton.

Taylor, R. (1985). *The death and resurrection show*. Anthony Blond.

Thompson, M. (Ed.). (2004). *Leatherfolk: Radical sex, people, politics, and practice* (3rd ed.). Daedulus. (Original work published in 1991)

Truscott, C. (2004). S/M: Some questions and a few answers. In M. Thompson (Ed.), *Leatherfolk: Radical sex, people, politics, and practice* (3rd ed., pp. 15–36). Daedalus. (Original work published in 1991)

Valens, A. (2021, May 19). Everything you need to know about pet play. *Daily Dot*. www.dailydot.com/irl/pet-play/

van der Berk, T. (2012). *Jung on art: The autonomy of the creative drive*. Routledge.

Winnicott, D. W. (1989). Review of memories, dreams, reflections. In C. Winnicott, R. Shepherd, & M. Davis (Eds.), *Psycho-analytic explorations* (pp. 482–492). Harvard University Press.

8

INTIMATIONS OF DEATH

Introduction

Throughout the preceding chapters, there has been a fantasy-figure partially hidden in the background of each discussion. Sometimes referenced in passing, sometimes implied, the fantasy-image of death has been quietly observing our exploration of soul's relationship to BDSM. The deep psychology of play includes the elements of boundaries, limits, edges, and secrecy, all of which recognize the death-image as the ultimate limit of ego consciousness and human existence. Suffering and degradation are contextualized by the existential terror of death's consciousness-defining presence. The specter of evil has a close connection to death through the perpetration of human atrocities as well as fantasy-images of the monstrous and the horrific. The ecstatic practices of shamanism include the ritual death and dismemberment of the mystic healer, and the ancient Greek cult of Dionysus has a similar special relationship with death. In fact, Heraclitus said that Dionysus and Hades are one and the same.[1] The enduring imaginal presence of death throughout these chapters suggests that the death-image is core to the nature of soul and has an inherent connection to BDSM.

Death can be a sensitive topic in the BDSM community. Although some kinksters may revel in the morbid and macabre aspects of leather and fetish culture, others may be reluctant to affirm the subtle or unconscious connection between death and the deep pleasure and spiritual meaning their activities and relationships afford. Still, others may bear the emotional scars

DOI: 10.4324/9781003223597-10

of encounters that went dangerously wrong or even ended in fatal catastrophe. Like rock climbing, skydiving, or other varieties of extreme recreation, BDSM's fascination with pushing physical limits in edgeplay is inherently risky. Sometimes the safety measures developed by the community are not enough to prevent a mishap.[2]

A few extreme cases of literal enactments of the sexual death fantasy are a grim reminder of the difference between fantasy role-play and the literalization of fantasy-images in physical acts of violence and death. But the collective BDSM community has no more interest in courting death than an afficionado of slasher films has an interest in committing actual murder. Nevertheless, death as an archetypal fantasy-image has a potent effect on the erotic imagination, and it is this fantasy aspect that will be the focus of the present discussion. The fact that a Google search for "Femdom Executrix" yields over 2,000 results for online videos is proof enough that the erotic death fantasy is an aspect of modern sexuality deserving psychological consideration.

The persistent intimation of the death-image throughout the preceding chapters has as much to do with the nature of the soul as with the interests or motives of BDSM. Throughout its history, depth psychology has privileged the spectral presence of death as an essential element of psychological life. The ethnic psychologist Edgar Herzog wrote, "To open oneself to death is to accept the aspect of 'becoming,' that is, of transformation, which is the very stuff of life, and to realize that the human condition transcends itself."[3] For depth psychology, death is more than a physical reality. Jung wrote: "Death is indeed a fearful piece of brutality, there is no sense pretending otherwise. It is brutal not only as a physical event, but far more so psychically."[4] Death poses an existential crisis for the psyche to reconcile the finitude of our human existence with the timelessness of the archetypal imagination.

Jung's[5] *Symbols of Transformation* provided a vast survey of world mythologies to support his claim that the individuation process consisted of integrating archetypal symbols from the collective unconscious into the personal psyche. Central to his argument was the mythic theme of the *katabasis*, or descent to the Underworld, as a symbol for one's personal reckoning with death. Shortly thereafter, Jung underwent his own personal *katabasis* into the spirit of the depths, the personal inner journey recorded in *The Red Book*. He encountered death and the dead in diverse forms that provided a phenomenological grounding for his mature psychology. Death and the dead appeared as personified figures, imaginal landscapes, nodal points for psychological reverie, and perhaps most importantly, as primordial symbols. The chronicle of his journey presents death as more than a source of horror and dread—it is also a source of deep existential meaning and regeneration.[6]

In his mature psychology, Jung contended that the underworld descent signified the death of heroic ego consciousness necessary to experience the reality of the psyche as a collective archetypal process.[7] He also recognized the fundamental relationship between the unconscious and death: "The unconscious corresponds to the mythic land of the dead, the land of the ancestors."[8] And the materiality of his own near-death experience notwithstanding, he imagined that the kingdom of death was a wholly psychological realm:

> If we assume that life continues "there," we cannot conceive of any other form of existence except a psychic one; for the life of the psyche requires no space and no time. Psychic existence, and above all the inner images with which we are here concerned, supply the material for all mythic speculations about a life in the hereafter, and I imagine that life as a continuance in the world of images. Thus the psyche might be that existence in which the hereafter or the land of the dead is located.[9]

By associating the world of images with the land of the dead, Jung found a connection that became central to Hillman's image-centered approach to archetypal psychology.

Hillman suggested that death is in fact a pure expression of soul. He argued that as soul enters into all things human, so, too, death is a psychic presence (a *soul-image*) contextualizing the meaning behind all our activities:

> To be human is to be reminded of death and have a perspective informed by death. To be human is to be soul-focused, which in turn is death-focused. Or, to put it another way: to be death-focused is to be soul-focused. This is because Hades' realm refers to the archetypal perspective that is wholly psychological, where the considerations of human life—the emotions, the organic needs, social

connections of humanistic psychology—no longer apply. In Hades' realm *psyché* alone exists; all other standpoints are dissolved.[10]

Both Hillman and Jung envisioned psychic reality as a world of autonomous living images, which extends well beyond the confines of ego consciousness and physical existence. In poetic terms, it is the soul's nature to lead all images through the portal of death back to their homeland, a place of pure imaginal reality in the Underworld.

The significance of death as an elemental characteristic of depth psychology extends beyond the work of Jung and Hillman. Sabina Spielrein,[11] one of the early female psychoanalytic pioneers, formulated the idea of the death instinct and linked it to sadomasochism. Freud[12] was impressed enough by her insights to develop them further in his book *Beyond the Pleasure Principle*. He posited the existence of a death drive to explain the phenomenon of *repetition compulsion* among trauma victims who unconsciously repeat unpleasurable experiences.

Death provokes uncanny, incomprehensible feelings of terror, helplessness, impotence, and dread.[13] Indeed, the record of human history illustrates our attempt to cope with these intolerable emotions, particularly through the emergence of a progressively personified death-image in folklore, mythic tales, and dreams.[14] In *The Denial of Death*, Ernest Becker asserted that the inability of the human community to face its feelings of terror and impotence in the face of death has resulted in a "hero system" of repressive denial with catastrophic consequences for modern society.[15]

Jung saw death as an archetypal image, as a living symbol of transformation.

The importance of the symbol to Jung's psychology can scarcely be exaggerated. It plays a crucial role in the economy of the psyche, bridging the gap between the primordial unconscious and the conscious personality.[16] The symbol consists of an image that combines rational and irrational elements. Robert Ryan provided a helpful summary of the symbol's importance:

> Though symbols cannot be completely encapsulated in rational thought, they do not entirely escape it. Moreover, they are experienced as somehow vitally meaningful. They appear as emissaries of a certain deep formal purposiveness of the psyche, and the mind recognizes this form as intimately significant for it. Such symbols are known by their effects. They are fascinating and feeling-laden

and are experienced as both spontaneous and necessary. A sense of vitality and yet inner orderedness [*sic*] accompanies their presence. They give hints of what lies latent and potential within the psyche; what the psyche must express if it is not to wither from the loss of its own roots and sustenance.[17]

The soul expresses itself through primordial images as symbols. The conscious mind struggles to find meaning in the irrational and unknown content that symbols provide. Jung[18] contended that it was important to allow meaning and understanding to emerge gradually into consciousness through a prolonged relationship with the mystery of the symbol. Thus, symbols function as generators of meaning by bringing the conscious personality into intimate contact with the primordial depths. The conscious mind learns about psychic reality by living in relationship with symbolic images, and this relationship lies at the heart of the individuation process by helping us to integrate that which is unknown.

From the symbolic viewpoint, death is essential to a cycle of regeneration and growth, which we can only partially grasp through the intellect. Experiencing death as a psychological reality allows a different kind of understanding and meaning to emerge. The secret to leading a fulfilling life involves learning how to live in alignment with the symbolic language of the deep psyche:

> There is a thinking in primordial images—in symbols which are older than historical man; which have been ingrained in him from earliest times, and, eternally living, outlasting all generations, still make up the groundwork of the human psyche. It is only possible to live the fullest life when we are in harmony with these symbols; wisdom is a return to them. It is neither a question of belief nor of knowledge, but of the agreement of our thinking with the primordial images of the unconscious.[19]

Jung considered the symbolic life to be the bridge between the images of the primordial past and our ultimate human destiny: our engagement with the living symbol brings greater consciousness into the world through our personal individuation. Death and the mythic Underworld confront us as great symbols of the unknown and the hidden, as symbols of the unconscious itself. Paradoxically, the soul expresses its vitality through the primordial symbol of death. Learning how to live in agreement with a death-oriented wisdom is one of the great psychological tasks of human life.

The discussion in this chapter will follow the mystery of the death-image to explore how the soul is present in the activities and relationships of kink and BDSM. We will look first at classical mythology and its depictions of the Underworld, which offers a metaphorical language to describe the intense inner journeys of many BDSM afficionados. We will then turn to the Gothic genre, which provides a second perspective on death as a source of horror and psychic destabilization familiar to many BDSM practitioners. Finally, the work of French philosopher Georges Bataille and psychoanalyst Jean Laplanche will provide a basis for exploring the mysterious relationship between eroticism and death, a relationship that lies at the heart of BDSM's numinous vitality.

Death and the Mythic Imagination

In Western culture, the mythic realm of the Underworld has been the symbol *par excellence* to contain and to develop our collective fantasies of death as a psychic reality. Hillman described the classical Underworld of Hades as both a place of imaginal origins and an ultimate destination:

> Because his realm was conceived as the final end of each soul, Hades is the final cause, the purpose, the very telos of every soul and every soul process. If so, then all psychic events have a Hades aspect. . . . All soul processes, everything in the psyche, moves toward Hades.[20]

The workings of the soul are intimately connected with death, and the mythic Underworld is the soul's imaginal homeland. When Thomas Moore referred to the psychology of the Marquis de Sade as "a conduit of an underworld mythology,"[21] he was recognizing a psychological interplay involving the roots of sadism, the soul-image of death, and the Underworld as its topographical symbol.

The Greeks referred to the ruler of the Underworld as the personification of the place, Hades. His primary characteristics were hiddenness and invisibility (his name has been translated as the "unseen or invisible one").[22] Hades was the faceless god of what cannot be imagined.[23] His name evokes the mysterious unseen and unknown qualities of death and the incomprehensible secrets of what happens after one's mortal existence. His name was taboo among the Greeks, so he was known by other epithets such as "the nourisher, . . . the receiver of many guests, . . . the good counselor, . . . [or wealth-giver]."[24] The etymological root of his name (*kolio*) has been traced back to an ancient word meaning "hider."[25] Linguistic research has found the same word throughout the Indo-Germanic world to describe various Death-Demons. The related word *kaluptein*, meaning "hide in the earth," or "bury," has given rise to a network of derivatives in Latin, Old Irish, German, and English, such as "cellar," "death," and "hell."[26] At the root of Hades's name are images of hiding underground, invisibility, and concealment.

BDSM and kink have an affinity for the hidden, the obscure, the concealed, and the invisible. The somber, ambient lighting of many dungeons and play spaces is reminiscent of the mythic darkness of the Underworld. In bondage and sensory deprivation play, blindfolds and hoods can obscure or completely block the vision of the submissive. Gimp suits evoke the uncanny by virtue of their capacity to conceal and to erase one's personhood. When we die, we are remembered less and less by the living, until the details of our lives and our accomplishments have been forgotten and erased. Is it perhaps a foretaste of our own eventual concealment and anonymity that gives the gimp its numinous effect as an unconscious symbol of death?

Perhaps the most vivid example of invisibility and concealment in BDSM is the fetish of mummification:

> The idea of complete mummification is to wrap the bottom, head to toe, in some material that will prevent any movement at all. As the wraps are installed, sensory overloading or sensory deprivation can also be arranged, the degree of breathing can be put in the Top's control, and other devices like catheters or tit clamps might be put in place under or through openings in the wrapping. All these variations carry with them their own safety demands and concerns, but the basic mummy wrap is as easy to learn as it is to enjoy.[27]

Another popular form of mummification uses a leather sleepsack, which can be adjusted to be form-fitting and completely immobilizing. When one is enveloped in the darkness of the bag and the outside world is completely concealed, one enters a twilight liminal consciousness, and one's vision opens inward. The submissive floats away from all daytime concerns into an attitude of complete surrender. The mysteries of inner space and oblivion are close at hand, depending on the wishes of the Dom. In such a twilight state, one senses why the Greeks regarded Hypnos, the divine personification of sleep, as the twin brother of Thanatos, the deity who carries the dead safely to the Underworld.

Hades's name is also connected to words that describe burying and covering with earth.[28] We bury our dead, and we also plant seeds in the earth that produce new growth. Thus, "Hades becomes associated with the fertilization of the ground, the burial of seeds, and care for the parts of plants that stay under the earth—those parts that transgress the border between his world and Demeter's."[29] The mythic connection between the Underworld and fertility supports a psychological insight that death has a cyclical relationship with regeneration and growth. The spiritual and ritualistic aspects of BDSM operate according to this same mythic theme. Pagan BDSM practitioner Raven Kaldera directly acknowledged employing "the archetypal Journey to the Underworld" as a framework for "intense psychological theater" in his ritual practice: "The top has to be both the psychopomp who gets [the bottom] in and out, and the stand-in for the implacable Death Gods who inhabit that dark place."[30] The partner in the Dominant position needs to learn to be ethically grounded for the responsibilities of scenes that are psychologically more intense. A ritualized encounter with symbolic death transforms the conscious personality and promotes psychological growth.

Hell Hounds, Pups, and Filth

As early human communities began to tell stories about death as the ultimate "other," the "Hider" was frequently "represented as a greedy, corpse-devouring wolf or a carrion-eating dog."[31] Herzog[32] compiled a detailed survey of world mythologies and anthropological studies that chronicled the connection between dogs and death as an archetypal pattern. The unrelenting jaws of a voracious hell hound personify the numinous power of death and the feelings of "impotent horror" it elicits.[33] The soul-image of death devouring the living was common in the ancient world. The Greeks referred to both Hades and Hekate (the goddess associated with the boundary between the upper and lower worlds) as "*pantophagos* (all-devourer) or *sarkophagos* (eater of raw meat or corpses)," and even the motherly Demeter was sometimes called "*adephagos* [gluttonous one]." The great devourer of raw meat, "*olophagos*," was the epithet given to the infamous three-headed hell hound, Cerberus.[34] Norse-German mythology also features hell hounds, such as Garmr, who guards the Underworld; the ruler Hel, who is a female deity, descended from wolves; and Fenris, a ferocious giant wolf, who luckily will remain captive underground until he escapes and helps bring about the end of the world. The Aztecs had a red hound of the dead, and the ancient Egyptians had the jackal-headed god, Anubis, who was "Lord of the Grave."[35] The primeval image of the corpse-devouring dog can be connected to the ritual practices of indigenous peoples in Mongolia and Tibet, who left their dead on open burial grounds, where packs of dogs consumed the bodies. Hillman[36] speculated that the historical connection between dogs and cadavers may have given rise to the epithet of the dirty dog and the human preoccupation with dogs as unclean.

The archetypal connection between dogs and death could be relevant to aspects of BDSM pup play. The canine qualities of devotion, obedience, and open-hearted exuberance are often evident in pup-identified individuals. However, pup play can also be a form of Domination and submission, and degradation can be part of the dynamic. The transition in identity from human to pup involves a lowering of consciousness to a more primal instinctual level. BDSM's fascination with disinhibition, transgressive pleasure, instinctual appetite, and the eroticization of filth and disgust are characteristics that are shared with the primeval dog, who is the mythic ancestor of the pup. Donning the pup mask, trading hands for paws, wearing a collar, being led on a leash, and eating from a bowl all signify that one's status as human has been blissfully surrendered to the status of animal. The fantasy-image of the dog has taken over (devoured?) ego consciousness. For the soul, the return of the animal becomes a journey to the Underworld and a restoration of imaginal possibilities. The dog knows what is hidden, buried, and concealed—it knows the mythic qualities of Hades. Psychologically speaking, Hades is a force that draws us inward and downward into the depths of underworld consciousness, places where the ego resists going.[37] The deep psychology of the pup has an ancestral connection to the Underworld, and it knows the hidden paths and warrens that lead to the homeland of the soul.

Role-Playing Death in BDSM

Katabasis was the Greek word that referred to the mythic journey to the Underworld, such as those undertaken by Herakles, Orpheus, and Aeneas.

Encounters with the land of the dead also appeared in the Mesopotamian myth of Gilgamesh, in the Egyptian myth of Osiris, and of course, centuries later in *The Divine Comedy* of Dante.[38] Viewing the shaman's initiatory illness as an underworld ordeal makes evident its connection to the archetypal pattern of the *katabasis*. Murray Stein[39] suggested that the imagery of both *The Divine Comedy* and *The Red Book* draws the reader into an immersive mystical experience of the underworld journey as an extended metaphor for the individuation process.

As in the older myths, those who journey to the Underworld face ordeals, gain knowledge, and return to the day world profoundly changed. Kaldera[40] specifically mentioned the underworld journey as an analogue of his own BDSM pagan ritual practice, but he is not alone in recognizing the symbolic death-image as an element in BDSM ritual and play. In their interview for this book, kinkster Moth Meadows (whose preferred pronouns are they/them) shared some of their experience exploring the theme of death in intimate fantasy role-play with their partner (their partner identifies as a trans woman, who uses the pronouns it and its):

> I was lucky enough to have an ego death experience on psychedelics a few years ago, which actually happened right before I got hit by a car, like several months before it happened. So, I had this really profound experience that allowed me to confront my anxiety around death and accept death as an inevitability but something that I could prepare for. So, I'm always aware of that and then having a near-death experience where I was hit by a car. I've had a lot of space in my life to sort of welcome my anxiety around death and not be so afraid of it, and I'm not somebody who's really afraid of dying. I feel very comfortable with the thought of death. It doesn't make me uncomfortable at all. And my partner, on the other hand, is extremely anxious about death and has like a lot of death anxiety. So, there was a couple of times where we explored sort of like, necrophile fantasies and things around bodies, and we couldn't really figure out what the right direction to go in for that would be. But my partner had sort of a breakthrough and discovered that its feelings as a Dom are really amplified by having total control over a body, and being able to not just dominate a body, but like fully having control. So, we wanted to explore a scene surrounding death,

that would kind of emphasize control, and wasn't putting emphasis on the idea of a corpse or a dead body.

So, we did this really intense CNC [Consensual Non-consent] scene that involves sort of a serial killer dynamic, where I played the victim to the serial killer, and we set it up to have it so that like, I would be killed during the scene, and then I could just be this body for my partner to use. And my partner discovered that it really, really likes that. And that that is what it can get out of playing with ideas of death around sex, and I discovered that I really, really liked the idea of just sort of getting to have this like, almost meditative experience of just pretending to be dead. It's like this nice grounding experience of just being fully present in my body, but not allowing myself to react to anything that's happening.

The fantasy role-play between Moth and their partner pushed the dynamic of Domination and submission to its psychological limit without literalizing the soul-image of death. Metaphorically speaking, death can be seen as the ultimate Dom, who exercises the final measure of control over all our lives. Ultimately, we all must submit to death's authority over the living. In taking on the role of the killer, Moth's partner functioned as death's agent. The specter of evil, which was the subject of Chapter 6, was fully present in the consensual scene the couple negotiated, yet its presence did not lead to physical or emotional harm. Moth's experience of "playing dead" illustrates several aspects of the underworld journey's relevance to BDSM.

First, Moth says that they felt comfortable with death. Two profound death-related experiences prior to the scene—an ego death during a psychedelic journey and a serious auto accident—helped them work through their initial anxiety and fear. As a result, they were able to give their consent to an extreme scenario in which they were to surrender their life because they had already accepted the inevitability of death as part of a natural cycle. The scene became an opportunity to explore the deeper dimensions of death as a soul-image. The integration of death's inevitability into our understanding of life is a major psychological accomplishment, as Herzog reflected:

Death cannot be eliminated! Should humans deny the reality of life, and try to understand and organize it in relation to death? Humans can only find a way of uniting death and life, or bringing them into harmony, if one is prepared to transcend the limits of existence. This task is only possible if humans can see that part of themselves reach into the unknown, and that it is from the unknown that order and meaning are given to their lives.[41]

Moth's voluntary participation in the scene allowed them to reach into the unknown of the Underworld because they were already prepared to transcend the limits of existence.

By contrast, one of the other epithets given to the Roman god of the dead was *Dis Pater*.[42] Dante adopted it for the monstrous lord of the dead, and according to Donald Kalsched,[43] the name has provided the prefix for English words such as distress, disease, and dissociation. He has said that people trapped in the hell of an unresolved traumatic experience joylessly (and unconsciously) reenact the core wound of the event again and again. This idea suggests that there is a risk that individuals with a history of physical and emotional trauma might use BDSM in an unexamined way to act out their pain without finding deeper meaning, resolution, or transcendence through their activities. In such cases, dissociation becomes a defense mechanism of the personal psyche to avoid the overwhelm and suffering that would come with conscious self-reflection. Psychotherapy with a kink-affirming professional can be a valuable resource to support BDSM activities as a path to healing and transformation from trauma. The way out of such a personal inferno would involve an engagement with the emotions trapped in the body, an acceptance of vulnerability as a fundamental part of the human condition, and a quest for meaning that emerges from the living symbols of the psyche.

Second, Moth described an experience of soul that was separate from the physical body. By enacting death as a fantasy role-play, they surrendered the daytime agency of the ego and its claim upon the body. Their physical being grew inert and lifeless as they descended into a deep meditative state. Their description suggests a quality of timelessness and suspended animation, consistent with Hillman's observation: "There is no time in the underworld."[44] Moth's imaginal encounter with death resembles the practice in ancient Greece of communing with the dead through necromancy. Scholars surmise that the most likely method in ancient times was to sleep overnight in a special sanctuary and converse with the shades of the Underworld through one's dreams.[45] Although Moth did not dream, their consciousness descended into a liminal state in which they became more familiar with the fantasy of death and the land of the dead.

Finally, Moth's experience illustrates how BDSM plays with the social construct of the heroic. Both Downing[46] and Becker[47] regarded our culture's obsession with heroism as a denial of the existential terror of death. When faced with the inevitability of our mortality, the prevailing cultural presumption is that we must wage a fierce, courageous battle against death, which has long been the ultimate test of heroic strength and bravery. When the mythic hero Herakles journeyed to the Underworld and captured the hell hound Cerberus, the exploit was regarded as one of his greatest accomplishments, although there was no ultimate triumph over death: Herakles immediately had to return Cerberus to his proper abode.[48] Becker was particularly pointed in his critique of what he described as Western culture's addiction to heroism. The heroic narrative opposes an acceptance of death as a natural part of the life cycle and refuses to see death as something that is inevitable and necessary. But the dangers of the heroic stance are more serious than simply the denial of death—heroism fuels a tragic obsession that requires each of us must prove that we are "an object of primary value in the universe."[49] Worse still, it can justify antagonistic impulses to fight, conquer, exploit, and destroy other people to prove our value. Heroism has the potential to become an agent of evil. Becker asserted that social and environmental calamities unfold because we are terrified to examine what we are doing to earn a feeling of heroic self-esteem, a feeling of primary cosmic value.

Becker's critique offers a unique perspective on the cultural significance of BDSM. In the activities and relationships of radical sexualities, a complex dialectic encircles the fantasy-image of heroism. In some instances, practitioners earnestly engage with the hero archetype: many Masters and Dominants find heroic meaning, purpose, and pleasure in experiencing themselves as powerful and uniquely important to the lives of those who serve them; submissives and slaves often experience similar feelings in their ability to undergo extreme challenges to their physical endurance and their mental and emotional fortitude. Many practitioners have turned to Joseph Campbell's[50] model of the hero's journey as a template that enables them to imagine BDSM ordeals as a mythic odyssey of transformation. In other instances, practitioners subvert the conventional fantasy of the hero:

excitement and fascination are associated with humiliation, degradation, filth, and cruelty, not virtue, purity, or justice; pleasure lies in the odd, the twisted, and the sinister, not in the courageous or the redemptive.

In some instances, the unconscious influence of the hero archetype can lead to ego inflation with destructive consequences. Dominants can exceed the limits of their own discernment and judgment and inflict serious harm on their submissives; subs can be seduced by their own heroic fantasies into thinking that they can endure more pain or punishment than they really can. Unconscious heroism risks "summoning the destruction that seems always to gather in the shadows of a scene, waiting for anything like an invitation."[51] BDSM plays with a dialectic between the heroic and the contra-heroic. It illustrates Becker's[52] contention that countercultural movements arise when groups of people no longer find existential meaning in established narratives of heroism. The pleasure and excitement of BDSM come from the intentional transgression of conventional norms. Paradoxically, the courage to transgress the established signifiers of heroism can itself become a heroic act. What is most germane to the present discussion is that the BDSM practitioner, like the hero in the Underworld, is always in close relationship with the soul-image of death.

Moth's experience with their partner demonstrates how BDSM can queer conventional narratives through transgressive acts. In contrast to the societal denial of death through the maintenance of a hero system, the couple's fantasy role-play was a direct acknowledgment and engagement with mortality through the enactment of two great cultural taboos: murder and the use of the dead for pleasure. Societal attitudes of horror and repugnance for transgressing the forbidden provided the dynamism of the scene. To the extent that there was any heroism present, it was characterized by a conscious and affirming attitude toward death's inevitability and necessity. As a mythic enactment, the scene paid tribute to Hades as the ruler of the dead and his ultimate domination over all our lives. In so doing, the role-play interrogated and deconstructed the conventional fantasy of the hero and its powerful hold on Western consciousness. The queer impulse within BDSM and kink leads to a pattern of challenging social norms by playing with the underlying presuppositions that structure daily life. Moth and their partner engaged in a queering of the heroic structures that underlie our larger systems of social order and meaning. The underworld encounter with murder, death, and necromancy became a peaceful affirmative meditation on existential truths that are less accessible to daytime consciousness.

The Legacy of the Gothic and the Macabre

Gothic is a genre that emphasizes intense emotion and pairs terror and death with transgressive pleasure. Horace Walpole's 1764 novel, *The Castle of Otranto*, which he sub-titled "A Gothic Story," introduced the use of the term in relation to literature and other cultural expressions.[53] Gothic also came to influence both the descriptive language of depth psychology and the peculiar combination of eroticism and terror that make BDSM and kink psychologically potent. Contemporary Gothic youth sub-culture draws much of its source material from previous eras of the Gothic, and there is extensive overlap with BDSM and kink.[54] Gothic's explicit relationship with the macabre contributes to a deeper understanding of how soul is present in the activities and relationships of kink and BDSM.

Gothic often expresses an uneasy dialectic between unexpected and often shocking binaries, such as horror and invigoration, sexuality and terror, or transgression and irrational delight. "You cannot have Gothic without a cruel hero-villain; without a cringing victim; and without a terrible place, some locale, hidden from public view, in which the drama can unfold."[55] The terrible place often conveys an ambience of breakdown and decay, such as medieval castles and dungeons, nocturnal graveyards, musty catacombs, and foreboding natural settings. The genre also typically includes a supernatural element in the form of ghosts, demons, or monsters that victimize the representatives of a seemingly rational and civilized moral order.[56] Incarceration is another frequent element of the Gothic: heroines typically are subjected to "terrors, persecutions and imprisonments."[57]

The Gothic idiom rose to prominence as a countervailing force during the Age of Enlightenment's celebration of reason and empiricism. The same era saw the horrors of the French Revolution and the subsequent Reign of Terror in which the technological efficiency of the guillotine created rivers of blood in the streets of Paris. From across the English Channel, the British aristocracy watched the rising specter of death in the French capitol with uneasiness and fear.[58] The horror of death threatened to overwhelm the triumph of reason. Gothic expressed the terror and instability of the era by personifying death as an incomprehensibly powerful and often sexually perverse monster.

Just as "the idea of death haunts us,"[59] so the phantoms and monsters of Gothic novels haunt the pages of their macabre tales. The Gothic monster brings to life Herzog's[60] notion that the specter of the demon arose from the depths of the psyche as a symbol to contain the inexpressible horror of the corpse. The taboo of death haunts the perverse body of the monster in works such as Mary Shelly's[61] *Frankenstein* (sometimes considered more science fiction than Gothic)[62] and Bram Stoker's *Dracula*.[63] The monster exists in an ambiguous, indeterminate state between life and death, simultaneously a deformed and degraded version of animate matter and an exalted version of the corpse. It is a liminal creature that transgresses the border between the dead and the living, and it can conjure feelings of fascination and repulsion because its numinous erotic power emanates from the archetype of death.

That *Fifty Shades of Grey* was originally a work of fan fiction inspired by the young adult *Twilight* vampire series indicates that BDSM has an inherent connection to the Gothic idiom and its liminal creatures.[64] In BDSM, the Gothic eroticization of pain and degradation can constellate primal fears of death's monstrous horror. The Top may appear as an other-worldly predatory transgressor, and the bottom may appear to be one of the entranced and tortured victims of a bygone era. Some practitioners may experience an inexpressible fascination with these archetypal Gothic figures.

The other supernatural figure popularized in the Gothic idiom was the double. Doubling is a recurring element throughout the Gothic genre and, in some cases, an explicit plot element in works, such as Robert Louis Stevenson's[65] *The Strange Case of Dr. Jekyll and Mr. Hyde* and Oscar Wilde's[66] *The Picture of Dorian Gray*. The double enabled Gothic writers to depict a phenomenology of the other, whether the other signified contemporary targets of antisemitism and xenophobia, perceived threats to modernity, or death itself as the ultimate unknowable double of life. The fantasy-image of the double is present in many of the traditional BDSM relational couplings: Dominant/submissive; Top/bottom; Handler/pet; sadist/masochist, etc. The Gothic double has a psychological counterpart in Sigmund Freud's[67] concept of the uncanny and Jung's[68] concept of the Shadow, both of which recognize the underlying significance of the double as a symbol of death.

Freud, Jung, and Hillman as Gothic Writers

Commentators on the Gothic idiom have referenced Freudian theory both to explore the psychological dimension of the genre and to illustrate the influence of the Gothic on Freud's model of the psyche.[69] Similarly, Susan Rowland[70] has referred to Jung as a Gothic author. These scholars make a strong case for the inclusion of Freud and Jung as contributors to the Gothic tradition. Hillman, too, can be regarded as a postmodern Gothic thinker.

Freud imagined the human psyche as an internal Gothic landscape in which the civilized ego was haunted and menaced by the monstrous sexual and aggressive appetites of the primal id on the one hand and tortured by the tyrannical restrictive judgments of the superego on the other. Freud moved the Gothic drama to the personal interior during the same era when writers of fiction were depicting the terror of the inner monster or the sinister double that turns out to be oneself.

Freud used the term "Uncanny" to describe the unsettling feeling of something strange and unfamiliar, which "arouses dread and creeping horror."[71] Experiences that typically evoke the uncanny involve death, the supernatural, epilepsy, and madness. Freud attributed the feelings of dread and horror not to unfamiliarity but to something remotely familiar that had been repressed, such as the primal separation from the mother and the primal fear of death. Freud's theory reflects the Gothic theme of a remote horror that returns to haunt the present and overwhelm the familiar world. BDSM has a particular talent for fetishizing and eroticizing the uncanny. The blurring of boundaries between human, subhuman, and nonhuman can arouse feelings of both delight and dread. The transgressive nature of BDSM (also a hallmark characteristic of Gothic) can provoke confusion and excitement but also anxiety and foreboding over liminal states of mind and emotion. The fetish of Dollification, in which the submissive participant is transformed into a living doll, is a perfect example of the uncanny in kink and BDSM activities. The human/nonhuman ambiguity of the living doll reminds us that dolls "oscillate between the material and the supernatural worlds, between the tangible and the ethereal. They represent the point of intersection between the mundane and the divine."[72] The gimp suit previously discussed is another example of the uncanny: the human form is familiar yet unfamiliar; it exists only as a non-person-object, an ambiguous negation of being, a shade. The double, which so frequently appears in BDSM and kink, has an uncanny effect that Freud believed was connected to our dread of death. When kinksters experience an undiscovered part of themselves, the effect can be exhilarating, but they will never fully return to the person they thought they used to be. In a sense, the "kinky double" has displaced (or dispatched) the person of the past. Freud's analysis of the uncanny may also offer a psychological explanation for the extreme negative reactions some people outside the BDSM community experience toward radical sexuality. Kinksters frequently have done personal work to integrate regions of the deep unconscious that arouse fear and dread in others. Outsiders may experience an uncanny reaction when exposed to the activities of BDSM and the profound pleasure and value that practitioners find in them; perhaps their discomfort betrays a recognition of something primal and familiar that they themselves long ago repressed.

Jung was fascinated by how the archetypal past continues to exert an influence on the present. He was especially interested in the Middle Ages as a point of reference in his psychology—as the presentation of *The Red Book* as an illuminated manuscript and his extensive studies in alchemy make evident. His comment in *The Red Book*, "I must catch up with a piece of the Middle Ages—within myself," is a thoroughly Gothic utterance.[73] The medieval past was present and active inside him, haunting him. Years later, in his autobiography, he wrote,

> The dead have become ever more distinct for me as the voices of the Unanswered, Unresolved, and Unredeemed; for since the question and demands which my destiny required me to answer did not come to me from outside, they must have come from the inner world. These conversations with the dead formed a kind of prelude to what I had to communicate to the world about the unconscious.[74]

The Gothic theme of a hidden, unredeemed ancestral past that claims the lives of its descendants is overt in the previous passage as is the notion that the dead continue to exert an effect upon the living. The present moment is forever ceding ground to the upswelling of unfinished business from the distant collective past.

Jung's concept of the Shadow is a second significant example of his Gothic style. Because the Shadow is the repository for all the psychic elements that are disowned or unrecognized by the conscious personality, it operates as a force that compensates for our habitual rational thinking in the daytime world. Like a supernatural monster in a Gothic novel, the Shadow can take on a nocturnal irrational character that overtakes us when we are undefended (for example, horrific nightmares when we are asleep). Gothic scholars refer-ence the Shadow without directly acknowledging Jung: "Gothic works invite the audience to acquaint themselves with, and to fear, the shadow that dwells within,"[75] and "Monsters have to be everything the human is not."[76] The Shadow is hidden and unseen by the conscious personality, and its hidden-ness has a relationship with death and mystery. Metaphorically, the Shadow hides in the obscure recesses of the psyche, spaces that correspond to the Gothic settings of catacombs and subterranean passageways. In a similar vein, Jung wrote of "penetrating into the blocked subterranean passages of our own psyches."[77] The Shadow can represent the unlived life or the life we refuse to live. In this regard, it operates in a psychological zone between life and death, similar to the uncanny Gothic monsters who are undead or who are constituted of parts both dead and alive. Many BDSM afficionados have personal experience with the ordeal of confronting the Shadow's unlived life, which can first appear during explorations into sadomasochistic play. Some leather Masters refer to "releasing the Beast" during intense scenes when they inflict the full force of their brutality on their submissives. It can be enormously helpful to practitioners to bear in mind the archetypal nature of such experiences as well as their Gothic pedigree. Often, what occurs in the world of BDSM transcends the personal—the play space is a haunted space populated by foreboding fantasy-images, by medieval costumes and devices, and by the ancestral traditions and protocols of leatherfolk and kinksters who have gone before.

As one of the major inheritors of Jung's legacy, Hillman was also sensitive to the Gothic element in archetypal psychology. His conviction that fantasy precedes reality as the origin of psychological life is compatible with the Gothic premise that our ordered rational existence is continually subverted by irrational mysterious forces that are as real or perhaps more real than we are. Hillman's particular commitment to pathology, degeneration, distor-tion, decomposition, fear, and death as processes of soul further reflects a Gothic sensibility. Finally, he displayed a distinctly Gothic attitude toward innocence, which he regarded as a superficial state of consciousness in need of sophistication through an initiation in the soul's underworld necessities.[78]

Shortly before his death, Hillman had a series of conversations with Jun-gian scholar Sonu Shamdasani regarding *The Red Book*. The interview tran-scripts were published posthumously as *Lament of the Dead*.[79] The following excerpt beautifully communicates the full measure of both Jung's and Hillman's affinity with the Gothic style:

> [*The Red Book*] is so crucial because it opens the door or the mouths of the dead. Jung calls attention to the one deep, missing part of our culture, which is the realm of the dead. The realm not just of your personal ancestors but the realm of the dead, the weight of human history, and what is the *real* repressed, and that is like a great monster eating us from within and from below and sapping our strength as a culture. It's all that's forgotten, and not just forgotten in the past, but that we're living in a world which is alive with the dead, they're around us, they're with us, they *are* us. The figures, the memories, the ghosts, it's all there, and as you get older your borders dissolve, and you realize I am among them, only it has that phrase living and partly living. You're living and partly dead, not dying but partly dead.[80]

The major characteristics of the Gothic are readily identifiable in the previous passage, which also succeeds in translating the Gothic genre into a new language for modern psychology. The subterranean monster is our own denial of death and an inability to recognize the presence of the dead in our psychology and in our current lives. Hillman envisions a cohabitation between their realm and ours, a synthesis of what they carry for us and what we carry for them.

The Sadeian Gothic

Some commentators have considered Sade as a Gothic writer.[81] During his many years of confinement in various asylums, he read and admired Gothic literature. Regarding the notorious novel *The Monk*, Sade wrote, "Let us concur that this kind of fiction, whatever one may think of it, is assuredly not without merit: 'twas the inevitable result of the revolutionary shocks which all Europe has suffered."[82] His comment supports the idea that the violence and slaughter unleashed by the revolution led to the Gothic genre as a necessary compensation for the era's valorization of reason and virtue. Sade's own writings contain many of the familiar characteristics of the Gothic style: isolated medieval castles in dramatic mountainous settings, subterranean dungeons and torture chambers, licentious monks running a secret brothel in the basement of their monastery, virtuous maidens in distress, and duplicitous libertines preying upon the innocent. The monsters of Sade's novels are most often of the human variety (he was more interested in the power of nature rather than the supernatural), and his flair for the obscene and extreme pushed the Gothic genre to the limits of absurdity.[83]

Sade's own incarceration for so many years can itself be seen as an inflection of the Gothic idiom, which links prison, dungeon, and tomb.[84] Michel Foucault has suggested that the French houses of confinement (the historical term for the asylums of Sade's era) locked up "a prodigious reserve of fantasy" (the language of the soul) along with the afflicted inmates.[85] In Sade's writing, particularly gruesome fantasy-images appeared under the conditions of physical incarceration. His stories express what the soul knows about captivity. Moore noted that prison can become a metaphor for a container that could hold the potentially destructive aspects of Eros and, by holding them, turn them "from complex to articulated fantasy."[86] In the modern era, bondage, restriction, and confinement are fundamental elements of BDSM, cherished by practitioners (B is for bondage). Many may not realize that the ropes, chains, padlocks, and cages of BDSM are all vestiges of Sade's own Gothic struggle with incarceration.

Given the innate theatricality of BDSM and kink, it is interesting that Sade was fascinated by theater as an extension of his Gothic sensibility. The Divine Marquis was raised by Jesuits from whom he learned to savor both corporal punishment and theater. During his personal forays into libertinage, he was said to have acted like "an apostate theater director" by ordering his prostitutes to utter sacrilegious lines.[87] Perhaps an unconscious thread of transgressive theatricality has made its way from Sade to modern BDSM role-plays. Although police reports from the time show that Sade was capable of extreme cruelty, his own letters suggest that he regarded his libertine exploits as fantasy play and not as literal abuse or torture. It appears his interest lay—at least in part—in *dramatizing* (not literalizing) the malevolent fantasies that animated his inner life. Perhaps Sade knew instinctually that eroticism is inherently theatrical—a dramatization of the soul's mad passions, what Foucault called "an insane dialogue between love and death in the limitless presumption of appetite."[88] Sade's love of theater continued into his later years when, as a patient at the Charenton asylum, he produced small theatrical productions with the other inmates.

The Theater of Horror

Roughly a century later, the city of Paris was host to a new form of theater, which could be considered a successor to the Marquis's perverse and macabre tastes in entertainment: the Théâtre du Grand-Guignol, otherwise known as the "Theater of Horror."[89] Each evening's program consisted of a variety of short pieces that featured "a peculiar blend of horrific violence, the erotic and fast-paced comedy."[90] The theater's name remains synonymous with "the display of grotesque violence within performance media."[91] The company's formula for intense shock-value theater performed at close quarters to the audience was so successful that the shows ran for 65 years, weathering two world wars, from 1897 to 1962.

The location of the Grand-Guignol in Pigalle near Montmartre was key to its success. The liminality of the experience began as one exited the metro station and walked through the seedy eroticism of the quarter's sex shops and bars. The theater of horror was housed in a converted convent chapel that had been sacked during the Reign of Terror in 1791. Two giant carved angels gazed down at the audience from the rafters. An evening of theatrical grotesquerie in such a setting would surely have aroused the envy of the Divine Marquis. One spectator said, "It felt like plunging into a tomb."[92]

The theater's small stage and the proximity of the performers to the audience created intimacy and intensity, at times oppressive and claustrophobic. The plays were sometimes tailored to the venue's ambience with settings such as prison cells, asylums, and execution yards.[93] Gory, violent crimes described in news reports were often the inspiration for the one-act plays, which included realistic effects, such as dismemberment, evisceration, burning and disfiguration from acid, hypnotism, murder, execution, and medical procedures gone horribly wrong. Elaborate special effects and lighting were intended to make the acts of violence as convincing and visceral as possible. The objective was to make the audience gasp and swoon in horror (the theater's management even hired a medical doctor to be on hand should any audience members experience too much distress). These moments of violence were the genre's "most defining and unique feature," although the violence in question was sometimes more psychological than physical (e.g., the emotional suspense of a prisoner's final anguished minutes before his execution).[94]

It is not clear why commentators on the Gothic tradition have often overlooked the Grand-Guignol in their cultural surveys. The gruesome dramas clearly employed many of the elements of the Gothic idiom: foreboding oppressive settings, cruel leering hero-villains, virtuous maidens in distress, and always the erotic dread of imminent violence or death.

Unlike the classic Gothic style, the Grand-Guignol avoided supernatural themes, largely because the theater had been founded with a commitment to Zola-inspired naturalism fused with popular melodrama. The works were "obsessed with death, sex and insanity" and were "dictated by primal instincts."[95]

The disembodied supernatural phantoms of an earlier age were now being replaced by the terror and savagery embedded in the body and the mind itself. This move toward an inner locus of horror is also evident in *Jekyll and Hyde*, where the ego was presented as the fortress or prison that degenerates and reveals the beast hidden inside.[96] By representing the monster as an inner evil that threatens the stability of our social identity, the Gothic literature of the era corresponded more closely to that of the Grand-Guignol productions.

Julia Kristeva wrote, "as in true theater . . . refuse and corpses show me what I permanently thrust aside in order to live . . . [and] the corpse is the utmost of abjection."[97] The immediacy and physicality of theater have a particular capacity to represent the unspeakable and unknowable psychic detritus of the abject. The Gothic productions of the Grand-Guignol and the modern theatricality of kink and BDSM engage in a psychic reclamation of the abject by dramatizing and representing the refuse and corpses of our inner lives. Perhaps we thrust aside the deepest horrors of the soul in order to live, but there is also evidence that we cannot live without them. We seek to destroy our monsters, but they always return. The Gothic theme of a present that is haunted by the unknown horrors of the past expresses the soul's need to keep us in relationship with what we have thrust aside. The Gothic impulse traveled from the literary page of the eighteenth century to the embodied performance space of the late nineteenth century and subsequently to the erotic enactments of modern BDSM play. Throughout each era, the pulsating horror of the abject and the soul-image of death have been essential features of the idiom.

The fantasy role-play that Moth Meadows shared in which they were the victim of a murder could easily have served as a lurid drama on the stage of the Grand-Guignol in which the evil murderer takes the life of its victim and then partakes of erotic pleasure with the corpse. Death and the corpse are the focus of the role-play. There is also liminality in Moth's state of consciousness, which interrogates the border between life and death. Role-playing a corpse becomes a form of confinement in which the body is the prison for the incarcerated victim who is still conscious. The murderer was the monster, and Moth's recollection of two near-death experiences posited a familiarity with death, which haunted the role-play in a distinctly Gothic style. The only features missing were a foreboding location and a more supernatural intrusion. However, Moth shared that on other occasions, they and their partner have enjoyed elaborate extended role-plays as vampires in various suspenseful scenarios, which further illustrates the extensive influence of the Gothic on modern BDSM play.

Since its emergence in the eighteenth century, the influence of the Gothic idiom on literature, media, and culture has been both extensive and enduring, from early scandalous novels to punk rock music, black leather fashion, and modern slasher movies. The preceding examples have shown that depth psychology and BDSM have both evolved under the effect of the Gothic imagination and the powerful archetypal symbols that have constellated around the genre. Those symbols include themes of transgression, degeneration, corruption, eroticism, violence, vulnerability, madness, incarceration, and liminality. On a deeper psychic stratum, there is the horror of the macabre, the abject, and the primordial archetype of death. What is perhaps most important to the present discussion is that the Gothic, depth psychology, and BDSM all acknowledge that the soul-image of death has an erotic aspect.

Death and Eroticism: Bataille and Laplanche

In the Gothic idiom, the Freudian formulation of Eros versus Thanatos becomes Eros *via* Thanatos.[98] The French philosopher Bataille and the post-Freudian analyst Laplanche developed more in-depth explanations for how psychic representations of death and eroticism operate in tandem. Their ideas enrich our understanding of how the archetypal soul-image of death insinuates itself into the activities and relationships of kink and BDSM.

Bataille, a close associate of Jacques Lacan, was active in the French intellectual world from the 1920s up to his death in 1962. He has been variously described as a mystic, an anthropologist, an author, a pornographer, and a philosopher.[99] His ideas have influenced subsequent generations of prominent philosophers, economists, and intellectuals, including Jacques Derrida, Gilles Deleuze, Jean Baudrillard, Foucault, and Kristeva.[100] His biographer, Michel Surya, has said, "All his life Bataille wrote with his eye on death, thinking of anguish and of ecstasy; inflamed, fascinated by death."[101]

Bataille's[102] book *Erotism* is a provocative treatise on the coextensive relationship between death and sensuality. He maintained that the meaning of eroticism is to be found in "assenting to life up to the point of death."[103] He found inspiration in a passage from Sade, who was one of his major influences: "*There is no better way to know death than to link it with some licentious image.*"[104] By eroticism, he meant any form of sexual enjoyment for purposes other than reproduction. *Erotism* investigates cultural patterns between religious philosophy, anthropology, and psychology to build the case that both eroticism and death offer a hypnotic, vertiginous form of existence beyond our individual lives.

Central to Bataille's argument is the concept of continuous versus discontinuous experiences. When we come into existence as an individual entity, we emerge from a state of wholeness and continuity with the rest of nature. As individuals, we are differentiated from our surroundings, and the continuity of being is lost:

> We are discontinuous beings, individuals who perish in isolation in the midst of an incomprehensible adventure, but we yearn for our lost continuity. We find the state of affairs that binds us to our random and ephemeral individuality hard to bear. Along with our tormenting desire that this evanescent thing should last, there stands our obsession with a primal continuity linking us with everything that is.[105]

Not only do we become separate from and discontinuous with the world outside—there is also discontinuity between us and other beings. Death restores our continuity, our wholeness with the rest of nature. Bataille contended that death and reproduction are equally fascinating because they both address the gulf between continuity and discontinuity and that "this fascination is the dominant element in eroticism."[106]

Bataille imagined that an inflection point occurred in the history of human evolution when early societies began to benefit from the structured collaborative activities that became work. Through work, humans further separated themselves from the rest of the animal kingdom, which resulted in a more vivid discontinuity with the world around them. However, humans have never been completely divorced from the more instinctual, chaotic, and violent world of nature. We live our lives torn between the conflicting inner forces of reason and the violence within us. As human communities found increasing value in work, it became necessary to restrict the destructive effects of violence by developing taboos that prohibited or prescribed potentially disruptive activities. The earliest taboos concerned sexual activity and death. Bataille defined violence broadly as any force that effects the transition from discontinuity back into the continuity of nature or, conversely, from continuity into the discontinuity of differentiated individual existence. For Bataille, the relationship between eroticism and death is innate to the structure of human existence: "We achieve the power to look death in the face and to perceive in death the pathway into unknowable and incomprehensible continuity—that path is the secret of eroticism and eroticism alone can reveal it."[107]

Bataille also recognized the numinous power of the erotic in relation to death. "All eroticism has a sacramental character," he wrote.[108] That is to say, the quest for continuity represents a longing to become one with God or with the divine cosmos. Eroticism, whether physical, emotional, or religious in character, always emanates from a nostalgia for a state of fusion and continuity. Both eroticism and religion are formed by the interplay of prohibition (taboo) and transgression. A transgression "suspends a taboo without suppressing it."[109] A paradoxical interdependent relationship arises between the taboo and its transgression. Because taboos prohibit the incursion of violence into the world of work, Bataille considered them as belonging to the secular and the profane. Transgression, on the other hand, "opens the door into what lies beyond the limits usually observed, but it maintains these limits just the same."[110] Transgressions violate taboos without negating them, which makes possible excursions into ecstatic experiences of continuity and a subsequent successful restoration of secular life upon the return. Therefore, transgressions belong to the numinous world of the sacred. However, the benefits of transgression are contingent upon maintaining the prohibition, which engenders feelings of anguish and terror. Bataille believed that the higher purpose of eroticism was to experience as much as we can bear of the divine continuity of nature, "assenting to life up to the point of death."[111] The power and meaning of eroticism are, therefore, dependent upon its transgressive character and its proximity to the mystery of death.

Erotism offers several philosophical insights that help explain how the archetypal symbol of death affects BDSM and kink. First, there is the significance of nakedness as it relates to death. Regarding eroticism, Bataille said that "stripping naked is the decisive action. Nakedness offers a contrast to self-possession, to discontinuous existence."[112] For BDSM enthusiasts engaged in various forms of authority exchange, stripping is a familiar element of domination and control. The celebrated erotic fiction author John Preston described the ritual of a submissive who stripped naked for his Master each weekend en route from a rural train station to the Master's isolated house: "The removal of each piece of clothing marked the advance of our journey. By the time he pulled into his own driveway I would be naked, sitting beside him in the truck, waiting to begin the weekend."[113] In our nakedness, "bodies open out to a state of continuity through secret channels that give us a feeling of obscenity," Bataille wrote.[114] In BDSM, the naked submissive surrenders his or her self-possession (a portion of one's discontinuous existence) to the authority of the Dominant. Stripping naked is a vivid act of submission to the authority and control of the partner—the submissive becomes continuous in being with the will and desire of the Dominant. In our nakedness, we are vulnerable and defenseless. Bataille wrote, "Stripping naked is seen in civilizations where the act has full significance if not as a simulacrum of the act of killing, at least as an equivalent short of gravity."[115] A corpse is stripped in preparation for burial or cremation. Readers familiar with mythology may recall the Sumerian legend of Inanna, who is forced to strip naked in order to enter the deepest recesses of the Underworld, where her sister, Ereshkigal, strikes her dead with the icy eye of death.[116] Our nakedness reminds us of the fundamental truths of our earthly existence, that archetypal state in which we enter and depart this material world, an elemental condition free of artifice or disguise in which the skin has become the symbolic surface of our mortality.

Two further examples of how Bataille's concept of continuity versus discontinuity applies to BDSM and kink are the practices of degradation and edgeplay. Degradation is a form of transgressive violence that is eroticized in BDSM—violence in the sense that one's loss of personhood effects a transition from discontinuity into continuity with nature through what remains of one's existence beyond the fantasy of the person. In edgeplay, partners experiment with the limits of what the human being can tolerate:

> Though all SM is concerned with boundaries, edgeplay is about negotiating *internal* boundaries—boundaries set within, for, and by

SM community members. In practice . . . these boundaries end up being those between consent and nonconsent, consciousness and unconsciousness, ethical and unethical, temporary versus permanent, and life and death.[117]

Consistent with the internal nature of edgeplay, Bataille wrote, "Human eroticism differs from animal sexuality precisely in this, that it calls inner life into play. In human consciousness eroticism is that within man which calls his being in question."[118] By playing at the edge of what the body, spirit, and mind can tolerate, BDSM practitioners engage in an erotic interrogation, which asks, "What is the nature of my existence, and what are its limits?" The edge between life and death is the ultimate limit that we the living encounter:

> Eroticism opens the way to death. Death opens the way to the denial of our individual lives. Without doing violence to our inner selves, are we able to bear a negation that carries us to the farthest bounds of possibility?[119]

Bataille's formulation corresponds in every detail to the erotic excitement and pleasure that BDSM afficionados find in edgeplay. His insight that the continuity of erotic experience leads to the ecstatic negation of our being helps explain the unique pleasure and meaning that people find in these extreme activities.

A final insight from Bataille that enriches our understanding of the soul's transgressive necessities in kink and BDSM concerns the religious or numinous dimension of the violence that belongs to eroticism. "Whatever is the subject of a prohibition is basically sacred. The taboo gives a negative definition of the sacred object and inspires us with awe on the religious plane."[120] Transgressive acts stimulate feelings of terror, awe, pleasure, and joy, which form the basis of religious feelings toward the subject of the prohibition (the taboo may be cruelty, suffering, degradation, objectification, or some other form of violence, for example). *The taboo creates the rule as well as the temptation to transgress it.* Bataille's formulation explains the numinous feelings that are a source of mystery and fascination for many BDSM enthusiasts. BDSM is inherently transgressive, and the range of activities habitually constellates around cultural taboos in order to violate them. Bataille affirmed that eroticism was based on transgressive violence and religious feeling:

> The inner experience of eroticism demands from the subject a sensitiveness to the anguish at the heart of the taboo no less great than the desire which leads him to infringe it. This is religious sensibility, and it always links desire closely with terror, intense pleasure and anguish.[121]

The convergence of eroticism, transgression, violence, and religious feeling facilitates the ecstatic transit from isolated discontinuity to the experience of continuous wholeness with the divine (i.e., a continuous existence in death). Psychologically speaking, the eroticism at the heart of BDSM and kink has an inherent connection to the transgressive mysteries of violence, religious experience, and death. Perhaps there is no better example of how these powerful forces converge in BDSM than fisting.

Fisting evolved in the gay leather community as one of the most physically intense and emotionally intimate activities of leathersex. The practice transgressed multiple cultural taboos, including penetration of the male body and eroticization of the anus and rectum. For anti-gay activists, fisting exemplified all they found horrific and repugnant about gay sex, while pro-gay activists distanced themselves from the transgressive practice because it weakened their efforts to present a sanitized version of gay life to a larger public.[122] As a form of eroticism, fisting is consistent with Bataille's formulation: the transgressive act breaks down the barriers of discontinuity and releases the Top and bottom into the ecstatic flow of continuous being. As leatherman Joseph Bean wrote:

> With all the longing that often precedes it and the nearly unparalleled intensity of pain and painless sensations that accompany it, it is no wonder that fisting is the route through which many men connect their sexuality and their spirituality. Fisting is a mind-altering experience. It is an opportunity to face and conquer any lingering traces of puritanical bias against sex and pleasure. And, it is a real test of a man's ability to connect on every level with another man, in a trusting intimacy that is not usually

possible with vanilla sex or necessary for most other forms of radical sex.[123]

Consistent with Bataille's definition of violence as that force which precipitates a transition between discontinuity and continuity, fisting is inherently violent. As Bean noted, it is also a convergence of transgression, sexuality, and spirituality resulting in a nearly unparalleled experience of trust and intimacy between the partners.[124] Ethnographer Staci Newmahr has also commented on the unique experience of intimacy that fisting affords: "The view of intimacy as accessing what is innermost approaches literal manifestation in fisting."[125] She noted that the transgressive nature of the activity "obliterates" the boundaries of self and other as well as "social, ethical, and sexual limits."[126] Fisting may provide practitioners access to intensity, intimacy, eroticism, and spirituality, but does it bring the partners into closer relationship with the soul-image of death?

A case can be made that fisting is indeed closely related to the archetype of death if we consider the cultural associations between the rectum and filth. Readers familiar with Jung's[127] studies in alchemy may recall that the symbolic visual language of the medieval treatises frequently linked sexual union (*coniunctio*) with subsequent death, filth, and putrefaction (*mortificatio*).[128] Bataille's assertion that there "exist unmistakable links between excreta, decay and sexuality" further suggests that fisting is a form of eroticism that connects us with the decomposition of our existence, our excreta, and the mysterious forbidden channels through which they pass.[129] The same pattern of eroticism and death gave rise to the popular fisting club in San Francisco in the 1970s, the Catacombs. The name had clear Gothic undertones, which "conjured up images of the underground tombs of ancient Rome, where early Christians fled to escape state persecution and practice their illegal religion in as much privacy as they could find."[130] The name of the club alluded to secrecy, hiddenness, and the necrotic, those archetypal characteristics of death. The anatomy itself corresponds to fantasies of depth and interiority, which is apparent in euphemisms that transfer the anatomical onto the planetary: "the bowels of the earth" and the place "where the sun don't shine." Fisting reaches into the depths of our psychic earth to know the innermost regions of another person.

The psyche habitually maps its fantasies onto our physical being, creating a topography of the soul in our flesh. The rectum carries our fantasy-images of deep interiority, secrecy, and mystery. Let us recall Kristeva's formulation of the abject ("dung signifies the other side of the border, the place where I am not and which permits me to be"):[131] our unwanted parts, our dirtiness, our expulsions, our dregs (the original Latin meaning of *feces*), the most unworthy parts of ourselves. The title of Leo Bersani's[132] essay "Is the Rectum a Grave?" alluded to the deaths of hundreds of thousands of gay men during the early days of the AIDS crisis, when the public response was characterized by silence and contempt due to a collective aversion toward anal sex. The title also described the deeper archetypal projection of the grave and the Underworld onto the nether regions of our anatomy. In a mythic sense, fisting reaches into the Underworld of our being. However, as the activity's name makes clear, the rectum is only one half of what is involved in fisting. The hand and forearm (and, on rare occasions, more) are the other half. A fist is different from a penis or a phallus or a dildo. It carries a different set of fantasy projections, which contribute to the unique archetypal value of fisting. The fist is a symbol of solidarity, power, and violence. The fact that the fist is formed from the hand connects it to other metaphorical qualities, such as reaching, feeling, and handling. All these characteristics are at play in fisting as one partner reaches deep into the hidden depths of the other to experience the wholeness that becomes available through the secret underworld regions, where the unknown and the unmentionable are carried. Fisting is a form of eroticism with a violent character that opens the partners to the divine continuity of nature and the mystery of death.

Jean Laplanche and the Sexual Death Drive

An exploration of how the soul-image of death operates as a psychic force in the activities and relationships of kink and BDSM would be incomplete without considering Freud's formulation of the death drive and the refinements brought to that concept by Laplanche. In *Beyond the Pleasure Principle*, Freud[133] credited Spielrein with anticipating the theory of the death instinct. Spielrein[134] in turn credited Jung with recognizing a proximal psychic relationship between sexuality and death. However, Freud's construction of the death drive is distinct from these forerunners. Professional appraisal of his theory over the years has been ambivalent at best.[135] Freud adopted a popular nineteenth-century fantasy of an original inanimate state of nature from which life materialized. He developed his ideas from the biological hypothesis of a primordial genesis and proposed that there are two competing forces at work in living organisms: one force impels life to build structures of increasing complexity, and the other force draws the organism back toward its origins in inorganic matter. The first force he characterized as *Eros* or libido, and the second force he named *Tod*, the German word for death.[136] The psychic dichotomy Freud mapped out has also been referred to as the life drive versus the death drive. Freud asserted that the potentially problematic and destructive aspects of sexuality— repetition compulsion, sadomasochism, and the paraphilias—could be attributed to the death drive.

The present discussion regards the psychic representation of death as a living symbol of the soul—one that presents a diverse range of potential meanings, including some that are generative and beneficial. From this perspective, death is neither inherently destructive nor exclusively antagonistic toward life. It is more than a force of negation. During the second half of the twentieth century, Laplanche both critiqued and revised Freud's original formulation of the death drive in ways that render it more compatible with Bataille's philosophy and more affirming toward expressions of radical sexuality.

Several of Laplanche's[137] post-Freudian contributions support a richer, more psychological understanding of death in the activities and relationships of kink and BDSM. First, Laplanche dismissed the metaphysical opposition of Eros and Thanatos (the other name sometimes given to the death drive). As noted earlier, there is much of life in death and much of death in life. As two principles that are ostensibly in opposition, they work through each other as much as they work against each other.[138] This cooperation between life and death brings to mind Jung's comment in *The Red Book*: "What you thought was dead and inanimate betrays a secret life and silent, inexorable intent."[139] Laplanche's revision regards the death drive less as a force pulling us toward annihilation and more as a liberator of repressed indecipherable messages stored within the unconscious. For kink and BDSM, the eroticism of the death drive, the excess of pain and pleasure, breaks down the conscious personality and liberates vital energy from the unconscious for a more expansive integrated identity.[140] A second point is that the life and death principles concern the reality of the psyche rather than the reality of biological facts. Sexuality belongs to the life of human fantasy, which is to say the life of the soul, and it is within the fantasy realm of sexuality that the Freudian principles of life and death operate. Therefore, Laplanche insisted that we speak of "the *sexual drives* of death and the *sexual drives* of life."[141] His distinction serves to separate the death drive from the biological processes of physical death, and he restores the impulses to destroy and destabilize to the realm of sexual fantasy. The eroticism of BDSM and kink dramatizes the fantasy-images that Laplanche designated as belonging to the sexual death drives. The restoration of fantasy to the life of the soul brings Laplanche's theory into closer alignment with the ideas of Jung and Hillman, and his formulation is also consistent with Bataille's assertion that eroticism "is assenting to life up to the point of death."[142]

There is an additional point of correspondence between Laplanche and Bataille that is relevant for practitioners of BDSM. Bataille's[143] idea that violence precipitates transitions between continuous and discontinuous modes of existence resembles Laplanche's[144] views on the psychic principles of unbinding and binding, which correspond to the sexual death drives and the sexual life drives, respectively. Bataille and Laplanche agreed that the unbinding of the psyche entails a primal erotic violence that breaks down the coherent (bound) structures of the personality and introduces us to the fantasy material that resides in the deepest layers of the unconscious. Laplanche referred to this region as "a 'pure culture' of alterity," where the deepest residues "are intimately related to sadomasochism."[145] He suggested that our deepest violent impulses to attack and destroy give rise to fantasies of hurting others or ourselves. The anarchic, erotic fantasies that the sexual death drives make available from these deep recesses become the source material for BDSM play. The unbinding properties of such psychic energy serve as catalysts that enable access to the intense joy and terror embedded in indecipherable messages hidden in these regions. Thus, for both Laplanche and Bataille, the transgressive necessities of the soul are intertwined with eroticism, violence, and death as pathways to ecstasy and transformation.

Discussion and Conclusion

Our intent throughout this chapter has been to approach death as a living symbol in the Jungian sense of the term. We have considered death through the ideas of Jung and Hillman, through mythic figures, through the Gothic tradition, and through the work of Bataille and Laplanche. It bears repeating that the significance of the symbol to the Jungian approach can scarcely be overstated. Death as a symbol rises out of the depths as the great hidden keeper of secrets in the unconscious. Because the symbol emerges from the soul, we have referred to death here as a soul-image to emphasize its primordial imaginal-symbolic origins.

"Death is indeed a fearful piece of brutality," Jung wrote.[146] He was referencing both the physical reality of death as a biological process and its wrenching psychological aspects, thus affirming Bataille's[147] assertion that death is the ultimate expression of violence. The symbolic approach to death as a soul-image has offered other dimensions of meaning beyond the existential dread of physical annihilation. A broader range of imaginal possibilities has helped demonstrate how death is deeply embedded in the depth psychological notion of soul. We have seen several examples of how the soul-image of death is present in the world of kink and BDSM. *Death's symbolic presence is arguably the great psychic force that brings radical sexuality into intimate relationship with soul.*

To review briefly, the mythic realm of the classical Greek Underworld has become a root metaphor in the Western imagination for all that is mysterious, hidden, buried, and forbidden. It has also become the imaginal reference point for symbolic journeys of initiation, including those undertaken by BDSM practitioners, especially those seeking spiritual growth through their activities. The Gothic tradition has evolved over two-and-a-half centuries in close relationship with the soul-image of death. It has influenced the metaphorical imagination of depth psychology as well as that of BDSM with its unique ambience of eroticism and suspense. Sade's pedigree as a Gothic writer affirms a particularly strong connection between BDSM and the Gothic idiom. The philosophical writings of Bataille and the post-Freudian insights of Laplanche both provide a stronger theoretical footing for understanding the connection between eroticism and death. Bataille's focus on transgression and taboo draws eroticism into the same sphere as the religious, an aspect that is understandably absent in Laplanche's work. BDSM enthusiasts can take heart that both men regarded the violence of eroticism and its proximity to death as a potential source of renewed vitality and meaning in our lives.

Following the living symbol of death through mythology, literature, culture, philosophy, and psychoanalytic theory has further illuminated how it is present in the world of kink and BDSM. Radical sexuality's fondness for concealment and hiddenness corresponds to the characteristics of the mythic Hades. The sadist's fondness for sleepsacks and manacles reflects the Gothic idiom's predilection for captivity and incarceration, which was further illustrated by Sade's turning his own incarceration into Gothic fiction. The theatrical aspects of kink and BDSM, which include a particular delight in preparing elaborate fantasy role-plays, express the same macabre impulse that gave rise to the Gothic-influenced Grand-Guignol Theater in Paris. Bataille's appreciation for nakedness as a vulnerable state that opens us to the wholeness and continuity of nature and death offers a deeper explanation for the pleasure and excitement that come from BDSM protocols involving stripping and nakedness. Finally, the leathersex practice of fisting involves the Bataillesque elements of transgression, violence, and eroticism that open the partners to the divine continuity of nature and the mystery of death. "To be death-focused is to be soul-focused," Hillman wrote.[148] To adopt a symbolic attitude toward the soul-image of death is to immerse oneself, as Laplanche said, "in 'a pure culture' of alterity."[149] In the activities and relationships of kink and BDSM, the soul enters with numinous intensity through its special relation with death as the ultimate *other*.

Notes

1 Hillman, J. (2007).
2 The National Coalition for Sexual Freedom published a survey in 2015 that had 4,598 BDSM- and kink-identified respondents. 55% of the respondents were women with another 10% identifying as gender queer, transgender, gender fluid, or agender. Among the findings regarding consent violations and physical injuries, the report stated, "96 people experienced an injury that required medical attention (2% of the total survey respondents and 7% of the people who reported a violation of safeword and/or pre-negotiated limits) in conjunction with BDSM activities. Only ½ of one percent of the survey respondents (23 people) reported receiving a serious physical injury that was life-threatening or serious enough to cause dysfunction in an organ or limb. In all, 33 people went to the hospital with injuries due to BDSM activities" (Wright, Stambaugh, & Cox, 2015).
3 Herzog, E. (1960/2000, p. 2).
4 Jung, C. G. (1961/1989, p. 314).
5 Jung, C. G. (1952/1967b).
6 The present discussion differentiates between Jung's insights into death and his own visionary experiences of the dead. Stephani Stephens (2020) has published a thorough treatise on Jung's encounters with the dead as ontologically real exchanges with "discarnates," or souls without bodies (p. 6). Jung recorded several such encounters in *The Red Book* and later in *Memories, Dreams, Reflections*. Jung's regard for the dead as living figures of the soul influenced his approach to active imagination and visionary experiences. The focus of the present discussion concerns the numinous effects of death as a soul-image and its psychological impact on BDSM and kink practitioners.
7 Jung, C. G. (1951/1969, p. 39 [*CW* 9ii, para. 72]).
8 Jung, C. G. (1961/1989, p. 191).
9 Ibid. (pp. 319–320).
10 Hillman, J. (1975/1992, p. 207).
11 Spielrein, S. (1913/1994).

12 Freud, S. (1920/1961).
13 Becker, E. (1973); Yalom, I. D. (2008).
14 Herzog, E. (1960/2000).
15 Becker, E. (1973, p. 6).
16 Jung, C. G. (1951/1968).
17 Ryan, R. E. (2002, p. 23).
18 Jung, C. G. (2009).
19 Jung, C. G. (1933/1955, p. 113).
20 Hillman, J. (1979, p. 30).
21 Moore, T. (1990/2022, p. 3).
22 Roberts, E. M. (2020, p. 41).
23 Herzog, E. (1960/2000, p. 35).
24 Downing, C. (1993, p. 37).
25 Herzog, E. (1960/2000, p. 35).
26 Ibid. (p. 35).
27 Bean, J. (2003a, p. 65).
28 Herzog, E. (1960/2000).
29 Roberts, E. M. (2020, p. 45).
30 Kaldera, R. (2006, p. 5).
31 Herzog, E. (1960/2000, p. 43).
32 Ibid.
33 Ibid. (p. 30).
34 Ibid. (p. 39).
35 Ibid. (p. 49).
36 Hillman, J. (2008).
37 Downing, C. (1993).
38 Graf, F. (2018).
39 Stein, M. (2022).
40 Kaldera, R. (2006).
41 Herzog, E. (1960/2000, p. 7).
42 Kerényi, C. (1951/1980).
43 Kalsched, D. (2013).
44 Hillman, J. (1979, p. 29).
45 Roberts, E. M. (2020).
46 Downing, C. (2007).
47 Becker, E. (1973).
48 Kerényi, C. (1959/1978).
49 Becker, E. (1973, p. 4).
50 Campbell, J. (1949/2008).
51 Bean, J. (1993/2003b, p. 19).
52 Becker, E. (1973).
53 Botting, F. (2014).
54 Ibid.
55 Edmundson, M. (1997, p. 130).
56 Botting, F. (2014).
57 Ibid. (p. 65).
58 Ibid.
59 Becker, E. (1973, p. xv).
60 Herzog, E. (1960/2000).
61 Shelly, M. (1818/2018).
62 Botting, F. (2014).
63 Stoker, B. (1897/2000).
64 Business Insider (2015).

65 Stevenson, R. L. (1886/2019).
66 Wilde, O. (1891/1993).
67 Freud, S. (1919/2003).
68 Jung, C. G. (1951/1969).
69 Botting, F. (2014); Edmundson, M. (1997); Halberstam, J. (1995).
70 Rowland, S. (2002).
71 Freud, S. (1919/2003, p. 1).
72 (Bittanti, n.d.). Similar fetishes to Dollification include Robot Fetishism, Dronification, and Stepfordization.
73 Jung, C. G. (2009, p. 457).
74 Jung, C. G. (1961/1989, pp. 191–192).
75 Edmundson, M. (1997, p. 11).
76 Halberstam, J. (1995, p. 22).
77 Jung, C. G. (1952/1967b, p. x [*CW* 5, para. 1]).
78 See Hillman's (1979) discussion of the rape of Persephone by Hades in *The Dream and the Underworld*.
79 Hillman, J., & Shamdasani, S. (2013).
80 Ibid. (pp. 83–84).
81 Tupper, P. (2018).
82 As cited in Botting (2014, p. 57).
83 Tupper, P. (2018).
84 Moore, T. (1990/2022).
85 Foucault, M. (1961/2009, p. 361).
86 Moore, T. (1990/2022, p. 27).
87 Tupper, P. (2018, p. 66).
88 Foucault, M. (1961/2009, p. 362).
89 Hand, R. J., & Wilson, M. (2002, p. x).
90 Ibid. (p. ix).
91 Ibid. (p. ix).
92 Ibid. (p. 30).
93 Ibid.
94 Ibid. (p. 33).
95 Ibid. (p. 33).
96 Botting, F. (2014).
97 Kristeva, J. (1982, p. 3).
98 The interdependent relationship between Eros and Thanatos is a notion that has been more clearly delineated in the post-Freudian era. See Gerber (2019).
99 Surya, M. (2002).
100 University Libraries (n.d.).
101 Surya, M. (2002, p. 490).
102 Bataille, G. (1957/1986).
103 Ibid. (p. 11).
104 As cited in Ibid. (p. 11, emphasis in original).
105 Ibid. (p. 15).
106 Ibid. (p. 13).
107 Ibid. (p. 24).
108 Ibid. (pp. 15–16).
109 Ibid. (p. 36).
110 Ibid. (p. 67).
111 Ibid. (p. 11).
112 Ibid. (p. 17).
113 Preston, J. (1984, pp. 1–2).
114 Bataille, G. (1957/1986, p. 17).

115 Ibid. (p. 18).
116 Wolkstein, D., & Kramer, S. N. (1983).
117 Newmahr, S. (2011, p. 147, emphasis in original).
118 Bataille, G. (1957/1986, p. 29).
119 Ibid. (p. 24).
120 Ibid. (p. 68).
121 Ibid. (p. 38).
122 Tupper, P. (2018).
123 Bean, J. (2003a, p. 51).
124 Two other writers in the radical sex community deserve mention: Geoff Mains (2002) and Purusha the Androgyne (Thompson, 2004) wrote with courage and vulnerability about similar profound spiritual experiences they accessed through fisting.
125 Newmahr, S. (2011, p. 171).
126 Ibid. (p. 171).
127 Jung, C. G. (1967a).
128 Jungian analyst Marybeth Carter (2022) has written about the positive teleological aspects of the anus as an archetypal image. Despite its associations with the demonic Underworld, referred to as "Satan's Mouth" in the 1600s, the anus also carries connotations of regeneration and discovery essential for psychic growth (p. 91).
129 Bataille, G. (1957/1986, p. 58). The cultural associations discussed in this paragraph concern the body as a psychic representation. With regard to the use of the literal anal canal and rectum in fisting, established practices prescribe meticulous preparation with cleaning and douching the area. As with all extreme radical sex practices, it is recommended to learn how to enjoy fisting from a trusted experienced partner and from reputable training sources (Bean, 2003a).
130 Rubin, G. (1990/2004, p. 119).
131 Kristeva, J. (1982, p. 3).
132 Bersani, L. (2010).
133 Freud, S. (1920/1961).
134 Spielrein, S. (1913/1994).
135 Kerr, J. (1993).
136 Although the name of the mythic Greek figure Thanatos is sometimes assigned to Freud's theory of the death instinct, Freud himself did not use it in his writings (Laplanche & Pontalis, 1973).
137 Laplanche, J. (2015).
138 Deleuze, G. (1967/1989) expressed a similar opinion that Eros and Thanatos (death) are forever combined.
139 Jung, C. G. (2009, p. 260).
140 Saketopoulou, A. (2014).
141 Laplanche, J. (2015, p. 170, emphasis in original).
142 Bataille, G. (1957/1986, p. 11).
143 Ibid.
144 Laplanche, J. (2015).
145 Ibid. (p. 174).
146 Jung, C. G. (1961/1989, p. 314).
147 Bataille, G. (1957/1986).
148 Hillman, J. (1975/1992, p. 273).
149 Laplanche, J. (2015, p. 174).

References

Bataille, G. (1986). *Erotism, death and sensuality* (M. Dalwood, Trans.). City Lights Books. (Original work published 1957)

Bean, J. W. (2003a). *Leathersex: A guide for the curious outsider and the serious player* (2nd ed.). Daedalus.

Bean, J. W. (2003b). The editor's introduction to the ties that bind. In J. W. Bean (Ed.), *Ties that bind* (2nd ed., pp. 19–22). Daedulus.

Becker, E. (1973). *The denial of death*. Simon & Schuster.

Bersani, L. (2010). *Is the rectum a grave? And other essays*. The University of Chicago Press.

Bittanti, M. (n.d.). *Prolegomena: Good luck*. Retrieved September 29, 2022, from https://cite-seerx.ist.psu.edu/viewdoc/download?doi=10.1.1.118.3867&rep=rep1&type=pdf

Botting, F. (2014). *Gothic* (2nd ed.). Routledge.

Business Insider (2015, February 17). *'Fifty Shades of Grey' started out as 'Twilight' fan fiction before becoming an international phenomenon.* https://www.businessinsider.com/fifty-shades-of-grey-started-out-as-twilight-fan-fiction-2015-2

Campbell, J. (2008). *The hero with a thousand faces* (3rd ed.). New World Library.

Carter, M. (2022). Satan's mouth or font of magic, what is it about the anus? *Jung Journal, 16*(3), 86–98. https://doi.org/10.1080/19342039.2022.2088993

Deleuze, G. (1989). *Masochism* (J. McNeil, Trans.). Zone Books. (Original work published 1967)

Downing, C. (1993). *Gods in our midst*. Crossroad.

Downing, C. (2007). *The goddess: Mythological images of the feminine*. iUniverse.

Edmundson, M. (1997). *Nightmare on Main Street: Angels, sadomasochism, and the culture of gothic*. Harvard University Press.

Foucault, M. (2009). *History of madness* (J. Murphy & J. Khalfa, Trans.; J. Khalfa, Ed.). Routledge.

Freud, S. (1961). *Beyond the pleasure principle* (J. Strachey, Trans.; J. Strachey, Ed.). W. W. Norton & Company. (Original work published 1920)

Freud, S. (2003). *The uncanny* (D. McLintock, Trans.). Penguin. (Original work published 1919)

Gerber, T. (2019, February). Eros and Thanatos: Freud's two fundamental drives. *Epoché, 20*. https://epochemagazine.org/20/eros-and-thanatos-freuds-two-fundamental-drives/

Graf, F. (2018). Travels to beyond: A guide. In G. Ekroth & I. Nilsson (Eds.), *Round trip to Hades in the Eastern Mediterranean tradition* (pp. 11–36). Brill.

Halberstam, J. (1995). *Skin shows: Gothic horror and the technology of monsters*. Duke University Press.

Hand, R. J., & Wilson, M. (2002). *Grand-Guignol: The French theater of horror*. University of Exeter Press.

Herzog, E. (2000). *Psyche and death* (D. Cox & E. Rolfe, Trans.; C. L. Sebrell, Ed.). Spring. (Original work published 1960)

Hillman, J. (1979). *The dream and the underworld*. HarperPerennial.

Hillman, J. (1992). *Re-visioning psychology*. HarperPerennial. (Original work published 1975)

Hillman, J. (2007). Dionysus in Jung's writing. In *Mythic figures: Uniform edition of the writings of James Hillman* (Vol. 6.1, pp. 15–30). Spring Publications.

Hillman, J. (2008). You dirty dog! In *Uniform edition of the writings of James Hillman* (Vol. 9, pp. 150–160). Spring.

Hillman, J., & Shamdasani, S. (2013). *Lament of the dead, psychology after Jung's Red Book*. W. W. Norton.

Jung, C. G. (1955). *Modern man in search of a soul* (W. S. Dell & C. F. Baynes, Trans.). Harcourt. (Original work published 1933)

Jung, C. G. (1967a). *Alchemical studies* (R. F. C. Hull, Trans.). In H. Read et al. (Eds.), *The collected works of C. G. Jung* (Vol. 13). Princeton University Press.

Jung, C. G. (1967b). Symbols of transformation: An analysis of the prelude to a case of schizophrenia (R. F. C. Hull, Trans.). In H. Read et al. (Eds.), *The collected works of C. G. Jung* (Vol. 5, 2nd ed.). Princeton University Press. (Original work published 1952)

Jung, C. G. (1968). The psychology of the child archetype (R. F. C. Hull, Trans.). In H. Read et al. (Eds.), *The collected works of C. G. Jung* (Vol. 9i, 2nd ed., pp. 151–181). Princeton University Press. (Original work published 1951)

Jung, C. G. (1969). Aion (R. F. C. Hull, Trans.). In H. Read et al. (Eds.), *The collected works of C. G. Jung* (Vol. 9ii, 2nd ed.). Princeton University Press. (Original work published 1951)

Jung, C. G. (1989). *Memories, dreams, reflections* (R. Winston & C. Winston, Trans.; A. Jaffé, Ed.). Vintage Books. (Original work published 1961)

Jung, C. G. (2009). *The red book, Liber Novus: A reader's edition* (M. Kyburz, J. Peck, & S. Shamdasani, Trans.; S. Shamdasani, Ed.). W. W. Norton.

Kaldera, R. (2006). *Dark moon rising: Pagan BDSM and the ordeal path.* Asphodel.

Kalsched, D. (2013). *Trauma and the soul.* Routledge.

Kerényi, C. (1978). *The heroes of the Greeks* (H. L. Rose, Trans.). Thames and Hudson. (Original work published 1959)

Kerényi, C. (1980). *The gods of the Greeks* (N. Cameron, Trans.). Thames and Hudson. (Original work published 1951)

Kerr, J. (1993). *A most dangerous method: The story of Jung, Freud, and Sabina Spielrein.* Vintage Books.

Kristeva, J. (1982). *Powers of horror, an essay on abjection* (L. S. Roudiez, Trans.). Columbia University Press.

Laplanche, J. (2015). *Between seduction and inspiration: Man* (J. Mehlman, Trans.). The Unconscious in Translation. (Original work published in 1999)

Laplanche, J., & Pontalis, J. B. (1973). *The language of psycho-analysis* (D. Nicholson-Smith, Trans.). Routledge.

Mains, G. (2002). *Urban aboriginals* (3rd ed.). Daedalus.

Moore, T. (2022). *Dark Eros, curing the sadomasochism in everyday life* (3rd ed., revised). Spring. (Original work published 1990)

Newmahr, S. (2011). *Playing on the edge: Sadomasochism, risk, and intimacy.* Indiana University Press.

Preston, J. (1984). *I once had a master.* Cleis.

Roberts, E. M. (2020). *Underworld gods in ancient Greek religion.* Routledge.

Rowland, S. (2002). *Jung: A feminist revision.* Polity.

Rubin, G. (2004). The Catacombs: A temple of the butthole. In M. Thompson (Ed.), *Leatherfolk: Radical sex, people, politics, and practice* (3rd ed., pp. 119–141). Daedalus. (Original work published in 1990)

Ryan, R. E. (2002). *Shamanism and the psychology of C. G. Jung.* Vega.

Saketopoulou, A. (2014). To suffer pleasure: The shattering of the ego as the psychic labor of perverse sexuality. *Studies in Gender and Sexuality, 15*(4), 254–268.

Shelly, M. (2018). *Frankenstein: The 1818 text.* Penguin Books. (Original work published 1818)

Spielrein, S. (1994). Destruction as the cause of coming into being. *Journal of Analytical Psychology, 39*(2), 155–186. https://doi.org/10.1111/j.1465-5922.1994.00155.x (Original work published 1913).

Stein, M. (2022). *The mystery of transformation.* Chiron.

Stephens, S. (2020). *C. G. Jung and the dead: Visions, active imagination and the unconscious terrain.* Routledge.

Stevenson, R. L. (2019). *The strange case of Dr. Jekyll and Mr. Hyde.* Keynote. (Original work published 1886)

Stoker, B. (2000). *Dracula.* Dover. (Original work published 1897)

Surya, M. (2002). *Georges Bataille: An intellectual biography* (K. Fijalkowski & M. Richardson, Trans.). Verso.

Thompson, M. (2004). Erotic ecstasy: An interview with Purusha the Androgyne. In M. Thompson (Ed.), *Leatherfolk: Radical sex, people, politics, and practice* (3rd ed., pp. 284–293). Daedalus.

Tupper, P. (2018). *A lover's pinch, a cultural history of sadomasochism*. Rowman and Littlefield.

University Libraries. (n.d.). Georges Bataille (1897–1962): Life and letters. In *Research Guides*. University at Buffalo. Retrieved September 27, 2022, from https://research.lib. buffalo.edu/bataille

Wilde, O. (1993). *The picture of Dorian Gray*. Dover. (Original work published 1891)

Wolkstein, D., & Kramer, S. N. (1983). *Inanna: Queen of heaven and earth*. Harper & Row.

Wright, S., Stambaugh, R. J., & Cox, D. (2015). Consent violations survey tech report. *National Coalition for Sexual Freedom*. https://secureservercdn.net/198.71.233.216/9x-j.1d5.myftpupload.com/wp-content/uploads/2019/12/Consent-Violations-Survey.pdf

Yalom, I. D. (2008). *Staring at the sun*. Piatkus.

EPILOGUE
THE FINAL WORD IS LOVE

Our exploration of soul's presence in the activities and relationships of kink and BDSM draws to a close. We have discovered traces of soul in the transgressive aspects of BDSM, which lie at the heart of radical sexuality's intense pleasure and excitement. Georges Bataille's[1] claim that transgression brings eroticism into close relationship with death helps explain in part BDSM's intimate connection to the mythic Underworld. Soul comes into the world through darkness, through coldness, through the cruel and the twisted, through debauchery and perversion, and through the sacrifice of innocence. Soul also comes into the world through love, and it is the mystery of love that concludes our journey.

The dictionary tells us that love is "a strong feeling of affection and concern toward another person," through kinship, close friendship, or sexual attraction.[2] This definition is a reasonable starting place and yet wholly unsatisfactory. It misses the quality of poetic expansion that love brings to life. It misses the ecstatic longing, the mystery, and the madness too. It is the irrational aspect of love that brings it into relationship with soul. Love, like soul as Hillman[3] defined it, is a deliberately ambiguous concept—its multifaceted power stems from this ambiguity. We pretend to understand it as a primordial force that is living through us, but at root, it is a mystery.

And love's emergence both as a subjective feeling and as an archetypal force in BDSM and kink is indeed a mystery. Some might find it counterintuitive to imagine that sadomasochistic relationships can also be loving

 DOI: 10.4324/9781003223597-11

ones. Yet many in the kink and BDSM communities testify to participating in deeply committed relationships of passion and intimacy precisely because they are engaged in the transgressive activities of authority imbalance and sensation play. Perhaps some within those communities would themselves avoid the word love because of its complex and ambiguous nature. However, the interviews featured in Chapter 6 with Mister Blue and BlueFrost and with Master Jess and boi Kaseem exemplify how fulfilling and intimate such committed relationships can be. Researchers who have studied BDSM and kink agree that "Through play SM participants construct deep feelings of intimate connection"[4] and that "Healthy BDSM relationships demonstrate trust, caring, and an ongoing commitment to mutual growth, which are all valid indicators of any positive mainstream relationship."[5] But any mention of the potential for the mystery of love to emerge from BDSM's transgressive margins is notably absent. To ignore love's presence is to ignore how deeply soul and numinosity enter into these relationships.

Indeed, participants themselves speak of the deep intimacy that arises from the chaotic margins of BDSM. When someone decides to enter this world, it can be a tremendous relief to find a partner who shares similar enthusiasms and compatible feelings of fulfillment and completion by engaging in these extreme activities and dynamics. Play partners develop a craft together as an attuned dyad. It requires skill on multiple levels as well as a finely calibrated awareness for what the other desires or needs (e.g., to focus on service and care rather than on submission and endurance, to be tested and pushed or to be allowed time to relax into pain, to urge a partner toward breakdown or to demand tenacity, to be held and praised or to be verbally or physically degraded).

The following description from a BDSM Top illustrates such a mysterious shared experience of deep intimacy:

> Through a singletail [whip], she shook, she gasped, she moaned, she cried, she screamed. And in all that shaking the real person came to view. The rawness of humanity came to vision . . . I looked into her eyes and could see everything. There was connection. There was oneness. There was the very essence of being. She was alive, and I was the conduit.[6]

An encounter of such intensity and naked authenticity requires two people who are unafraid to meet each other in the essence of being. It is a numinous experience of eroticism that disrupts the couple's perception of themselves as separate discontinuous persons, and it is inherently violent, "assenting to life up to the point of death."[7]

It should, therefore, not be surprising that in encounters of such vulnerability and trust, love sometimes emerges. The love in question is suffused with paradox: violence and tenderness, cruelty and affection, degradation and respect, dread and desire, presence and oblivion. It is a form of love born in the mysterious unknown of the Underworld. The paradoxical irrational nature of this mystery is best expressed indirectly through myth and perhaps most powerfully by the classical myths surrounding the god Eros, who personified the primordial origins of eroticism.

Eros as a Primordial Force

The classical world had several different myths about Eros. All are "true": they complement rather than replace one another. The earliest appears in Hesiod's[8] *Theogony*, the mythic account of the coming into being of not just the divine cosmos but also of the physical world. To begin with, there is Chaos, which is not disorder, or confusion, but most literally a yawn, an opening, a nothingness that signifies possibility. Eros and Gaia, Desire and Earth, are the first entities to emerge out of the yawning void of Chaos. Eros is a cosmic primordial force—divine and numinous—not as a personified figure capable of love himself.

Without Eros, there would be no movement, no growth, no development. Placed at the beginning of creation, he is imagined as the force that generates the subsequent union of divine powers.

> Eros is the connecting principle, not so much in the sense of going from place to place, realm to realm (as does Hermes), but in the sense of bringing together in union at any level realms that otherwise are apart, separate, disconnected, and unrelated.[9]

The emergence of Eros out of Chaos helps explain the archetypal relationship between eroticism and death. As a mythic symbol of love, Eros is familiar with the depths of oblivion, yet he is also able to connect, relate, and unify, which make him the great symbol-maker.[10] Eros is the figure that holds the tension of opposing forces: pleasure and suffering, creativity and destruction, domination and submission, bondage and liberation, beast and lover, life and death. From the chaos and tension of opposition, Eros produces the living symbols of transformation.

Eros brings together Gaia and Ouranos, Earth and Sky, and all subsequent couplings, couplings that are creative and reproductive although not necessarily harmonious. Gaia becomes so resentful of Ouranos's attempts to control her that she persuades her youngest son to castrate her husband. When the severed genitals are tossed into the sea, full-grown Aphrodite, goddess of sensual love, of the feeling side of love, of a more personal kind of loving, emerges from the waters. The energy that she represents long predates the much more anthropomorphic Zeus-dominated Olympian gods with whom we are more familiar. In Hesiod,[11] when she first steps on earth, crocuses and violets grow where her feet have trod. In the *Homeric Hymn to Aphrodite*,[12] her very presence awakens desire.

Homer's Aphrodite is a very humanlike figure, the child of Zeus and his first wife, Dione, associated primarily with the kind of passionate, obsessive love that provokes strife and enmity. In Homer, Eros is now a personified figure, the son of Aphrodite, but his power is also reduced. He is little more than a pawn his mother uses to advance her own meddlesome intrigues. But his parentage is important; he is the child of Aphrodite and Ares, the god of war, of aggression, a death-bringer (a figure well-acquainted with the primal violence of BDSM). Once again, in BDSM so also in myth, we find a connection between love and chaos, love and death.

In Plato's[13] *Symposium*, we see for the first time a connection between Eros and soul (Eros and psyche) in reference to a higher form of love. But there is still no personification of psyche—no story of a personal relation between Eros and Psyche. For that, we have to wait for a story invented by a Latin writer, Apuleius, in the second century CE, in which for the first time, Psyche is personified as a human female.

Psyche and Eros

Russell Lockhart[14] has referred to the tale of Psyche and Eros as the great myth of relationship. Among its best-known versions is the one Erich Neumann[15] provided for his psychological commentary on the story. Neumann transformed the myth into a deep meditation on the relation between love and the soul.

As James Hillman[16] said, a story about soul, about psyche, must be a story about love. However, "neither psyche nor eros can be identified with our [own] souls and our [own] loving."[17] These mythic figures transcend our personal circumstances—they are archetypal energies that we engage imaginally. The two together form a *syzygy*: Psyche/Eros. The story of Psyche is, must be, a story about Eros.

As the story begins, we learn that Psyche is a wondrously beautiful maiden. When her father petitions the oracle of Apollo to find her a husband, the instruction is to prepare Psyche for a funeral ritual to offer her to a divine being. The myth supports Bataille's[18] assertion that the experience of eroticism (Eros) is always filled with intimations of death. Unbeknownst to Psyche, she is regarded as a contemptible rival by the beautiful Aphrodite, the goddess of love. Aphrodite instructs her son, Eros, to destroy the maiden by pairing her with a wretched and vile suitor. However, the young god finds himself smitten, and he transports Psyche to a secret enchanted palace, where he consorts with her only in the obscure darkness of night to conceal his identity. Neumann[19] regards this episode in the tale as representing an undifferentiated state of psychic merger in which two lovers are united yet strangers to each other. Although Psyche lives in luxury, she is in fact a prisoner in her enchanted palace. Eventually, Psyche's jealous sisters convince her to expose the identity of her mystery lover under the pretext that he might be a hideous predatory monster. When Psyche approaches the sleeping Eros with a lamp in one hand and a knife to slay her captor in the other, she inadvertently pricks her finger on one of the fated arrows of the god, and she is hopelessly smitten with him. Having been revealed, Eros retreats to the abode of his mother, Aphrodite, who, in utter fury, separates the lovers. Desperate to recover her beloved, Psyche surrenders herself to Aphrodite. In an episode with vivid sadomasochistic elements, the goddess of love turns her rival over to Trouble and Sorrow, who torment her with whips and other devices of torture. In order to reunite with her beloved, Psyche must carry out a series of impossible tasks set forth by Aphrodite, who intends to lead the maiden toward her own destruction. In BDSM, when a submissive is forced to perform seemingly impossible tasks in the hopes of earning a longed-for reward, the dilemma is called predicament play. The same sadomasochistic pattern is at work between Aphrodite and Psyche. Consistent with the mythic theme of eroticism and death, Psyche's final challenge is to obtain a Beauty Box from Persephone, the Queen of the Underworld. She is almost successful at completing the task, but on her return to the land of the living, she disobeys the stern instruction not to open the divine casket. Hoping to steal a small bit of beauty for herself, she is overcome by a deathly slumber. Having escaped from his mother, Eros rescues Psyche, and in the end, the couple is granted a divine marriage with the gods on Mount Olympus. Their union produces a child known as *Voluptas*, or Pleasure.

This story beautifully demonstrates that erotic love has a necessity to be with soul (Psyche). "I discover that *wherever* eros goes, something psychological is happening, and that wherever psyche lives, eros will inevitably constellate."[20] *Eroticism, therefore, always has a psychological aspect.* The intimate relationship between *erotic love* and soul creates true intimacy in all relationships:

> One tells all at great risk; one exposes one's true reality, reveals it to the other in all its horror and delight, the full range. No barriers, no walls, no hidden prisons for secrets. It is holding nothing back; it is nakedness to another. If one can do that in relationship, Eros will be there.[21]

In erotic love, we come to know the innermost depths of another person's subjective truth. "I looked into her eyes and could see everything. There was connection. There was oneness. There was the very essence of being."[22] The logos of Psyche in union with Eros compels the telling of the deepest necessities. The telling is not always with words—Psyche also speaks through gesture, breath, gaze, pulse, tears, and inner vision. We have also seen that she speaks through slaps and blows, gasps and cries, restriction and confinement, and the other countless ecstasies of torment and subjugation. The telling itself is a transgression—an erotic boundary-crossing between contrasting realms of inner and outer.

When erotic love emerges through the chaotic edge of BDSM, it summons the mysterious intimacy of Psyche and Eros, who speak each other's innermost truths. In such instances, the experience of kink and BDSM can feel like an initiation into soul. Hillman wrote, "*Initiation as a transformation of consciousness about life involves necessarily a transformation of consciousness about sexuality.*"[23] When we recognize that eroticism is also psychological and that psychology is also erotic, a new form of consciousness is born. We discover that sexuality is about more than genital pleasure, coital union, and orgasmic release. Sexuality is also about curiosity, desire, overwhelm, suffering, dread, and ambivalence. When Psyche joins Eros, the birth of pleasure signals a new form of sexual consciousness that can integrate the transgressive necessities of the soul.

The tale of Psyche and Eros is a myth about love, suffering, degradation, cruelty, power, submission, transgression, eroticism, and death. Thematically, the story constellates the same archetypal forces that have emerged through our exploration of the soul's presence in the activities and relationships of kink and BDSM. The union of Psyche and Eros is a particularly apt image to invoke at the conclusion of our journey. In contrast to the dictionary definition of love, we find the erotic love of Psyche and Eros to be irrational, inherently chaotic, secretive, covetous, and elusive. Erotic love is also potentially deadly, perhaps more so in its greatest necessity. With its churning primordial energy, it is the love that emerges from the chaos of BDSM ordeals.

Love in Persephone's Realm

The final challenge Aphrodite gives Psyche is to journey to Hades to bring back to the goddess a small Beauty Box from Persephone, the Queen of the Underworld. This task suggests, of course, that there is a kind of beauty familiar to the Underworld goddess that Aphrodite envies. Hillman (1960/1972) reflected on the deeper implications of this quest for underworld beauty:

> The ultimate beauty of psyche is that which even Aphrodite does not have and which must come from Persephone, who is Queen over the dead souls and whose name means "bringer of destruction." The Box of Beauty which Psyche must fetch as her last task refers to an underworld beauty that can never be seen with the senses. It is the beauty of the knowledge of death and of the effects of death upon all other beauty that does not contain this knowledge. Psyche must "die" herself in order to experience the reality of this beauty, a death different from her suicidal attempts. This would be the ultimate task of soul-making and its beauty: the incorporation of destruction into the flesh and skin,

embalmed in life, the visible transfigured by the invisibility of Hades' kingdom, anointing the psyche by the killing experience of its personal mortality.[24]

To understand the particular beauty, the particular power, that belongs to Persephone, we must look at her own story of struggle, suffering, and erotic transformation. She was not always a powerful divine sovereign. Her tale is intimately acquainted with the same transgressive necessities that emerge thematically in BDSM and kink.

The most important ancient source for Persephone's myth is the Homeric *Hymn to Demeter*.[25] There we learn that Persephone is a divine maiden, daughter of Demeter and Zeus. Hades desires a consort and queen, and one day, as the maiden plucks a beautiful narcissus blossom from the earth, she, too, is plucked by Hades, who erupts from the Underworld in a golden chariot and carries her back into the depths. Much of the subsequent *Hymn* concerns the distraught suffering of Demeter, who searches everywhere for her daughter and who allows the plants and fruits of the Earth to wither. Little is said in the *Hymn* of what happens to Persephone as a new arrival in the Underworld, but in a pivotal episode, she eats a few pomegranate seeds, which secures her place as an inhabitant of Hades's world. The living things of the upperworld are doomed unless Demeter can recover her lost daughter, so a compromise is reached in which Persephone spends a third of each year with her husband in the Underworld and the other two-thirds above ground with her mother.

Whereas Psyche and Eros express the archetypal aspect of love in intimate relationship, Persephone draws us toward a deeper appreciation for the love of primordial mysteries—the archetypal love for the unknowns of the soul. Often, interpretations of Persephone's story emphasize the mother-daughter bond and its inevitable metamorphosis in which a "maiden" grows into a mature woman, but such interpretations view the myth from the maternal perspective of bereft Demeter.[26] Persephone, in her more somber aspect as underworld divinity, offers a different perspective to anyone who seeks to understand the complex archetypal relationship between transgression, transformation, authority, and love. "Persephone is regarded as the secret, hidden, ineffable goddess, related to things beyond, not even to be named except as Thea. She is, as Freud called her, the silent goddess of death."[27] It may well be that no mythic figure offers deeper wisdom and insight for the practitioners of kink and BDSM.

The theme of transgression, so essential to the world of BDSM, is prevalent in Persephone's tale. There are the more overt examples, such as the abduction itself, which is often referred to as a rape, but her seizure is also an initiation into sexual experience. Christine Downing[28] has noted the overt symbolism of Persephone's plucking the virginal flower, Hades's phallic eruption from the depths, and the womb-like red of the underworld pomegranate as representations of Persephone's sexual initiation. The *Hymn* says that the maiden herself is a flower.[29] Ellie Mackin Roberts[30] regarded flowers as having a fundamentally transgressive nature because they grow between the worlds of Demeter and Hades—blossoms in the upperworld, seeds and roots hidden in the lower. Her insight offers a more rudimentary vision of transgression that recalls its fundamental characteristic of crossing borders and traversing the space between disparate states or identities. Through her ordeal, Persephone gains a unique and powerful gift to move with the seasons from one dimension of her being to another. Jungian scholar Elizabeth Nelson wrote, "Having suffered and returned, Persephone's freedom of movement—a genuine and remarkable kind of power—now exceeds even that of her dread mother Demeter, her formidable husband Hades, and every other god except Hermes the messenger."[31] Persephone's gift offers valuable support to BDSM practitioners, who must learn to navigate between the worlds of transgressive belonging in authority imbalance and impact play and other worlds they inhabit as professionals and family members.

Regarding the pomegranate, different versions of the myth assign varying levels of agency to Persephone, which has led to speculation that she may have made a conscious choice to eat the seeds. The transgressive act of tasting the forbidden fruit that transforms her from maiden to queen is itself a psychological necessity. Persephone cannot remain a maiden, innocent and virginal. By transgressing, she gains authority and power. Her inviolability as a maiden takes on a deeper dimension of insight: "the quintessence of bottomless depth in which arriving is simply not possible because there is no final understanding, only an endless cascade of deeper and deeper understandings."[32] Persephone reveals the intimate relationship between transgression and individuation that is so deeply implicated in the activities and relationships of BDSM. Through transgression, we are transformed, and we become more deeply aligned with the archetypal forces that shape our unique being. We come closer to "the realization of [our] individual and unique wholeness."[33] Queen Persephone is the personification of the individuation process in its shadowy and destructive aspect. She is in fact a goddess of individuation through transgression.

Persephone introduces a love that is different from the relational love of Psyche and Eros. Hers is a love for the depths and the invisibles of the Underworld. Downing has written, "I now understand Hades' realm, the underworld, the depths, to mean the realm of souls rather than of egos, the realm where experience is perceived symbolically."[34] Downing came to love the mystery and the richness of this realm through Persephone. Without question, there is a relational kind of love between Persephone and Hades. He brought her to her deep subjective truth, and she brought to him a gentle dignity and wisdom that his somber world previously lacked. However, it is Persephone's devotion to her underworld kingdom, the place where all soul-images find their ultimate expression and their final destination, that makes her love unique.

Persephone teaches us to love the beauty of the Underworld and its transgressive necessities. In kink and BDSM, practitioners find beauty in unexpected places—it is an irrational beauty that defies conventional standards. There is beauty in a bruise and its deeper erotic meaning ("I surrendered, I descended, I belonged"); a cry, a scream, a sob caught in the throat can all be beautiful in their ambiguous fusion of pain and pleasure; a seductive oscillation between pinching, slapping, spanking, caressing, and the sudden withdrawal of contact that can lead one into complete stillness can be beautiful; and holding the stern and steadfast gaze of a partner in unwavering care and attunement can be a timeless descent into the beauty of Queen Persephone's mysterious world. When one adopts the mindset of an initiate, a transgressive experience of suffering, degradation, confusion, disorientation, or breakdown can be transforming and beautiful. It can be equally profound and beautiful to serve as the conduit for such experiences.

The intimacy that we discover through Persephonic love is the interiority of the soul itself. The Queen of the Underworld knows the transgressive path that leads from the upperworld of daytime concerns down and inward to the secret, hidden places, where the restrictions of ego identity must be surrendered to encounter the soul-images that dwell below. "In Hades' realm *psyché* alone exists; all other standpoints are dissolved."[35] Love in Persephone's realm is a love for the absolute otherness of the autonomous image liberated from all the utilitarian stratagems we employ that treat images as objects for our consumption and advantage. *Persephone teaches us to love the inner life of the image in its deep mysterious alterity.* In kink and BDSM, the naked, raw truth that practitioners discover in a scene is the truth of what lives as "the Other" beneath the surface identities of ego and persona. Intimacy refers to the innermost.[36] Sometimes the intimacy of kink and BDSM transcends the personal—it touches the inner life of "the Other," appearing as animated fantasy-image (e.g., the archetypal figures of Master, slave, pup, penitent, or mystic). One learns to love the reality that lives inside these figures. One learns to love as Persephone does.

Every life experience of intensity and meaning is animated by an archetypal figure from the depths, a figure that guides and forms the contours of the experience. As we conclude our journey, honor is due the archetypal presence of Persephone. Perhaps all along, she has been leading, and we have been following. She knows the power of play to de-literalize material reality and restore imaginal possibilities; she knows the value and necessity of suffering and degradation for true psychological transformation; as the bringer of destruction, she knows the potential of intentional malice and cruelty to break lives asunder; as one who journeys between worlds, she knows the paths of ecstasy; and as Queen of the Underworld, she is intimately acquainted with the relationship between eroticism, chaos, and death. If we allow a bit of poetic reverie, we can find her deep in the imagination in the abysmal palace of Hades. Roaming the shadowy corridors from dungeon to boudoir, she watches over the pristine soul-images that source the world of kink and BDSM. "Fantasy first, then reality," she whispers. The sweet, pungent taste of pomegranate still lingers on her sovereign lips. She enters the throne room. Here is the chain of transgressive necessity in her hand. And here is something shimmering in the obscure half-light, barely visible. We begin to trace the silhouette of her wondrous crown.

Notes

1 Bataille, G. (1957/1986).
2 American Heritage (2011, p. 1039).
3 Hillman, J. (1975/1992).
4 Newmahr, S. (2011, p. 168).
5 Shahbaz, C., & Chirinos, P. (2017, p. 15).

6 As cited in Newmahr, S. (2011, p. 173).
7 Bataille, G. (1957/1986, p. 11).
8 Hesiod (1988).
9 Lockhart, R. (1983, p. 126).
10 Hillman, J. (1960/1972); Lockhart, R. (1983).
11 Hesiod (1988).
12 Homer (2003).
13 Plato (1999).
14 Lockhart, R. (1983).
15 Neumann, E. (1956).
16 Hillman, J. (1960/1972).
17 Ibid. (p. 105).
18 Bataille, G. (1957/1986).
19 Neumann, E. (1956).
20 Hillman, J. (1960/1972, p. 91, emphasis in original).
21 Lockhart, R. (1983, p. 128).
22 As cited in Newmahr, S. (2011, p. 173).
23 Hillman, J. (1960/1972, pp. 63–64, emphasis in original).
24 Ibid. (p. 102).
25 Foley, H. (1994).
26 Downing, C. (1981/2007).
27 Ibid. (p. 44).
28 Ibid.
29 Foley, H. (1994).
30 Roberts, E. M. (2020).
31 Nelson, E. E. (2016, p. 15).
32 Ibid. (p. 8).
33 Ibid. (p. 8).
34 Downing, C. (1981/2007, p. 45).
35 Hillman, J. (1975/1992, p. 207).
36 Newmahr, S. (2011).

References

American Heritage. (2011). Love. In J. P. Pickett (Ed.), *American Heritage dictionary of the English language* (5th ed., p. 1039). Houghton Mifflin Harcourt.

Bataille, G. (1986). *Erotism, death and sensuality* (M. Dalwood, Trans.). City Lights Books. (Original work published 1957)

Downing, C. (2007). Persephone in Hades. In *The goddess: Mythological images of the feminine* (pp. 30–50). iUniverse. (Original work published 1981)

Foley, H. (Ed.). (1994). *Homeric hymn to Demeter: Translation, commentary, and interpretive essays* (H. Foley, Trans.). Princeton University Press.

Hesiod. (1988). *Theogony and works and days* (M. L. West, Trans). Oxford University Press.

Hillman, J. (1972). *The myth of analysis*. Northwestern University Press. (Original work published 1960)

Hillman, J. (1992). *Re-Visioning psychology*. HarperPerennial. (Original work published 1975)

Homer. (2003). *The Homeric hymns* (J. Cashford, Trans.). Penguin.

Lockhart, R. (1983). Eros in language, myth, and dream. In *Words as eggs* (pp. 113–146). Spring.

Nelson, E. E. (2016). Embodying Persephone's desire: Authentic movement and underworld transformation. *Journal of Jungian Scholarly Studies, 11*(1), 5–17. https://doi.org/10.29173/jjs37s

Neumann, E. (1956). *Amor and Psyche: The psychic development of the feminine* (R. Manheim, Trans.). Princeton University Press.

Newmahr, S. (2011). *Playing on the edge: Sadomasochism, risk, and intimacy.* Indiana University Press.

Plato. (1999). *The symposium* (C. Gill, Trans.). Penguin.

Roberts, E. M. (2020). *Underworld gods in ancient Greek religion: Death and reciprocity.* Routledge.

Shahbaz, C., & Chirinos, P. (2017). *Becoming a kink aware therapist.* Routledge.

INDEX

Printed in Great Britain
by Amazon